Jeremy Thorpe was a colleague, and remains a close and respected friend; if what happened to him had happened to me I would have lost my courage, my faith, probably my life. Jeremy's account of the good times and the bad, written with unique insight and humour, is an arresting story — a book no-one who has ever considered voting Liberal should miss.

Sir Clement Freud

Jeremy Thorpe brings to life the events and issues of the sixties, with his inexhaustible fund of anecdotes and sharp recollections of many leading personalities of the time. His contribution to the long struggle against racism and apartheid in southern Africa should be remembered and honoured today.

Lord Avebury (Eric Lubbock)

Jeremy's section on Europe is clear, succinct, illuminating and, as ever, amusing. He contrasts the Liberal commitment, from the start, to the practical idea of Europe with the evasive reluctance of the Conservative and Labour parties, in a precise but not unkind way.

Lord Russell-Johnston

Jeremy Thorpe's book is fascinating reading. I have said many, many times, in talks I've given, that: 'There is no-one you'd rather have round a dinner table than Jeremy Thorpe. He is brilliant at conversation and anecdotes.' This book will prove my point. His campaigning skills in Rochdale were a major contribution to my success, and I have always admired his wit and humour, and always will.

Sir Cyril Smith MBE

This book is an interesting contribution to twentieth-century history. Selective in its approach, it is an anthology rather than an autobiography. A wide range of characters are introduced in a witty and often amusing fashion. Having met Jeremy as an undergraduate in his Oxford years, and having seen him many times since, through music at Aldeburgh, I have greatly enjoyed reading on paper some of the stories which I have heard before. They all deserve to be recorded for the future.

Lord Briggs

In My Own Time

In My Own Time

*Reminiscences
of a Liberal Leader*

Jeremy Thorpe

First published in Great Britain 1999
by Politico's Publishing
8 Artillery Row, London, SW1P 1RZ, England

Tel. 0171 931 0090
Email politicos@artillery-row.demon.co.uk
Website http://www.politicos.co.uk

A catalogue record for this book is available from the British Library.

ISBN 1 90230 121 8

Printed and bound in Great Britain by St Edmundsbury Press.
Cover design by Ad Vantage.

Picture acknowledgements
Cover photo and facing page, and page 220: Rupert Thorpe.
Pages 18, 64, 80: Sir Rupert Hart-Davis
Page 30: Devon News Agency
Page 44: Associated Rediffusion Ltd
Page 92: R.L. Knight, Barnstaple
Page 120: R. Forester Smith, Edinburgh
Page 191: The *Times*
Page 217: Waverley Photographic, Barnstaple
All other photographs and cartoons taken from Jeremy Thorpe's own
collection.
The cartoon on page 98 is reproduced with the kind permission of
the *Guardian*. The cartoon on page 118 is reproduced with the kind
permission of Punch Ltd.
Every effort has been made to trace the copyright holders of the
pictures reproduced in this book. The publishers apologise to any who
have not been contacted.

Contents

Richard Lamb

Foreword

With the publication of Jeremy Thorpe's recollections from his life in politics, the time is ripe for a reassessment of his dramatic and unparalleled impact on the British political scene. In welcome contrast to the reminiscences of other former party leaders, Jeremy does not blow his own trumpet. Let me do it for him.

In the 1959 general election, Jeremy was the only Liberal to gain a seat, and only two others out of the six elected (Jo Grimond and Clement Davies) were victorious in three-cornered fights. Thus Jeremy won North Devon against the general trend, and this was a great tribute to his exceptional talents. His experiences in the Oxford Union, at the Bar and as a television commentator had made him a fluent speaker and given him enormous confidence. On top, he was always humorous and good-tempered, with a flair for instant communication with his fellow beings. He went about electioneering with genuine gusto and enjoyed it, showing an aplomb which was all his own; he was an extremely attractive candidate.

There had been some Liberal revival in Tory-held seats in the wake of the Conservatives' humiliation over Suez in 1956 and Anthony Eden's enforced resignation as Prime Minister. Then, in early 1958, Jeremy's and all Liberal hopes were ignited by remarkable performances in two by-elections. On 12 February, at Tory-held Rochdale, uncontested by Liberals for several elections, the charismatic Ludovic Kennedy, much helped by his attractive wife, shocked the Conservatives by pushing them down into third place and coming within 3,000 votes of defeating the Labour victor. On 27 March, the Liberals did even better, winning Torrington in Devon with Mark Bonham Carter by 219 votes — the first Liberal by-election victory since 1929. Mark was a good candidate, but the star of this by-election was his mother Violet, daughter of Asquith, who seized on the easy publicity available to exploit her charisma to the full, with great effect.

The Rochdale and Torrington by-elections convinced Jeremy that with charismatic candidates, Liberals could win seats.

It is well established that charisma can be exploited more easily in by-elections than in general, and this makes Jeremy's performance in 1959 in defeating a pleasant aristocratic sitting Conservative quite unique.

Once in Parliament, Jeremy was an instant success, wisely refusing a suggestion that he should mimic Harold Macmillan in his maiden speech. However, appreciating the limited opportunities for a party of six in Parliament, he threw most of his efforts into his own constituency and making Liberals an efficient fighting force. His speciality was by-elections. He had an eerie eye for forecasting which MPs would die and making preparations in advance.

This strategy paid off. In November 1960, six by-elections on the same day showed a strong swing towards the Liberals, especially at Tiverton, close to Jeremy's own seat; while Frank Byers, breaking the long-standing electoral pact with the Tories at Bolton East, scored a respectable 24.8 per cent.

In the spring of 1961, there was a Liberal breakthrough at Paisley, the scene of Asquith's dramatic by-election victory after the First World War. The charismatic John Bannerman, immensely popular in Scotland, came within 1,600 votes of victory, pushing the Tory share down from 43.8 per cent to 13.2 per cent, although the Liberals had not contested the seat since 1951. Jo Grimond, the Liberal Leader, was tremendously encouraged by this result, declaring that he: 'wrung his hands that Bannerman had not got in.' Although popular nationally, Grimond had until then been rather a dilettante leader; now, prodded by Jeremy, he began the most active political campaigning of his leadership. Then, when Orpington fell vacant six months after the Paisley by-election, Jeremy realised that here was a golden Liberal opportunity. Liberals were in third place in 1959, only one per cent behind Labour, but since then they had had considerable success in local government, with twelve Liberal councillors.

At the time of Orpington, the Macmillan Government was in disarray. The pay pause and rising prices, together with high and demonstrably inequitable taxation, were making the Conservatives unpopular, and opinion polls soon showed Labour had no chance in this by-election. The sound Liberal candidate, Eric Lubbock, cleverly exploited electoral dissatisfaction over Schedule A property tax in a community of 75 per cent owner-occupiers. The by-election was long delayed, and as opinion polls showed the likelihood of a Liberal win, Jeremy threw everything into the campaign.

He galvanised Liberal supporters all over the south of England to canvass there, persuaded Liberal candidates to allow their agents to work full time, and personally spent long hours on the doorstep. The Liberal by-election majority was 7,855 against a former Tory majority of 14,760, and the victory was almost as much Jeremy's as Lubbock's. There might even have been a double Liberal triumph. For technical reasons the by-election in Blackpool North was held the day before Orpington, and the Liberals with a tiptop candidate came second, only 973 votes behind the successful Tory. Had Blackpool North polled the day after instead of the day before Orpington, Liberal credibility would surely have been high enough to produce another victory.

Macmillan noted in his diary: 'we have been swept off our feet by the Liberal revival and made the world safe for Liberalism.' Although the Liberal upsurge in Orpington is still largely unexplained, one thing is clear — it was a triumph for Thorpe. The Liberals followed up by nearly winning Derby West on 6 June with a weak candidate. With an even weaker candidate in Leicester North East on 12 July, where the Conservatives had been only 1,431 votes behind Labour in the general election, the Liberals ended a close second to Labour, pushing the Tories down into third place with 6,578 votes against their previous 17,990. However, while Leicester North East was polling, Macmillan, in his 'night of the long knives,' sacked seven of his Cabinet colleagues, including the Chancellor of the Exchequer — whereupon Jeremy made his famous comment: 'greater love hath no man than this, that he lay down his friends for his life.'

Unfortunately for the Liberals, Macmillan's medicine worked. In spite of the Profumo scandal and the substitution of Alec Home for Macmillan as Prime Minister, the Conservatives, both in opinion polls and by-election votes, won back the ground they had lost to the Liberals. After nearly winning by-elections at Chippenham and Colne Valley in 1963, Liberal support tailed away drastically. Abolition of Schedule A tax — due entirely to the Liberal resurgence — contented traditional home-owning Tory voters.

The 1964 general election was a grave disappointment after the heady days of Orpington. By now Jeremy had collected funds which he put into winnable constituencies, and in the case of Russell Johnston, he created the post of Director of Scottish Liberal Research, based in Inverness. In this way, Russell was able to devote the required time to winning the seat.

Gratifying increases in the Liberal vote were notched up in most of Jeremy's other winnable seats. However, the overall result was frustrating; the two Liberal enclaves at Bolton West and Huddersfield West, no longer protected by local pacts, fell, and there were only four gains — Bodmin and three Highland seats. Bodmin owed much to Jeremy being a neighbour. Still, the Liberals were second in fifty-four seats, while in 1959 they had been second in only seventeen, and polled over three million votes, a considerable advance.

Following the 1964 general election, Jo Grimond disclosed in private that he wanted to resign as Liberal Leader and for Jeremy to take over. With another general election only a few months off, Jeremy was appalled and managed to persuade Jo to carry on until after the votes were counted. In 1965, there was a false dawn when the future Liberal Leader David Steel won the by-election in Roxburgh, Selkirk & Peebles. As soon as the seat fell vacant Jeremy used his 'winnable' funds to install four full-time agents and spent a considerable time himself in the constituency, even canvassing on the doorstep. Thus David Steel owes a debt to Jeremy for the help he received to win his first and crucial election.

In the 1966 general election, Jo Grimond suffered the tragic loss of his son during the campaign, and as a result his impact was muted. Jeremy gallantly battled in the 'winnable' constituencies, distributing largesse from his funds to the most deserving, including myself in North Dorset. Chippenham, Cardigan, Caithness and Banff were unluckily lost by the narrowest of margins, but consolation prizes were surprise wins at Aberdeen West, Cheadle, Cornwall North and Colne Valley. All those constituencies, as those narrowly lost in 1964, had benefited from Jeremy Thorpe's special financial treatment and encouragement.

Jeremy had become Party Treasurer in 1965, and Party Leader in 1967. He raised considerable sums for the party but the 1970 general election was not a happy hunting ground for him. The nation was choosing between a Conservative and a Labour government and the Liberals were squeezed. After giving generous time to winnable constituencies, Jeremy saw his own majority in North Devon drastically reduced and the number of Liberal MPs fall from thirteen to six. Jeremy, still under the shadow of the death of his charming first wife, may not quite have played himself in as yet as a party leader; irresponsible behaviour by Young Liberals also dented the Liberal image and was not stopped by firm management at party headquarters.

February 1974 was to be a different story. By then Jeremy, happily married again, had achieved considerable stature as a major political figure. He raised impressive sums of money and stepped up his work in the 'winnable' constituencies. By-elections soon told the tale. The Heath Government's honeymoon with the electorate was short-lived, and this time discontented Tory voters turned to the Liberals, as they had eleven years earlier at Orpington. In by-elections in 1973, Liberal candidates won more votes in total than either Conservatives or Labour. Jeremy was convincing in asserting that the Liberal resurgence in these by-elections showed the electorate believed the Liberals were now a practical alternative to the two big parties.

Varied types of seats — Rochdale, Sutton & Cheam, Isle of Ely, Ripon and Berwick-upon-Tweed — became startling Liberal by-election victories. Dedicated attention to local grievances and community politics fostered by Jeremy played a big part, and in August 1973 opinion polls showed Liberal support reaching 30 per cent. It was clear the Liberals would be a major force in the coming general election.

Jeremy, now defending a 300 majority in North Devon, decided to conduct his campaign mainly from Barnstaple, using helicopters to visit some of the winnable seats and a closed-circuit television link to London for the daily press conference. Opinions differ as to whether this paid off or not; it clearly muted hostile questions and emphasised how different was the Liberal campaign from others. 517 Liberal candidates took the field and produced enormous public exposure. Each night on television, Jeremy skilfully and with ready wit projected an attractive and constructive image which was compared very favourably in the national press with those of Heath and Wilson. A poll showed that 40 per cent would vote Liberal if the party had a chance of holding the balance of power, and 48 per cent if the party could be the next government. Jeremy had made the Liberal Party a credible alternative government for the first time since 1929 under Lloyd George. Liberals had surpassed all their expectations; obviously they were about to harvest their largest total vote since the war.

The 1974 result, while hugely rewarding in terms of total votes cast, was bitterly disappointing for Jeremy in the number of seats won. He recounts in this book how, after the result, Ted Heath asked him to join a coalition so that the Conservatives could continue in government. The Liberal Party would not agree, and anyway the numbers were wrong. Lobby correspondents almost to a man have criticised Jeremy for not accepting Heath's offer. In fact it was just not on.

Still, in 1974 an overwhelming case had been made for a change in the voting system. A Labour government had been returned with only 37 per cent of the votes cast — less than the Tories; while the Liberal vote, which had gone up by nearly four million to six million, had produced only 14 MPs. Jeremy immediately appointed a strong Liberal committee to conduct an all-out campaign for voting reform, and provided considerable funds. One of his ideas was a nationwide ballot like the Peace Ballot of 1935 (this caused a complete change in government policy); another, an exit poll after the next general election to show what percentage of the voters favoured a change. Either would have been effective. When Jeremy gave up the leadership, his successor did not follow his lead and the strong case for voting reform made in 1974 was largely allowed to go by default.

The second 1974 election was an anticlimax. The Liberal vote, at five and a quarter million, more or less held in spite of a marked swing to Labour; Jeremy personally got 46 per cent of the votes in North Devon. However, the total Liberal vote was high enough to reinforce the case for voting reform which Jeremy pursued vigorously in his last months as party leader.

Then disaster struck him. Because of widely publicised allegations, Jeremy was forced to resign in May 1976. David Steel was elected Leader in his place and took on a difficult inheritance. Within a very short time he negotiated the Lib–Lab agreement, which enabled the Prime Minister, Jim Callaghan, to remain in office. It is a mystery how Steel got his parliamentary party to agree, because Jo Grimond and John Pardoe were opposed.

Because of this pact the Liberals were taunted by the Tories as being responsible for all Labour mistakes and in the 1979 general election the Liberal vote fell drastically to 4,300,000 — a far cry from February 1974 — and Jeremy himself, although polling 23,000 votes, was defeated in North Devon. Not until the alliance with the SDP in March 1981 did the Liberal phoenix arise from the ashes again.

Between 1959 and 1976, Jeremy had been the life and soul of the Liberal Party. He brought eloquence, humour and compassion into politics and had a flair for picking out the issues which mattered to the nation. With the odds stacked against him by the first-past-the-post voting system, his inspired leadership brought the Liberals to the brink of breaking the two-party system in 1974. His like will not be seen again.

Richard Lamb was a prominent Liberal in the Grimond and Thorpe revivals, and the author of eight books, including The Macmillan Years *(John Murray, 1995).*

Introduction

Time and again when I have recalled a political situation, friends and colleagues have said: 'I hope you will write it down somewhere'. This is a modest attempt to do just that. Having been involved in politics for the past fifty years, it has become clear to me that many of the things I could write about from first-hand experience were merely part of history to those who were later entrants into politics.

So, I have written about Lloyd George, whom I was privileged to know. With Churchill, my contact was limited to two encounters, each of which for me was memorable; a fair sprinkling of British and foreign personalities; events in the Commonwealth, some humorous, some less so; developments in the UK; I refer to my trial; I go in some detail into two political issues which dominated my life — the European Community and Rhodesia.

This is not an autobiography. It is more of an anthology. If any part of it stimulates enthusiasm for politics, I shall be content.

Acknowledgements

My warm thanks to Richard Lamb for his introduction, and to him and Richard Moore, my gratitude for reading through my manuscript and making valuable suggestions. My thanks also to Eric Avebury, Asa Briggs, Clement Freud, Russell Johnston and Cyril Smith for their commentaries; to Trevor Jones, Jenny Day, Liz Cocks, Yvonne Keer and Laura Wallace, for their help; to the British Library at Colindale, for their efficient and courteous assistance; to my editor, Duncan Brack, and Iain Dale and John Simmons at my publishers, Politico's, who, whilst highly professional, have been a delight to work with; to Judy Young, who has patiently typed each page of the book and supplemented my recollections with her own; and to my son Rupert, some of whose photographs are included and whose idea it was that I should draw extensively on the photographs in my collection.

Above all, to Marion, who has been a constant source of advice and inspiration — which comes as no surprise.

Jeremy Thorpe
March 1999

To
HJL
in memoriam

Chapter One

Relations

My maternal grandparents

Since this is not an autobiography, I shall pick out only one or two of my relations. Undoubtedly, the matriarch of the family was my maternal grandmother, Lady Norton-Griffiths, who died, in full possession of her faculties, at the age of 101 in 1974. There is a record of longevity in her family, since her mother died aged ninety-nine and her grandmother, whom she remembered well, and who was at her wedding, was born in 1797 and died in 1901, having lived in the eighteenth, nineteenth and twentieth centuries and five reigns. My own mother died in her ninetieth year.

My grandmother was short of stature but had a commanding personality. Throughout her long life she was to experience some appalling tragedies. These she met with calm and amazing courage and faith. She obviously adored my grandfather and was a tremendous encouragement to him in his career. During her long period of widowhood she travelled extensively. I remember staying with her in Rome in her high eighties — the sightseeing schedule kicked off with two churches and a picture gallery before lunch. At one of the churches, she said that she had not visited it for seventy years; there was, however, a family connection with the church since her uncle, a civil engineer, had drained the foundations, which had become waterlogged and threatened the stability of the building.

Her husband, my grandfather, Sir John Norton-Griffiths, was also a civil engineer, and she frequently accompanied him on his projects abroad. In 1905 she was with him in Angola where he was building the Benguela Railway. The labour force went down with yellow fever and it was necessary for someone who was fit to go down to Johannesburg to arrange for replacements. My grandmother volunteered and was advised that she should negotiate with a labour lawyer who was an Indian called Gandhi. If his agreement was obtained, all would be well. They had three days of talks

Sir John and Lady Norton-Griffiths crossing the Andes by mule, 1909

and she returned to Angola triumphant. I once asked her what she thought of Gandhi, to which she replied: 'Such a nice little man. I never thought he would give us so much trouble later on!'

On another trip from the Argentine to Chile in 1909, she refused to take the boat round Cape Horn, being a very bad sailor. It was pointed out to her that the only land route was over the Andes, and winter was approaching. She promptly decided to make the journey and she and my grandfather set off with a pack of mules and some twelve thicknesses of clothing. Somehow they arrived.

She was intensely musical and as a girl studied singing in Germany, where she met Brahms. When I asked her what Brahms was like, she replied: 'long flowing beard and fat fingers like sausages'.

I was particularly pleased when, in her eighties, my grandmother came down to North Devon and sat on the platform at a mass Liberal rally in the Barnstaple Pannier Market. Her last visit had been in 1926. I looked up the mayor's visitors' book which contains the signature of my grandfather, Sir John Norton-Griffiths, accompanied by my grandmother, on 13 November 1926. He had come to speak in support of the sitting Tory MP, Sir Basil Peto. The opposite page of the visitors' book recorded the signature of David Lloyd George on 16 October 1926, who likewise had come to speak at a rally in the Pannier Market in support of the Liberal candidate, D.M. Mason. He was accompanied by his younger daughter Megan. On 21 August 1989 my mother, Sir John Norton-Griffiths' elder daughter, and Lady Olwen Carey-Evans, Lloyd George's elder daughter, called on the mayor and both signed the book, bringing the two families together in the common cause.

At her hundredth birthday party, Sir Harry Brittain, who was himself ninety-nine, bellowed at my grandmother: 'Good evening, Gwladys'. She called me over and said: 'Please tell that old man that I may be older than he is but I am not deaf!' At a later stage she said to me: 'Darling, please take me home, I am slightly tired and very tiddly!'

My grandfather, being an engineer, was asked to found the Tunnellers' Regiment, which played an important part in the First World War in burrowing under enemy lines. He was also a Tory Member of Parliament. As an engineer, he was ordered by the British military authorities, at the height of the First World War in 1916, to blow up

Lady Norton-Griffiths

the Romanian oil wells at Ploesti, to deny oil to the advancing Germans. He asked King Ferdinand of Romania for permission to destroy the oil wells and told him that Romania would be compensated by the British government after the war. When asked by the King what guarantees could be offered, he said: 'Sir, I am a British Army Officer and a British Member of Parliament, shouldn't that be sufficient?' 'Yes', said the King. 'It is. But on what basis shall we be compensated?' 'Where are your accounts and company books?' asked my grandfather. 'They are at St Petersburg for safe keeping. The accountant involved in their preparation was Sir Harmood Banner, a British MP.' My grandfather suggested to the King that he, my grandfather, should collect the books from St Petersburg and take them back to the UK, where they would form the basis of a claim for compensation. Agreement having been reached, my grandfather carried out over a period of three days the wholesale destruction of the Ploesti oilfields.

He was described as the great god Thor, wielding a massive sledgehammer, causing a vast amount of damage. A great volume of black cloud was generated which made it impossible to tell whether it was night or day.

Lady Norton-Griffiths' 100th birthday, 2 January 1973: from left, front row: Ursula Thorpe (daughter), Johanna Butt (granddaughter), Rupert Thorpe (great-grandson), Lady Norton-Griffiths; back row: Michael Norton-Griffiths (grandson), Sir Peter Norton-Griffiths (son), Jeremy Thorpe (grandson)

The Germans did not get a drop of oil. With unusual generosity towards someone carrying out such destruction to his economy, the King decorated him with the Order of the Grand Star of Romania, after which my grandfather set out to collect the Ploesti company books, commenting that he knew Sir Harmood Banner as a fellow MP and would accept his figures without argument.

In St Petersburg, my grandfather was received by the Tsar and was created a Count of the Order of St Vladimir. He was probably the last man to be so decorated since the Russian Revolution broke out a few days afterwards. According to my uncle Peter (Sir Peter Norton-Griffiths), he also brought back the last letters from the Tsar to our Royal Family.

In February 1967, I met Kosygin, the Soviet premier, when he was on an official visit to London from the USSR. I told him that my family had played a great part in the Russian Revolution. His eyes lit up like light bulbs and he asked for more information. I told him about my grandfather's audience and decoration and said that for the Russian people, this was the last straw which sparked off the revolution. This was greeted by a rather wintry smile. The next evening Kosygin asked me about the decoration and whether the Soviet government could have it for the Kremlin museum. I told him that I thought it very unlikely. As it happens, my cousin has the decoration and I keep the ceremonial sword which goes with it in an umbrella stand to be used against burglars.

My father and grandfather were both in the House of Commons as Conservative MPs. My grandfather sat for Wednesbury, and subsequently Central Wandsworth. My father won the Rusholme Division of Manchester in a 1919 by-election. Ironically, he was defeated by a Liberal, Charles Masterman, in 1923.

My grandmother had a bizarre experience when campaigning in Wednesbury. There was terrible poverty, and a woman living in the poorest area had given birth to stillborn twins. My grandmother went to sympathise with her. The poor woman invited my grandmother to come into the front room, where, propped up on the settee were the two dead babies, each wearing a red rosette, which was the local Conservative colour. The mother commented: 'You can see — loyal in life and loyal in death'.

I am certain that I would have found the political views of my father and grandfather to be very much to the right of my own. However, they both enormously enjoyed politics, and this is something that I share.

My grandfather used to campaign in a balloon and once persuaded his hapless opponents to come for a ride. Unfortunately, the balloon ended up twenty miles off course and they were not very pleased! He was known in the constituency as Empire Jack, or the Monkey Man. This was sparked off by a heckler who shouted out: 'You do not know what it is to be hungry'. 'Oh yes, I do', replied my grandfather. 'During the South African war we were so short of food that I ate monkeys!'

I share my grandfather's enthusiasm for what is now the Commonwealth. However, my activities revolved round the movements for independence in the colonial territories, whereas his approach was that of an Empire builder — hence his name, 'Empire Jack'. In 1911, the Liberal government entertained delegates attending the coronation but nothing had been arranged for the delegates by the Conservative opposition. My grandfather decided to take steps and leased Temple House, near Maidenhead. There he offered hospitality to forty people over the weekends and invited 200 more for the day. The Tory Chief Whip was to draw up a list of MPs and Sir Harry Brittain was to provide the list of Empire guests. It must have been a glittering season.

My paternal grandparents

My paternal grandfather was a Protestant Irishman from Cork. He was Vicar of St George's, Stockport, and become Archdeacon of Macclesfield. He was appointed to the former by Wakefield Christie-Miller, who had donated the land and helped build the church. With a romantic touch, his son (Geoffry Christie-Miller), married the vicar's daughter, my Aunt Olive, who was my father's sister.

My grandfather's everyday uniform was a frock coat, top hat, apron and gaiters. I get the impression that he was intensely intolerant. On one occasion when his daughter, Ella, was entering into marriage with a groom he considered inadequate, he remained in the vicarage with all the blinds down at the time the ceremony was taking place. Special family prayers were always held before anyone went on a journey, to pray that if they were not to meet again in this world, they would meet in the next. The advice which I most cherish was that given by him to a daughter: 'You are going on a long journey. My advice is, put your faith in God and change at Clapham Junction!'

In contrast to the Archdeacon, my grandmother, whom I also did not know, apparently had lovely Irish charm and vagueness. When she wanted to catch a train, she would go down to the station and wait till the right train turned up, saying: 'There is plenty of time'.

My father

I adored my father. Our relationship was almost that of two brothers, and I was intensely proud of him. I remember him once telling me by the sea at Criccieth that he was frightened of his father, who subjected him to a harsh discipline, and he never wanted me to be frightened of him. I can honestly say that we never exchanged a word in anger. He was tremendous fun and had a great sense of humour.

When my father was in the House, on 18 April 1923 he sought leave to bring in a bill by which ministers in either House were to be allowed to speak but not vote in the Other House. This was defeated by 244 votes to 100. Although it would not have been the ideal reform needed in our parliamentary system, it would have enhanced the chances of a peer, like

Lord Curzon, to become Prime Minister and speak in the House of Commons, and it could likewise have been of use in the case of a peer of the calibre of Lord Carrington. I think I can claim to share with my father a deep interest in constitutional reform.

In 1967 I was a member of the Inter-Parliamentary Conference, whose members were drawn from both houses, which sought to reform the House of Lords. Ironically, we all reached agreement, but when the report reached the House of Commons, it became clear that we would not be able to carry our backbenchers with us. The opposition to our proposals was spearheaded by an unique coalition of Michael Foot and Enoch Powell. As Viscount Samuel was to remark: 'Mr Asquith said that the reform of the House of Lords brooks no delay. My Lords, we have been brooking ever since!'

As a barrister, my father's commitment to the Bar was total. He chose to practise at the Parliamentary Bar. This involved appearing before a Committee of MPs when he would be piloting or objecting to a private bill. He could not 'appear before himself', and had to make a choice between regaining his seat and pursuing a Parliamentary career or concentrating on his legal practice. The law won. In his full bottom wig he looked immensely distinguished.

J.H. Thorpe

The Bar had its complications. On one occasion my father was travelling on a non-corridor train. He was conscious of a man sitting opposite him fixing him with a stare. The man ultimately leant forward and said to my father: 'Excuse me, sir, are you the Recorder of Blackburn?' 'Yes', said my father. The man said: 'I have just come out of Preston jail, where you sent me three years ago'. 'I never like sending a man to prison', said my father; 'did you have a fair trial?' 'Yes', was the reply. 'I want to go straight. My wife has kept the building business alive, but I am worried that I may be victim-

J.H. Thorpe KC in 1935

ised by the police. Can you help me?' My father gave him a letter to the Chief Constable. He also suggested that the man should call on my father in his room in the Law Courts after court hours to report upon his progress. This he did. He kept in touch with my father, who was delighted that the man had managed to remake his life. The word got around and several 'old lags' called on my father for advice.

In 1940, at the beginning of the war, I was evacuated, aged eleven, along with my sister Camilla, to stay with my American aunt, Kay Norton-Griffiths, in the USA. My parents took this precaution as my father was on the German blacklist. and in the event of a German invasion, which at the time was a real possibility, he and the family would have been at risk. My father was vulnerable because of his work (with Norman Birkett) on alien tribunals, which had the difficult task of determining who were genuine asylum seekers and who were under-cover spies.

I was in America for three years. I was extremely happy at my school, the Rectory School, Connecticut. We all had some responsibility for the domestic side of the school — my privilege was to look after the pigs. My aunt came down to visit me during my first winter there just after a heavy snowstorm. By way of a compliment, I invited her to come with me on my toboggan, taking the food down the hill to the pigs. Rather nobly she accepted and, wrapped up in her mink coat, sat behind me whilst I clutched between my knees a pail full of swill which I had collected from the kitchens. The worst occurred. We hit a rock hidden by snow and Kay, myself, the garbage and mink coat were thrown off the sledge and landed in a heap! Needless to say she was not best pleased.

My aunt lived in West Newton, near Boston, and in the summer we would go to her mother's house on Lake Squam in New Hampshire. I had my own outboard motorboat and the place was idyllic. Before I left America

I had developed an American accent and am therefore able to know what the English sound like to the Americans, which is rather prissy!

By 1943 my father thought it was high time I returned home; otherwise I would become a complete American and lose contact with my country. A number of parents who had also sent their children across the Atlantic took the same view. The Royal Navy agreed to take on board a number of schoolchildren, although it was emphasised that the German U-boat threat was still very real and all ships had to travel in convoy. I was told that I had been accepted to be one of the ten children to be taken aboard HMS *Phoebe,* a light cruiser sailing from Norfolk, Virginia to an unnamed British port, which turned out to be Liverpool. An additional twenty-five children were to travel on the battleship *Queen Elizabeth,* which was part of our convoy.

The Captain vacated his cabin and moved to a much smaller cabin near the bridge, which was the normal procedure on leaving port. I am ashamed to say that by mistake we flooded the Captain's bathroom and were therefore relegated to communal plumbing on that deck. We did four-hour stints on the bridge on watch duty. This suited me, since the bridge was the least turbulent place in rough weather, and I was therefore marginally less likely to be sea-sick. We put in for the day at Bermuda and half the ship's crew, in which we were included, went ashore for a picnic and a swim on a beautiful, totally deserted beach. Before disembarking in Liverpool, we settled up our mess bills — mine, I think, if my recollection is accurate, was £6 7s 6d.

J.H. Thorpe KC in full bottom wig, 1928
(drawing, Peter Castelle)

J.H. and Ursula Thorpe at a pre-war wedding

On the last lap of my journey from America I caught a train from Victoria station bound for Oxted, which was the station for my home. Just before the train left I saw my father boarding the same train. I cannot analyse the reactions that followed, but although I was desperately keen to be reunited with him, I simply could not face the emotional situation in a carriage full of people, and decided to wait to speak to him when we reached Oxted. Because there were complications with my luggage I was a little late getting off the train and I missed him. There were not many cars around because petrol rationing was very tight, but I did manage to get a lift and arrived at home ten minutes after my father. I rang the doorbell and both my parents came to the door. I had been away for three years and was tremendously excited to be back home.

My father was involved in an immense amount of war work: in addition to tribunal work, he was Chairman of the vitally important Price Regulation Committee. This workload took its toll, and he suffered a stroke in 1944, aged fifty-seven, and died of a cerebral thrombosis. On my return from America, I was blessed with less than two years of his companionship.

Mother and father

My mother and father met in rather romantic circumstances — in Westminster Abbey at the wedding of Princess Mary, daughter of King George V, in February 1922. Strictly speaking, they were not entitled to be there. The ballot for tickets took place in the House of Commons and an old bachelor MP drew tickets, one for himself and one for his wife. Rather than surrender the ticket, he offered it to my father. My maternal grandfather, Sir John Norton-Griffiths, drew tickets for himself and my grandmother. She for her part nobly suggested that Ursula, who was still in her teens, would enjoy the ceremony and gave her her ticket. My mother was in her place in the Abbey when she saw a handsome man in military uniform, 'with every button doing its duty', and swore that she would die if he didn't come and sit next door to her. As luck would have it, that was precisely where he was ushered. That same evening there was a ball at the Royal Albert Hall to celebrate the wedding. My father rudely abandoned his party's host and hostess and spent the rest of the evening in Joynson Hicks' box where my mother and grandfather were guests. They never looked back. One strange coincidence was that Princess Mary and my mother were both to become mothers-in-law to my wife Marion.

My parents' marriage plans received a severe jolt a few days before the wedding ceremony was due to take place. My father had visited a leading insurance company in order to take out a life insurance policy, and underwent all the conventional tests. He was asked whether he would call in to see the senior doctor in charge of the department, and the doctor, obviously shaken, said they were very sorry but they could not issue a life insurance policy on his behalf. My father asked why and was told that they did not regard him as a good risk. He pressed them further but the doctor declined to indicate on what basis they had formed this judgement. The doctor did say that my father's life expectancy was not very good. My father went to see his mother-in-law to be (my grandmother) and asked her whether he should tell my mother the news; should he call off the wedding; should he go abroad? 'No,' said my grandmother: 'get a second opinion.' This my father did. The company rather sheepishly provided him with a life policy. They had by then discovered that they had muddled up the specimens of two applicants. The other applicant was granted a policy on the basis that he was A1. In practice he died within the year.

My mother

Relations with my mother were more complex than those with my father. She was a woman of strong character, fearless in her convictions, outspoken and often tactless. She was a disciplinarian, whereas I and my sisters regarded our father as a safe haven. In my early childhood, before the war, the family led a comfortable, conventional and — I suppose I should say — privileged existence. We had a living-in staff of five — cook, scullery maid, parlour maid and housemaid, and a nanny. Some years before the war the chauffeur was stood down as an economy measure.

My earliest canvassing was experienced at my mother's ladies' luncheon parties, which were followed by a rubber of bridge. I was directed to go round the table, shake hands and be polite to each lady in turn. The house was run like clockwork; my mother's first business of the day, following breakfast in bed, would be a conference with the cook, Mrs Macey, to plan the menus. The other staff were appropriately instructed. Ursula's appearance was made more formidable by the fact that she wore a monocle. Her father thought that spectacles, as then designed, were unbecoming. Therefore, for this reason and due to the fact that she only had one bad eye, he offered her an additional £100 a year on her allowance if she wore a monocle. The monocle won. She wore the monocle at her wedding, attracting the headline: 'Britain's first monocled bride', and prompting a small boy to ask his mother why the lady wore her ring in her eye and not on her finger!

One of her quirks was that she firmly wore her conventional spectacles when swimming in the sea. These were safer than the monocle, and when people from far and wide would swim over to her to point out that she had forgotten to take off her glasses, she would reply: 'Thank you. But you see, I have bad eyesight, and need them to see where I am going!' She passionately enjoyed swimming in the sea and until she was well into her seventies she would take a regular dip.

Children's parties followed a well-established pattern. The children arrived with their nannies, who went into a huddle and expected to be entertained. One complained that none of them had been offered any sherry. My mother was furious, and promptly rang up the nanny's employer, saying that their nanny had behaved very badly and she, Ursula, had given her notice on behalf of the employer.

Sometimes her shock tactics worked: at a toll gate at Borth-y-Gest in North Wales, the toll gate lady had an unenviable reputation of

Ursula Thorpe (1930s)

being surly and unhelpful. On this occasion, she muttered how difficult life was if people didn't bring the right change. Few people spoke to her, so she was somewhat taken aback when being thus addressed by my mother: 'My husband and I have been coming to Wales for the last fifteen years, and we have come to the conclusion that without any doubt you are the most disagreeable woman in the whole of North Wales'. The effect was electric: from that moment the woman was transformed, and became well-disposed to mankind and polite. It was a good day's work, and I am sure the woman was happier for it.

Another incident which I have never forgotten occurred when I must have been about five years old: my mother rang the bell in the first floor drawing room and asked the parlour maid, who had to come up two flights of stairs from the basement, to put some coal on the fire. When the maid had left, I asked her why we couldn't do it ourselves, to which she replied that she would get her hands dirty. In fairness to her, come the war, she would willingly get her hands very dirty, not least in cutting up several hundredweight of raw horsemeat for which the local dogs formed an orderly queue.

Wartime brought the compassionate side of her character to the fore, accompanied by a social conscience and a sense of duty which shone through in all her activities. She threw herself into war work: she was a forceful local billeting officer for evacuees from London's East End, and would not accept a refusal of shelter for children. Learning that the driver of the local grocer's van at Limpsfield in Surrey had been called up, she took on the delivery round, covering a large rural area. As a result of my father's voluntary withdrawal from the Bar, in order to concentrate on a variety of wartime jobs, his income had plummeted. By the time of his death in 1944 the family was very hard up. My mother coped with the changed circumstances with courage, never compromising on her standards. One lady in Limpsfield Chart was heard to say that: 'Mrs Thorpe has come down in the world better than any lady I know'.

Ursula was superb in a crisis, and totally loyal. In the 1955 election she was still a Conservative. It took the Suez crisis in 1956, when she was Chairman of the local branch of the United Nations Association, to bring about her resignation from the Tory party and join the Liberals, working tirelessly on their behalf. In the 1955 general election (my first), she collected her Conservative subscriptions in the East Surrey constituency and set off for North Devon to back my campaign. Or, to quote the civilised advice of her local Tory MP's wife, she should indeed go down to North Devon, 'to drive and cherish'.

During the campaign in North Devon, local Tories distributed a red leaflet, naively asking whether the recipient was a Labour donkey or a Liberal mule, with appropriate drawings. I didn't take it very seriously. Not so my mother. She stormed into the Tory office in Barnstaple, and asked to see the agent, having established that he had been responsible for the publication. She told him that it was disgraceful. She had been on her own Conservative committee, appointing their Tory agent, and she and her fellow Conservatives would not have tolerated such behaviour. Somewhat chastened and sensing possible trouble, he asked her to leave her name and address so that the divisional Tory chairman might contact her. 'Ursula Thorpe', was the reply, 'my son is your local Liberal candidate. It will be sufficient if you wish to contact me to do so care of the Liberal headquarters in Barnstaple.' It was not for nothing that she proudly claimed to be daughter, wife and mother of Members of Parliament. Her support in all my eight elections was invaluable.

A wonderful tribute was paid to Ursula at her memorial service by my close friend from my schooldays, Simon Barrington-Ward, who became Bishop of Coventry. He spoke of her with personal warmth and affection, mentioning many public services she had performed during her life. She sat on Surrey County Council as an Independent; she was Chairman of Oxted County School, and took particular interest in Nutfield School for the Deaf; she served on the bench as a JP. She was Chairman of the Medical and Special Schools Committee of the County Council in Surrey. He also spoke of her compassion for individuals who had fallen on hard times, whom she would regularly visit and support.

Although in my early years I found her somewhat awesome, and we had some stormy interludes in my teens after my return from three years in America, we grew much closer in later years. Her enormous energy, her integrity, loyalty and support sustained me in good and difficult times. I remember her with great affection and gratitude.

George

I cannot make reference to the closer members of my family without mentioning George. George was a brown and white fox terrier of immense character. I was given him by my godfather after I had a long illness. He was chosen by my godfather's wife, from Harrods. Originally he was intended for clients in Nigeria, but she insisted that they should be sent a substitute. We lived in London before the war and used to exercise George in Hyde Park. One of his delights was to find an enormous branch broken off a tree which he would pick up in his mouth and charge ahead — unfortunately on several occasions laddering the silk stockings of unsuspecting pedestrians!

George was also capable of being a thief. My family had taken a furnished house in Woolacombe before the war for a holiday and the landlady had unwisely placed a leg of lamb on the lower shelf of a trolley. The temptation was too great for George — he rushed out of the house carrying our Sunday joint with him! On another occasion he visited Mrs Horney's bakery in Limpsfield and after a lot of noise, appropriated a large cream bun with which he ran out of the shop, with Mrs Horney in hot pursuit!

George was very amorous. He had a long-standing relationship with a certain Georgina, who was also a smooth-haired fox terrier. He would visit her almost every day of his life and they had several litters. He was not averse to fighting over other ladies, but as he got older his battles were less and less successful. He would somehow drag himself home and lie on his back outside the back door letting out the most blood-curdling howl, which meant he wanted tender lov-

George

ing care. He usually had a torn ear which needed to be bathed, or a wound to be cleaned. To round off the treatment, he would be wrapped up in a blanket with a hot water bottle and revived with a drop of brandy, to which he was very partial. Within three or four days, if the door was open, he would shoot out in quest of further battles.

I only found him bad-tempered on one occasion. During the war we were in Doodlebug Alley. This involved a great cluster of barrage balloons in our area, designed to intercept V1s and V2s before they reached the heavily populated area of London. The V1s cut out their engines and gave one a few seconds' notice that they were liable to explode. On one such occasion a V1 cut out overhead and my mother dived into the cupboard under the stairs, where there was just room for two people to squat, and grabbed George by the tail and pulled him into the cupboard — whereupon, from a combination of shock and pride, he bit her. In fact he had cause to be grateful since the whole of the kitchen floor was covered in splintered glass.

George had one distressing complaint from an early age, namely that he had terrible wind. On one occasion in mid-winter, we were driving in the car with all the windows up when George gave us a really fruity one. My family turned on him and said: 'You filthy dog'. I, aged six at the time, unswervingly loyal to my dog, was alleged to have said: 'As a matter of fact, I rather like it!'

Uncle Mumpy and Aunt Violet

A great eccentric in the family was my great uncle Mumpy, my grandmother's brother, Ralph Wood. He lived in a Queen Anne cottage, known as Flint Cottage, on Box Hill. He was a great collector: almost every object in the house was worthy of a place in a museum, but that would not prevent him from using them. So you might find yourself eating off a Ming plate with a James II silver spoon.

One slightly macabre acquisition was a burial vault in the church at Mickleham. The local squire had a row with the parson so, in high dudgeon, he decided to open his family vault and take all the coffins down to Cornwall to be placed in his wife's family vault. Although the Mickleham vault was large in size, Uncle Mumpy insisted that its use be restricted to my grandmother and grandfather, my great aunt and himself. In this way they could have an undisturbed rubber of bridge!

Uncle Mumpy was a great defender of Box Hill, and woe betide any cyclist who dared to bicycle on the sacred slopes. On one occasion, he thrust his stick into the spokes of a cyclist's wheel, causing him to be jettisoned over his handlebars! 'I shall have you prosecuted', said the cyclist. 'And I shall have you prosecuted for breaching the bye-laws', retorted Uncle Mumpy. His heart condition was not particularly well suited to these encounters. After a few more exchanges they both decided to call it a day. The threats were duly withdrawn.

However, he did have a brush with the law. One of his peccadillos was to travel for a few stations on the railway without holding a valid ticket: if he was travelling from stations A to Z he would buy a ticket from stations A to L; he then travelled without a ticket for the next few stations and then purchased a ticket to cover the remainder of the journey. He was only denying the railway a few shillings but was in due course discovered and was to be prosecuted before a stipendiary magistrates' court. In panic he came to see my father asking him to defend him. My father wanted to give the matter some thought, since the appearance of a KC at a magistrates' court could well produce unwelcome publicity. Eventually he agreed, with one proviso: that Mumpy mustn't mind what was said about him

Ralph Wood, drawn by Max Beerbohm in 1943

in court. He agreed. My father opened: 'Sir, before you is a very silly old man having a rather pathetic, you may think, last fling before settling down to obscurity. He is so shocked at what he has done that he has already received his own punishment.' At this Mumpy jumped to his feet, shook his fists and cried out that this was outrageous. Calm was eventually restored. Either due to my father's pathos or Mumpy's eccentric outburst, he was bound over and in the course of time my father was forgiven.

One joy of Flint Cottage was that my great aunt and uncle gave shelter in the war for a time to Sir Max and Lady Beerbohm, who had been bombed out of their home at Abinger. Sir Max was entrancing. One of my prize possessions is his cartoon of the Liberal front bench of 1910, which years later I was to show to Churchill — as I mention elsewhere. One breakfast when the news from the front had been particularly bad, Max put down his newspaper with a groan and said to his wife: 'Oh, Florence'. 'What is it, Max?' she replied. 'Florence, the toast is cold.'

Flint Cottage had previously belonged to George Meredith, and the chalet in which he did much of his writing stood in the garden. Max was fascinating when reminiscing about Meredith, the Rosettis and pre-Raphaelites generally. I have referred elsewhere to Max's lifestyle in Rapallo, to which he returned after the war.

My great aunt Violet was no less a character than my great uncle. I remember being taken one afternoon to a cinema in Dorking. Aunt Violet bought 1s 3d tickets, which plonked us down in the very front rows. My aunt protested that it was much too close to the screen for her liking, so she moved back and sat in the 2s 9d seats, which were infinitely superior. She was asked by an usher to show her tickets, and when it was pointed out to her that she was sitting in a 2s 9d seat for a 1s 3d ticket she replied that she couldn't see in their beastly seats in the front, and was compelled to move further back. If they didn't want her custom, they must say so. Since the cinema was virtually deserted, they did not feel that this was an issue on which they were disposed to do battle then, and, as far as I know, on her future visits.

On an occasion during the war she was rung one evening by the Dorking police station to say that a sergeant was on duty on Box Hill and was needed urgently. Could she try to find him? She thought this was rather a tall order but would do her best. She proceeded to take down all the blackout curtains and blinds, put on all the lights and waited. Within next to no time an irate sergeant appeared and said, did she want the Germans to land, or at the very least come over on a bombing raid? 'No', said Aunt Violet, 'I am not expecting the Germans, but was waiting for you to tell you that you must go down to the police station at once'.

Uncle Geoffry Christie-Miller

I knew aunts and uncles on my mother's side better than on my father's. One notable exception was my Uncle Geoffry, who, as I have already mentioned, married my father's sister, Olive. When my father died we were very hard up, since for several years he had not been earning fees at the Bar, having given up his practice in order to devote himself full time to war work. Uncle Geoffry immediately volunteered to see me through Eton, Oxford and my call to the Bar. I once said to him: 'Uncle Geoffry, I can never thank you enough for what you have done for me.' 'Yes, you can', came the reply. 'I am a director of the family business, Christy's, who make hats. Always wear a hat, it is a good advertisement for the trade.' I always have, *in piam memoriam*. And for not the least of reasons, the fact that one loses twenty-five per cent of one's body heat through the head! A hat is more important to me than an overcoat.

Uncle Geoffry was a great stickler for people being on time. On one occasion Queen Elizabeth (now the Queen Mother) visited the hat factory and was shown round by Uncle Geoffry. She stopped on several occasions to talk to the workers and Uncle Geoffry was heard to cry out: 'Come along, come along, Ma'am, or you will be late for the Mayor of Stockport!'

He was keenly involved in the affairs of the Territorial Army and as an ardent Conservative was particularly chuffed to receive a KCB on the recommendation of the Labour Defence Minister, Emmanuel Shinwell.

Caroline

Gate-crashing a royal event
Caroline and I announced our engagement on 1 April 1968. That evening I was due to attend a government dinner at Lancaster House to mark the

fiftieth Anniversary of the RAF. I had visions of my being photographed in white tie and tails whilst Caroline, deserted, would be cooking over her stove in her flat. A recent innovation was that after a government dinner there would be a reception for spouses and others invited to attend. I was pretty sure that this would apply on this occasion and so I arranged to meet her at the front door just as soon as the speeches were over. I sought out Denis Healey, who was Defence Minister, to clear the arrangement with him. Denis told me that it was not that sort of event — no wives had been invited. The only ladies who would be there were the Queen, the Queen Mother, Princess Margaret, the Duchess of Gloucester and Princess Marina of Kent and their ladies-in-waiting. Additionally, there would be a few WAF officers representing the main RAF Stations. I asked him what I should do in the circumstances, and he nobly replied: 'She has probably had her hair done and got out her frock, she'd better come', for which I have always been grateful to him. Caroline duly arrived. She was, of course,

'I know your family are Conservative, dear, but this is a bit much!' The *Sun* envisaged Conservative leader Ted Heath playing the organ at the Thorpes' wedding (April 1968)

even more conspicuous than usual by reason of the absence of other spouses or future spouses. The Queen Mother was first and said: 'We needn't ask who this is'. Next the Queen arrived and said: 'Is this …?' 'Yes, Ma'am, it is.' The other royal ladies followed suit. I said to Caroline: 'Since we had only announced our engagement that afternoon, a royal presentation the same evening was pretty good going!'

Time and again in tributes paid to Caroline she is summed up in one word, 'radiant', to which I would add, 'serene'. She brought warmth to every situation in which she was involved. We were married in the Chapel at Lambeth Palace by the Bishop of Crediton, Wilfred Westall, and given the blessing by the Archbishop of Canterbury, Michael Ramsey. Both were treasured friends, which brought an added happiness to the event, and Joan Ramsey became our son Rupert's godmother. We were then generously lent the Royal Academy of Arts for our reception, which was 1,500 strong, a month after the wedding.

Caroline was blessed with countless gifts. Her knowledge of birds and plants gave added joy to being in the country. Her job at Sotheby's under-pinned her love of the fine arts. From her experience with a firm of interior decorators, she had become an accomplished seamstress and made most of the furnishings in our homes at Higher Chuggaton and Ashley Gardens. She took great delight in Rupert and although he was not old enough to remember her, he is very conscious of the part she has played in his life and cherishes this.

Politics was a new experience. When we were on our honeymoon in Elba, a ham-fisted attempt was made to stage a coup against me as Liberal Leader. We learnt of this incredibly ill-timed operation by seeing a banner headline in the

Jeremy and Caroline Thorpe, fishing off Brighton pier — Liberal Assembly, September 1969

Jeremy, Caroline and Rupert Thorpe, 1970

English newspapers. Caroline innocently asked: 'Is it always like this?' 'No', I replied, 'just sometimes'.

Twenty-five months after our marriage Caroline was killed in a car accident. It felt as if my life had come to an end. Thank God I had Rupert, and met Marion who bound up my wounds. It is seldom given to a man to be blessed with two such matchless women.

Before I remarried, one of the more daunting problems was to organise my life, involving, as it did, a busy parliamentary career, to enable me to

Michael Ramsey, Archbishop of Canterbury, at Jeremy and Caroline Thorpe's wedding, Lambeth Palace, May 1968

give sufficient time and attention to my son. This involved trying to finish committee meetings at a reasonable time, and in debates I tried to be called as early as possible. This would normally enable me to get back to the flat to put Rupert to bed and read him a story. I tried to find an hour during the day when I could take him to Lambeth Palace gardens, where Michael Ramsey, the Archbishop of Canterbury, generously allowed us to roam freely, which gave us some privacy.

I was very fortunate that, immediately following Caroline's accident, help was at hand. One of Caroline's closest friends, Vivienne Franklin, who grew up with her during the war and was virtually her sister, arrived on the scene and offered to help look after Rupert and run the flat. I had met her once when she came to stay in Devon. She was a dedicated teacher and wonderful with children, and I am always grateful to her for the security and affection which she gave him. It is good to know now that she is married, with her own son, Charles.

Marion and musicians

For once the press got it right! In January 1972, the pianist Moura Lympany, who is an old friend, telephoned me to ask whether I would like to go to a concert at the Festival Hall the following week to hear Nathan Milstein play the Beethoven violin concerto. The business of the House was fairly free on the night in question, so I accepted the invitation gladly. Moura told me that we were invited to supper afterwards at Marion Harewood's. In the car, Moura boldly announced her object was to bring together Marion and myself, since it was her view that we should get married. When I recovered my equilibrium I said that I hoped Marion hadn't been told the same thing, since the evening would be rather embarrassing as I had only once briefly met her, in 1952. Moura assured me that she hadn't been so informed. The evening was to prove not only memorable, but eventful as well. Marion and I married in 1973, and our silver wedding was celebrated in 1998 with a reception in the National Liberal Club. The evening was even more enriched by Moura Lympany's presence.

One of the many joys of being married to Marion is that of attending musical events, which before I had very often turned down on the grounds of parliamentary duties. As a child, I was often taken to Sunday concerts at the Queen's Hall, alas destroyed by bombs during the war. My earliest encounter with musicians was probably my meeting with Sir Thomas Beecham. I wrote to him saying that I was aged eight and was one of his fans — might I be allowed to come round and see him after a concert to pay my respects? The message came back that Sir Thomas would be very pleased to see me. My mother and I duly arrived in his dressing room, where he gave me a warm welcome. He asked whether I was attending the following Sunday concert as well and if so, where would I be sitting. I said, rather precociously: 'In my usual place in the front row'. On the following Sunday Sir Thomas mounted the podium with tremendous dignity — turned round, saw me, and gave me an enormous wink. My day was made.

The stories about Beecham are legion and most of them true. I like particularly the one of Beecham travelling in a non-smoking compart-ment of a train when a lady asked whether Sir Thomas would mind if she smoked. 'Provided', replied Beecham 'that you don't mind my being sick!' 'Sir', replied the lady, 'I don't think you know who I am. I am one of the director's wives'. 'I don't mind, Madam, if you are the director's only wife, I should still be sick!'

Throughout my life, music has always played an important part. Marion's dowry included her close friendships with many leading musicians. She herself had grown up in Vienna in a musical world, as the daughter of Erwin Stein, an eminent musicologist, and was herself a pianist. Amongst her early recollections are her father's colleagues and friends, the composers Alban Berg and Anton von Webern, and indeed Schoenberg, the founder of the Second Viennese School. When the Stein family sought refuge in the UK in 1938, she came to know Benjamin Britten, who was to be a life-long inspiration. I first met Ben at a gala concert at Covent Garden, 'Fanfare to Britain', in 1973, to celebrate our joining the European Community. Marion introduced us, and I noticed that he was wearing his Order of Merit back to front. I had the temerity to point this out, to which he replied that he was aware of this, but if the decoration was worn the other way round, it carried the words 'For Merit', which he found somewhat embarrassing!

Sadly, I only really got to know him after he had had major surgery, shortly after our wedding. He never fully recovered from the operation, and therefore I did not have the privilege of hearing him either as a conductor or as a pianist. Over the years, I have come to know and love his music, and I have heard all his operas in many parts of the world. Ben was blessed with many qualities in addition to his musical genius. His hatred of war and violence led him to write 'War Requiem', which was first performed in the rebuilt Coventry Cathedral, which had been destroyed in the war. He and Peter Pears showed great courage in returning from the US at the height of the war in 1942 on the first available boat, knowing that as conscientious objectors, he and Peter would have to face a tribunal, which could, as in the case of Michael Tippett, involve being sent to prison. Given the short time I knew him, I was aware of his powers of perception and his compassion for people and causes.

Peter Pears was not only a great singer, but unlike all too many of his colleagues, he was conspicuous in his clear articulation of words. Certainly, there was never any doubt in what language he was singing! His superb technique, which had exemplified his long career, enabled him to make his debut at the Metropolitan Opera in New York at the age of sixty-four, in Britten's opera 'Death in Venice'. Amongst his many interests he had a flair for collecting pictures, often by as yet unknown young artists. He and Ben amassed a large library of scores and books, which formed the nucleus of what is now the Britten-Pears Library at Aldeburgh. Most importantly, the Library contains a unique collection of the composer's manuscripts. After Ben's death, the Treasury accepted a proportion of the manuscripts in lieu of death duties, vesting their ownership in the British Library. Through the persistence of two of Britten's executors, Isador Caplan and Donald Mitchell, and to the credit of the British Library and the Treasury, the manuscripts were allowed to remain on permanent loan in Aldeburgh at the Britten–Pears Library. As a result, the Library now houses a unique concentration of the work of one composer, to the great benefit of scholars and students of his music.

The great Russian cellist and musician, Mstislav Rostropovich, and his wife, the soprano Galina Vishnevskaya, are also close friends. Apart from his musicianship, Slava is a man of immense courage. He gave shelter to Alexander Solzhenitsyn at a time when he was *persona non grata* with the Soviet authorities. For this and his opposition to the totalitarian regime, he himself fell from favour. He and his wife were granted temporary leave of absence to perform abroad, but learned from a radio broadcast that they had been stripped of their Soviet citizenship. With the advent of Yeltsin, Slava flew into Moscow unannounced to play his cello as an act of solidarity. Their citizenship has now been restored.

As a musician he is superb — the sound that he is able to draw from his cello is magical and almost has the variety of a full symphony orchestra. I once asked him how he had acquired the scratch mark down one side of his Stradivarius. 'Oh', said Slava, 'Napoleon'. At the time before spikes were fitted to the base of the cello, the player had to hold the instrument in place with one foot wedged into the waist of the cello. The story goes that Napoleon had asked Duport, the owner of the Strad, whether he might be allowed to play the instrument, which was readily conceded. But Napoleon forgot that he was wearing spurs, hence the scratch mark.

I mention two examples of Slava's immense sense of humour. On Peter Pears's seventieth birthday, there was a concert at the Snape Maltings Concert Hall in his honour. In the course of the concert Murray Perahia, who was taking part in the programme, announced that although Rostropovich's commitments made it impossible for him to fly over from America to play at this special concert, nevertheless he had sent one of his most promising pupils to play on his behalf. The most drab looking woman in a faded green dress, straw hat and never-to-be-forgotten yellow plastic shoes appeared on the stage. She sat down to polite applause and after what seemed

Peter Pears, Galina Vishnevskaya, Benjamin Britten,
Mstislav Rostropovich and Marion, Red Square,
Moscow, March 1963

like an eternity, took off her hat, started to unbutton her dress and lo, underneath, dressed in a dinner jacket, was Rostropovich! It was a total surprise to everyone.

After the Aldeburgh Festival in 1968, Slava, Ben and Marion were driving to Rose Hill in Cumberland, where Ben and Slava were due to give a recital. They planned to spend the night on the way up at Harewood House. Slava was most anxious to know how protocol indicated that he should address the Princess Royal, who would be at Harewood. 'I take it I curtsy', said Slava. He was told that this was quite the wrong thing to do and that she would be acutely embarrassed. The next day or so before leaving Aldeburgh, Slava was seen walking up the High Street, stopping every now and then practising his curtsy. When the party, en route for Harewood, reached Lincoln for lunch, Slava reverted to his intention to curtsy to the Princess Royal. At that stage Ben realised that there was a very real likelihood of Slava doing just this. He entreated Slava to put the idea out of his head and said: 'I'll do anything within reason if you promise not to curtsy'. 'Anything?' said Slava. 'Then will you write me six unaccompanied cello suites in return for my agreeing not to curtsy?' Ben agreed, and a contract was drawn up on the back of the hotel menu. Three cello suites were written before Ben's death.

When the Benjamin Britten opera theatre was opened at the Royal College of Music, various bigwigs were invited to place some contemporary object or document under the foundation stone. Slava's contribution was a copy of the Lincoln hotel contract.

Slava was invited to play at our musical evening at Covent Garden, which was generously lent to Marion and myself to celebrate our wedding in 1973. The authorities in Moscow deliberately prevaricated and in essence refused him permission to travel to the UK despite the fact that a senior member of the Foreign Office had personally spoken to Gromyko about the invitation. When Slava was eventually to come to the UK he offered to give a charity concert to make up for our disappointment. We were lent Exeter Cathedral, and I chose the Barnstaple Parish Church Appeal Fund and the Caroline Thorpe Children's Fund as the benefiting charities. The cathedral was packed out on a glorious September evening to hear Slava play a programme of three unaccompanied Bach suites. He took the West Country by storm.

Another landmark in my life was Yehudi Menuhin, whose death is deeply mourned by the countless number of people who knew and loved him. The first soloist I heard was Yehudi with his sister, Hepzibah, at the Queen's Hall in 1937, when I was eight. Exactly forty years later at the Albert Hall, Yehudi played at the Liberal Party centenary concert, when my son, Rupert, also aged eight, heard his first soloist, who again was Yehudi.

To celebrate his twenty-first birthday on 14 November 1969, Prince Charles held a musical evening at Buckingham Palace, at which Yehudi played. Driving home, my wife Caroline remarked: 'I suppose one of the great advantages of being the Prince of Wales is that you can get Yehudi Menuhin to play for you specially'. After her death, I received a letter of sympathy from Sir Robert Mayer saying that if ever he could be of help I must let him know. Recalling our

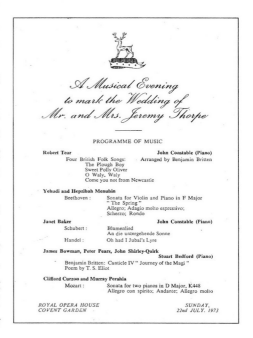

A Musical Evening to mark the Wedding of Mr. and Mrs. Jeremy Thorpe

PROGRAMME OF MUSIC

Robert Tear   John Constable (Piano)
     Four British Folk Songs: Arranged by Benjamin Britten
         The Plough Boy
         Sweet Polly Oliver
         O Waly, Waly
         Come you not from Newcastle

Yehudi and Hepzibah Menuhin
     Beethoven :   Sonata for Violin and Piano in F Major
         "The Spring"
         Allegro; Adagio molto espressivo;
         Scherzo; Rondo

Janet Baker   John Constable (Piano)
     Schubert :   Blumenlied
         An die untergehende Sonne
     Handel :   Oh had I Jubal's Lyre

James Bowman, Peter Pears, John Shirley-Quirk
               Stuart Bedford (Piano)
     Benjamin Britten: Canticle IV " Journey of the Magi "
     Poem by T. S. Eliot

Clifford Curzon and Murray Perahia
     Mozart :   Sonata for two pianos in D Major, K448
         Allegro con spirito; Andante; Allegro molto

ROYAL OPERA HOUSE   SUNDAY,
COVENT GARDEN   22nd JULY. 1973

Jeremy and Marion Thorpe with Yehudi Menuhin at Chuggaton, July 1981

conversation following the Palace concert, and on a sudden impulse, I picked up the telephone and rang Sir Robert to ask him whether it would be thought very presumptious for him to inquire whether Yehudi Menuhin would be able to play at Caroline's memorial service. Within ten minutes Yehudi was on the telephone to me to ask very diffidently whether I would like him to play at the service. It was a wonderfully generous offer; Yehudi played Bach's unaccompanied Chaconne, and, with Robert Masters, the slow movement of Bach's Double Violin Concerto. It was a sublime and moving experience.

Yehudi, with his sister Hepzibah, also played at the Covent Garden wedding concert, and chose Beethoven's Spring Sonata for Violin and Piano. It was an evening of the giants, with Clifford Curzon and Murray Perahia playing Mozart's Sonata for two pianos in D major; James Bowman, Peter Pears, John Shirley-Quirk and Steuart Bedford (piano), sang Benjamin Britten's Fourth Canticle — 'The Journey of the Magi'; Janet Baker sang

Schubert and Handel and Robert Tear four British Folksongs arranged by Benjamin Britten. The evening was a great tribute to Marion, that so many of her friends should have readily agreed to take part in that marvellous musical occasion.

During Marion's presidency of the South West Arts Association, it was suggested that to mark the Association's twenty-fifth anniversary there should be an event known as 'President's Choice' — the President to decide whom to invite and where to stage the concert. It was against this background that a packed parish church at South Molton in North Devon had the privilege to hear Yehudi play. Yehudi and Slava, in their different ways have espoused great causes outside and beyond music. I doubt whether there are any personalities in the world of music who are more beloved in their lifetime for their artistry, compassion and humanity.

One of the first events in my marriage is that within six months Marion made me a grandfather (albeit a step-) without any intervening generation. There are now eleven grandchildren, each of whom is devoted to their grandmother, who in turn takes an intense interest in the life of each one of them. The same deep affection is felt by the four sons — the three Lascelles, David, James and Jeremy, and the Thorpe — Rupert. I am a very lucky man.

Marion has a great gift of adapting herself to new situations. Within less than a year of our marriage she was pitched into the February 1974 general election, with the intensive campaigning, principally by helicopter, all over the UK, which this involved. There was also the North Devon constituency which was highly marginal and needed tending. Throughout the campaign Marion gave out warmth and friendliness, warmly appreciated and returned in full measure.

Throughout our marriage there have been many many happy moments and some less so, but there was always the background of music: Aldeburgh, with its coastline and Festival; Chuggaton and its garden, and above all we are blessed with some very wonderful and supportive friends.

Marion is now chairman of the Britten-Pears Foundation. This takes an increasing amount of her time, but it is a labour of love. She brings to this, as to everything else that she touches, a calm, imaginative and wise counsel. For my part no man could have a more perfect companion.

Chapter Two

Early Years

The violin

I started learning the violin at an early age. My teacher was Ruth Araujo, herself a pupil of Jelly d'Aranyi, who was the great niece of the renowned violinist Joachim. I therefore had distinguished ancestry to instruct me. My mother would practise with me and accompany me on the piano. At my pre-prep school (Wagner's) in Queensgate, the headmaster announced at a school concert: 'Thorpe will play', and then 'Mrs Thorpe will accompany'. The curtains were drawn back. She always swore that her nerves were worse than mine. I continued studying the violin during my years at school in America. But it was later at Eton that there were real opportunities for progress.

Edward Boyle, who was amongst the best informed people on almost every subject, long felt that there was insufficient encouragement given to string playing at Eton, and therefore presented a cup to be competed for annually by string players. There were three of us, all first violins in the school orchestra, who were level pegging: Eustace Gibbs, who went on to the Foreign Office; Simon Streatfield, who went on to play the viola in various internationally known orchestras, and myself. In 1944 I won the cup, playing one of the Beethoven Romances. In 1945 I over-reached myself by playing the slow movement of Mendelssohn's Violin Concerto. I still do not know how I managed the double stoppings — maybe I didn't! Eustace won. In 1946, I played a real old teashop piece by Wieniawski and won back the cup.

The school orchestra took itself very seriously, but looking back as dispassionately as possible, I think in fact we were surprisingly good. We tackled Beethoven's Symphonies numbers 1, 5 and 8; once, for a glorious orgy without audience and solely for our own self-indulgence, we played all three symphonies one after another. What was the most exciting event for me was when Simon and I played the first two movements of the Bach Double Concerto with orchestra.

We had a variety of conductors. Dr Henry Lee, the precentor, used to mortify us by referring to us, the orchestra, as 'Band'. This was in part a Freudian slip, because although he was one of the finest organists in Europe, he was criticised for playing too loudly. Matters came to a head — literally — when a large piece of plaster under the organ loft broke off while he was playing at his very loudest, and fell to the ground, narrowly missing an elderly beak (master). The situation was saved by the daughter of a previous provost, who said that when she went to church she did like a holy hullaballoo, and Dr Lee must keep up the volume! We were also conducted by Dr Thomas Dunhill; I particularly remember his Sea Shanties and reflecting what an experience it was to learn the innermost thoughts and feelings about a piece which the conductor had composed himself. Dr Sidney Watson was another maestro. I am afraid we were rather unkind to him. He had a terrible stutter, and for some unknown reason he was always stumped when trying to say 'double bar'. At rehearsal we made a point of making some mistake, which would inevitably require him to instruct us to go back to the double bar!

Mention must be made of music in my House at Eton, attributable to my dame, Norah Byron, who was in charge of the well-being of the boys in the House. She was an accomplished musician and viola player and however esoteric the combinations of instruments in the House — for example two bassoons, one French horn, a clarinet and a violin — she would make a brilliant arrangement of an existing piece of music to bring in all the players available.

I wondered whether I should take up the violin professionally, but early on decided that I would not be good enough to succeed either as an orchestral player or, still less, as a soloist.

My violin, an early instrument by the English maker William Hill, has upon occasion been lent to young musicians who lacked an adequate instrument. This leads me to mention a campaign which I intend to wage to persuade museums who have priceless instruments in their collections to lend them out to reputable performers who cannot afford to buy an instrument worthy of their talents. Instruments need to be played, and deteriorate if not put to use. Perhaps as a compromise, great museums who have these rare possessions should stage concerts on their premises, drawing on their own collections.

Chinese ceramics

My interest in Chinese art began at an early age. I admired and coveted three paintings on rice paper which hung in my parents' bedroom. One was of a Chinese junk and the other two of an Emperor and an Empress. With those pictures happily hanging in my own room, having been surrendered by my parents, I started collecting. I gave a talk to the Eton College Archaeological Society, on the T'ang Dynasty (960–1279 AD). This was arguably the greatest period of the flowering of the arts in China. It produced China's greatest painter, Wu Tao Tzu, the court poet; Li Tai Po and the poet/painter, Wang Wei, of whom it was said that his poems were paintings and his paintings poems. It was a period which produced some of the most magnificent pottery objects such as horses, camels, warriors, lady instrumentalists, birds and farm animals — some glazed, some unglazed. These figures were buried with the dead to attend to their needs.

The Han Dynasty (206 BC–220 AD) was more severe but also produced superb funerary objects. The Sung Dynasty (96–1280 AD) produced celadon and very fine jade and with the Ming Dynasty (1358–1643 AD), one immediately thinks of blue and white china.

One of my great excitements was to be invited by the Greek, British-born banker, George Eumorfopolous, to see his superb collection of Chinese art. It must have certainly been one of the greatest private collections of all time. An indication of its breathtaking dimensions was that he sold the entire collection jointly to the British Museum and the Victoria and Albert Museum. Being a generous benefactor, he sold the collection for a nominal total of £100,000, it being worth millions even in those days.

His collection was displayed in large glass cases on a whole floor of his house in Cheyne Walk. He would hand me some priceless object and with great modesty would say: 'Some people think this is rather beautiful'. His whole collection was photographed and published in catalogue form by Benn Brothers. He gave me several pieces of Han pottery, all of which featured in the catalogue. At one stage my mother wrote to George Eumorfopoulos to say he mustn't feel that he had to give me something every time I went to visit him; it was bad for me and an imposition upon him.

Another mentor was Peter Sparks of John Sparks, Chinese Art Dealers in Mount Street. When I was in my late teens he told me that there would always be a place for me in the Gallery and that in due course I would inherit the business from him. It was a great temptation.

Bagatelle at Dorneywood

One of the prize outings from Eton was to bicycle over to Burnham Beeches to call on Lord Courtauld-Thomson, who lived in a very splendid Queen Anne house called Dorneywood. Having no heirs, and being a rich man, he left the house and its contents to the nation for the use of a cabinet minister. The Prime Minister had his official residence at Chequers. The Foreign Secretary now uses Chevening and the present occupant of Dorneywood is the Chancellor of the Exchequer.

I bicycled from Eton on several occasions and more often than not, Simon Barrington-Ward (subsequently the Bishop of Coventry) came with me. Courtauld, welcoming our arrival, would say: 'You two gentlemen are two of the most remarkable travellers in Buckinghamshire'.

In his dining room there was a case of richly bound leather books, one of which stuck out slightly from the rest, and had inscribed on its spine the title: 'The Way to the Billiards, by Courtauld-Thomson'. It turned out to be a door handle, which did indeed lead to the billiard room. Amongst his possessions in the games room was a bagatelle board, attached to which was the Golden Book, recording those who had exceeded 1,000 points at bagatelle. In December 1942 Churchill came over from Chequers to lunch with Courtauld and to see the house. He tried his luck at the bagatelle board, and having failed to score 1,000 points, asked if he could borrow the board, so that he could practise at Chequers. There is a certificate at Dorneywood from Chequers, Butler's Cross, Aylesbury, Bucks., which says: 'This is to certify at 16.00 on Sunday 6 December Mr Churchill scored 1015 (one thousand and fifteen) points at bagatelle in our presence. Signed Louis Mountbatten. Certified as to addition: Lord Cherwell, Averill Harriman. Received 8 December 1942'.

It is of some comfort to know that Churchill was able to relax at the height of the war.

This was part of the general tour of the house which Simon and I found fascinating. I remember that there was a Georgian cabinet which was a *trompe l'oeil,* depicting a variety of objects, from silver spoons to crystal jam pots. He had a matching but real cabinet made, and spent years collecting objects to match the painted ones. In the hall I remember a particularly fine landscape of Dorneywood by Rex Whistler, who was tragically killed early in the war. In the bedrooms, there was a printed notice saying: 'It's particularly requested that no gratuities be given to the indoor or outdoor staff'. We asked Lord Courtauld-Thomson the reason for this, to which he replied: 'Firstly, there is often embarrassment as to how much and to whom tips should be given. Secondly, I want to invite people who might not be able to afford wholesale tipping. And thirdly, I am a rich man, and do not deserve to keep a staff if I do not pay them properly, so that they are not dependent on tips for their income.'

Simon and I presented him, and hence the house, with a mother-of-pearl card case, which matched one already in his possession, as a small token of our gratitude for his hospitality. I gather both still exist, but are locked in a cupboard for safe keeping.

One of Courtauld's rather charming follies was to commission a series of stained glass windows in a converted barn, to tell the story of his life, 'so that in the future people would know who the old gentleman was who left the house to the nation'. The windows therefore include his coat of arms, his places of education and his livery company. The last time I saw him he asked me to come and help him advise the stonemason on drawings for his tomb in the local churchyard. It should require no upkeep and not be too grand.

He was an instructive and enchanting person for whom I have retained great gratitude and affection.

The Bar

I was called to the Bar in 1954 and served a pupillage with Rodger Winn. Later I gained experience in criminal law in the chambers of Edward Cussen. I started with the usual mix of magistrate's courts and county courts and once made the rarefied atmosphere of the Court of Appeal, presided over by Lord Goddard. I joined the Western Circuit and built up a practice which involved appearances in Exeter and Plymouth.

It became apparent to me when I was elected as MP for North Devon in 1959, as one of only six Liberals in the House of Commons, that the job would be full time. Solicitors upon whom one depended for briefs would realise my preoccupation with politics, which was hardly the climate in which to build up the practice. I therefore retired within a matter of a few weeks after my election.

I remember very vividly a case before Bridgwater Sessions when I was appearing for a man accused of drunken driving. The undisputed evidence was that he hit a car containing the Superintendent of Police and his Deputy, followed by another car containing four police constables. All six gave evidence against him. After a two-day fight the jury must have obviously felt: 'But for the grace of God, there go we'. And he was acquitted. I felt this was a suitable moment to retire and remind myself to be very careful when driving through Bridgwater.

A really hair-raising attempt to combine my Bar practice with my television commitments occurred when I was appearing before the stipendiary magistrate in Bow Street. I asked him at the beginning of the hearing whether he would be following the usual procedure of rising at four o'clock that afternoon. Were it otherwise, I would find myself in difficulty. He was helpful in indicating that he would rise at the usual time. As four o'clock approached (3.58, to be precise) he showed no signs of calling it a day. So I respectfully reminded him of his declared intention. He agreed to adjourn the case and asked when it would be possible for me to return to the court, so that he could continue the case. I thanked him and said I would be back in between thirty-five and forty minutes. This was accepted. I left the court as rapidly as I could and grabbed a taxi and made for Associated Rediffusion Television in Kingsway. I was in the studio by 4.25 P.M., interviewing Lady Mountbatten on world relief. Back in the taxi, I made for Bow Street and was back in the court taking part in the adjourned hearing of the case. The whole incident showed the extreme difficulty in combining two, if not three, careers at the same time.

Committee of Privileges

Before becoming an MP, I was retained to advise the editor of a local newspaper whose case was referred to the Committee of Privileges of the House of Commons. During the Suez crisis a strict rationing regime was introduced for petrol. MPs received a special allowance which, to put it mildly, was regarded as generous. True to form, John Junor for the *Sunday Express* weighed in to castigate MPs for their behaviour, and was promptly referred to the Committee of Privileges. The Committee ruled that he was in contempt of the House of Commons and was duly required to appear at the Bar of the House to apologise, which he did. At the same time a Mr Dooley, the Editor of the *Romford Recorder,* had made his criticism manifest and was likewise referred to the Committee of Privileges. I took the view that MPs had been looking after themselves rather generously and that he might consider running the defence of justification. I advised that he should petition the House for leave to be represented by counsel before the Committee of Privileges and, if necessary, at the Bar of the House. We lodged our petition, which was an exact copy of that of John Wilkes in the eighteenth century, which we obtained from the Public Record Office.

The Committee met and obviously decided that this thing had gone far enough and recommended no action. Dooley was in favour of having a press conference to mark this outcome. I advised him that, as a matter of courtesy, he should write to the Chairman of the Committee of Privileges that he intended to make known the recommendation of the Committee. By return a messenger arrived with a note pointing out that by resolution of the House of Commons in 1837, all matters referred to the Committee of Privileges are themselves privileged unless and until the report of which they are a part has been considered by the House. The House never considered the Dooley case and therefore the outcome was not generally known. Nonetheless it was a valuable corrective for Parliament in its relations with the citizen.

Twelve writs for libel

One of the most memorable cases in which I was involved related to Colonel Douglas Roe — a larger-than-life personality, with infinite charm and a bubbling sense of humour. He had founded a co-operative egg packing station and was a pioneer in date-stamping eggs, as well as the number of the operative who examined the eggs to see that they had neither bloodspots nor any other imperfections. This was years ahead of its time, although now it is common practice.

Having reached his mid-seventies, he was prepared gradually to hand over responsibility to his younger colleagues at the marketing association known as 'Supremo' (Somerset Poultry Marketing Association). A clash was inevitable. If common sense had prevailed, they should have made him president with a pension, and listened to what he had to say, in return for which he would have relinquished executive activities.

At one board meeting he was asked if he would kindly mind leaving the meeting, as they wanted to discuss his pension. The minutes secretary was ill, so they decided to tape the whole meeting and omitted to turn it off while he was out of the room. Another secretary typed up the record of the proceedings, and sent a copy to each of the directors, including Colonel Roe. The chairman of the meeting asked: 'How do we get rid of the old man?' to which a colleague replied: 'We've got to be jolly careful since when we need an overdraft, he is the only one the bank will listen to'. Another member said: 'It looks as if we will need to stage a coup'.

Being fully informed of the intention of the board, I was retained by the Colonel to advise and act for him. He called an Extraordinary General Meeting. A leaflet was prepared and approved by me for distribution to all the members, which said: 'What they say in public and what they say in private about Col. Roe'. Our leaflet was in red, and the board reacted by issuing a reply on a blue leaflet, which I advised was highly defamatory. In my view, he would win a libel action but would need to sue eleven directors and the company secretary. If he lost, the costs would be astronomical and would break him. Before taking the final decision I would ask a QC, who was an old friend, to give us his assessment without a fee. I therefore approached Archie Marshall (who subsequently became a High Court Judge), and he agreed to express his opinion, which concurred with mine. I also advised the Colonel that the board would wait until the last minute to settle the action, hoping that he might withdraw. His reaction was: 'I am an old soldier; this is a battle which must be fought'. The day before the action was to be heard in the High Court, they settled and the battle was won.

ITV

I must confess that prior to the introduction of Independent Television (ITV) in 1955 I had serious apprehensions that advertisers would sponsor programmes that would lead to the lowest common denominator. Mercifully the Conservative government, with a degree of imagination, proposed that TV companies should produce and provide the programmes and merely sell advertising time in the slots which were known as 'natural breaks'. Another aspect on which ITV should be commended was the insistence that the consortia applying for franchises should have a fair sprinkling of local interests to ensure that in the case of small companies they would not be swamped by the giants. What I find incredible is the move by a Conservative government to allow existing companies to take over, and/ or swallow whole, the smaller companies. In my view this is a serious challenge to regional minority interests, and it is to be hoped that this policy will be reversed.

Early on, ITV struck a blow for freedom of speech. By the rule known as the 'Fourteen Day Rule', the government prohibited discussion by the broadcasting authorities of any subject which would be raised or might be raised within the next fourteen days in the House of Commons. Imagine the effect of that today. What was staggering was that not only was the rule obeyed but that it was introduced in the first place. I was asked how ITV should react to this restriction. My advice was: 'Ignore it, it will die a natural death' — which it did.

I first appeared on BBC television with Gilbert Harding in 1952 in a programme called 'Teleclub' for young people. Gilbert horrified the BBC by asking me questions of a political content which the producers were determined to exclude on this kind of programme. I was not invited again for a long time.

ITV, however, was enormously exciting, and at its inception I would appear on two or three different programmes a week. I gave a series of law lectures for schools for Rediffusion but inadvertently the recording tapes were wiped, so that no record exists. I chaired the scientific brains trust, 'The Scientist Replies'. I remember on one occasion I chaired a panel of four Fellows of the Royal Society. One of them, whose blushes I will spare, travelled up to London overnight by sleeper from Penzance. Outside

Falmouth he sensed an overpowering smell of burning and pulled the communication cord to stop the train. The railway people conceded that there was an acrid smell, but could find no trace of burning. The train proceeded on its journey and safely delivered the Professor, who went to take breakfast at the Athenaeum (where else?!). On opening his briefcase he got a horrible shock: two chemicals in glass phials had leaked and joined forces to render the contents a soggy mess of illegible burnt-out paper, including his notes for the programme!

Another alarming incident I recall on the programme was when one of those giant cameras operated by a seated driver got out of control and, like some mechanised dinosaur, bore down on me where I was seated at a table, with my scientists either side. The red light was off which showed that the camera was not being used for filming. I resolved that I would carry on, concentrating on cameras one and three as if nothing was wrong. Only when the camera actually hit the table would we beat a retreat. When it was within inches of the table, some benefactor pulled out the plug and the camera halted in its tracks! Another memorable instance was when I was conducting an interview during which a pneumatic drill came through the ceiling! We just carried on.

'This Week': King Hussein dispenses justice

In 1958 I was asked by 'This Week' to go to Jordan. Apparently there were three known assassination plots against King Hussein, and although it sounded ghoulish, the programme wished to cover any such possible crises. One trouble spot was Irbid, which the King included in his speaking tour. I was positioned on the balcony of the town hall, from which the King was to address the crowds. The King arrived, preceded by the Household Cavalry in their red tunics and astrakhan caps. He received a tumultuous welcome from the men in the street and from the women, separated from the men on the roofs opposite. There were two exceptions: two women had positioned themselves by the main door, and I learnt that they were the mothers of two young men who had been caught gunrunning across the Syrian-Jordanian border, and were involved in a plot against the King. They were due to be executed the following morning. The mothers had come to plead for their sons' lives. The head of Arab Radio, Abu Zeld, told me that the King would be making a dramatic statement.

In the course of his speech, the King said: 'At this moment there are two young men who have plotted against the Hashemite dynasty and against the best interests of my people. They will be executed at dawn tomorrow.' At this, all the women started wailing, and Hussein then ordered the two men to be brought before him from the central jail. They duly appeared handcuffed. Hussein proceeded to address them: 'You have been discovered smuggling guns across the border, with the ultimate object of overthrowing the regime. Tomorrow you will be executed. What a waste of human resources. If I spare your lives, will you dedicate yourselves to the service of my people and to the greater glory of Jordan?'

To put it mildly, they hadn't got much option, and swiftly agreed. Then Hussein said: 'Remove their handcuffs. They are free.' The crowd went wild and started shouting: 'Long live Hussein, long live Hussein!' He had shown panache and, as it turned out, had made a shrewd decision. Whatever assassination plans had been made must have been swiftly abandoned.

'This Week': The Shah of Iran bites on the bullet

'This Week' was a constant source of excitement. I would be rung up and asked whether, at a few hours' notice, I could go out with a camera team to some part of the world currently in the news. One such visit was to Iran in July 1961 to interview the Shah. He started off his reign as a reformer, dissolving the ultra-conservative Majlis (Parliament), and actively distributing title deeds of royal lands to peasants.

On arrival in Tehran, we were told that the Shah would be flying to Azerbaijan to give out land titles, leaving his private airfield at seven the next morning. He would give us an interview before take-off. I insisted that in view of the earliness and limited time made available to us, it was essential to get all the equipment in place and fully tested the night before.

The next morning, the Shah drove up on the dot of seven o'clock and said: 'I gather you want an interview. Do you need to use the cameras?' Somewhat puzzled, I replied: 'Yes, Your Majesty. The alternative would be

Interviewing the Shah of Iran for the Rediffusion programme 'This Week', July 1961

your voice over a still photograph.' 'When were the cameras brought down?' he asked. 'It was last night, sir', I replied. The Shah turned to the head of security for a private discussion seemingly arising from our presence. After a few moments, the Shah agreed to give us a filmed interview. Following his departure, I asked the head of security what on earth the discussion had been about. He asked me whether I had noticed a hairline crack by the Shah's mouth. He went on to tell me that the Shah had been photographed opening a new extension to the university, and amongst the battery of cameras was one containing a revolver, which was fired at him. One bullet went through his mouth and one through his shoulder. The Shah was immediately driven off to the hospital and the incident was hushed up. He was, therefore, not unnaturally somewhat inhibited about facing cameras. Our decision to bring down the cameras the night before was therefore wiser than we thought, since it had given the authorities the opportunity to inspect them for security.

Chief commentator for the network

About this time, Paul Adorian of Associated Rediffusion told me that the programme companies were considering creating the position of chief commentator for the network. Would I be interested? If so, he would like to put forward my name. I asked him how this would affect my position as a prospective parliamentary candidate. He replied that, amongst other things, I would be expected to mastermind the the presentation of the general election results on television, and therefore I would have to relinquish my candidature. In fact, if I were returned in any subsequent election I would have gained a lot of national publicity; I would therefore be more likely to get elected and to get office. I told him that I did not belong to that sort of party. Then he said: 'If that means you are a Liberal, surely you won't ever get elected?' I told him that I was likely to win North Devon even though it might be the only gain in the whole country, but if I was wrong, I would be tempted to reconsider his offer. In practice the North Devon and Torrington constituencies, next-door neighbours, represented the one Liberal gain and one Liberal loss of the whole 1959 election.

I was in fact signed up to do the commentary covering the route for Churchill's funeral, whenever that might occur. At the time he died I had been elected to Parliament and it was not felt right that one MP should take up such a role.

Chapter Three

Personalities

Lloyd George and his family

My family took holidays fairly regularly at Criccieth where Lloyd George and his wife, Dame Margaret, lived. My parents would stay with the Lloyd Georges at Brynawelon, whilst we children were farmed out to various boarding houses nearby, usually with the Lloyd George grandchildren. We therefore saw a lot of the previous generation, namely Olwen, Megan and Gwilym, all of whom were our honorary aunts and uncle. The friendship between the Thorpe and Lloyd George families has spanned five generations. It originated with the friendship between my mother and Megan who, as young girls, were launched on the London scene. Megan was to become my mother's bridesmaid, my sister's godmother and, in a different context, a parliamentary colleague. As an economy measure my grandfather let his London house 'one season', so my mother used No. 10 Downing Street as her London base. This could involve responsibilities — one evening Lloyd George came up to see the girls and announced that Mr Albert Thomas, the French Minister of Defence, was coming to breakfast the next morning; the Foreign Office interpreter was ill; that the two girls had had an expensive education and therefore would they please report at eight o'clock the next morning to act as interpreters in the discussions.

Years later, Megan and my mother went to Downing Street when Harold and Mary Wilson were the incumbents. Photographs of former Prime Ministers had previously been placed on the staircase but Lady Dorothy Macmillan, disliking their positioning, had had them moved to a corridor leading to the reception rooms, where they remained throughout the Macmillan and Douglas-Home periods. Harold and Mary Wilson had tried to get the photographs reinstated on the staircase, but the Ministry of Works would not react. When Megan and my mother reached the staircase, Megan asked why the Prime Ministers were no longer there, and, in particular,

J.H. Thorpe and Gwilym Lloyd-George dressed as the Emperor and Empress of Abyssinia seeking asylum, summer 1936 (photo taken by Ursula Thorpe with Box Brownie camera)

why her father's was behind the green baize door, hidden when it was hooked back. Mary Wilson welcomed this additional pressure and successfully had the Prime Ministers reinstated, where they now happily remain.

There was a family tradition of practical jokes involving much fun and laughter, which made the Lloyd George house in Wales such a delight to visit. My first meeting with Lloyd George took place on one such occasion in the summer of 1936 at the time of the Abyssinia crisis. Italy had annexed this country and the Emperor and Empress had fled into exile and were therefore in the news of the moment. My father, an eminent silk, and Gwilym, who subsequently became Home Secretary, decided to dress up as the Emperor and Empress of Abyssinia seeking political asylum. Lloyd George's arrival from his farm at Churt was awaited. The families lined up and as the youngest person present, I was deputed to hold aloft the flag of Wales. I doubt whether the Emperor would have been pleased with the charade, but Lloyd George thought the joke hilarious. I remember Dame Margaret giving me a prize apple from the crate which Lloyd George had brought from his farm and I thought at the time how much it matched her beautiful rosy complexion.

On another occasion, when I was not present, my father dressed up in a red wig, red beard and clerical collar and, accompanied by Megan, who was togged out in her nanny's bonnet and black 'go-to-chapel dress', called on Dame Margaret. The purpose of the visit was to invite her to open with prayers a series of children's services which were to be held on the beach at

Lloyd George arriving at Brynawelon — family lining route, Jeremy Thorpe holding flag; summer 1936 (photo: Ursula Thorpe)

Criccieth. Surprisingly, she did not recognise either of them and appeared somewhat flustered, apologising for the state of the room, and saying: 'Papers, papers everywhere. That's the worst of being married to a politician.' At this point, Lloyd George, who was hiding behind the screen, exploded with laughter, in which Dame Margaret joined!

My father and Dame Margaret were great fishermen. Occasionally she would knock on my parents' bedroom door early in the morning and say 'Thorpey, shall we go mackerel fishing?' They were both excellent sailors and impervious to rough seas. On one occasion, claiming the weather was very calm, they persuaded some family members to join them. However, the sea turned out to be much rougher than expected and everyone bar my father and Dame Margaret was beginning to feel very queasy, and exercised iron control not to be seasick! At that moment my father decided to put on a most awful, lurid green sweater. This was too much for the Lloyd George/Thorpe crew and they finally succumbed to an all-round bout of seasickness!

One Christmas the traditional game of charades was played. The subject matter is now forgotten, but the acting of the scene remains vivid. Sir Thomas Carey Evans, Lloyd George's son-in-law and husband of Olwen, and a distinguished surgeon, 'operated' on his wife and after much grunting and gesticulation triumphantly extracted from her an entire leg of lamb, which he held aloft!

Two dinner parties

The Carey Evans had moved into a house called Elsteddfa, a home which years before had belonged to the Carey Evans family. They had planned their first dinner party after moving in. Megan was miffed that she had not been included amongst the guests. My mother and I were staying with Megan, and she decided that we would make our displeasure known. Accordingly, our car was parked down the drive, and the three of us climbed into the house through an open window. We made for the room on the first floor directly above the dining room, where the dinner party was in full swing. On a signal from Megan, we jumped and jumped and jumped on the floor. Downstairs there was pandemonium; the chandelier in the dining room swung backwards and forwards; the floor sagged and the ceiling looked decidedly fragile. Uncle Tom Carey Evans rushed out with his two sons, Robin and Bengy, and dispersed in different directions on the first floor. Megan was hiding in a clothes cupboard and started to giggle. We hid ourselves as best we could, but Megan was discovered and the truth was out. The Carey Evans family was not best pleased, but the Lloyd George family sense of humour prevailed.

Lloyd George arriving at Brynawelon, summer 1936 (photo: Ursula Thorpe)

A slightly less dramatic dinner, but nevertheless one I shall not readily forget, was a dinner at Megan's house, Brynawelon, with my mother and myself. We had been served Jerusalem artichokes in a thick white sauce. My first bite was incredibly bitter, and I spat it out. I felt reminded of Dr Johnson, who spat out a mouthful of hot potatoes and glared at his neighbouring diners, saying: 'Yes, and any other fool would have swallowed it and ruined his digestion for life!' The artichokes were abandoned. After dinner we went into the kitchen to investigate. Megan saw a brown paper bag, in which there was one artichoke left. To her horror, she discovered that they were not artichokes, but Amaryllis bulbs, priced £1 each. They had been a recent present to Megan, unbeknownst to the cook! Our leftovers were fed to the chickens, who, I regret to say, all died.

One of the most fascinating political discussions which I remember involving Lloyd George took place in my mother's house at Limpsfield. Our guests were Field Marshal Viscount Slim, who had been Commander-in-Chief Burma, Major-General Fuller, who invented the tank, and Megan Lloyd George. Megan and Fuller, both of whom had met Hitler, compared their recollections of him.

The occasion when Megan met Hitler arose out of Lloyd George's meeting with Hitler at Berchtesgaden in 1936. Lloyd George had been anxious to make an assessment of Hitler and for his part, Hitler had a great admiration for Lloyd George and had many of his speeches translated into German. At the end of the morning meeting, Lloyd George told Hitler that he had two of his children with him, both of whom were MPs, who very much wanted to meet him. Hitler replied: 'Of course, let them come up for tea. Will they want music [which would have meant laying on a string quartet] or do they want to talk?' Not surprisingly they opted for the latter. Megan well remembered the scene. The tea was not to be at the Eagle's Nest, but at the Lower House. There were three large Mercedes, one of which was for Lloyd George, one for Megan and Gwilym and one for the guards. There was a long flight of stone steps from the house to the approach road and the sun was setting behind the mountain. Hitler started to walk down dressed in khaki uniform; Lloyd George advanced, cape and white hair flowing in the wind. They met half way. At the end of tea Lloyd George turned to Schmidt, the interpreter, and said: 'Would you remind the Führer that he has very kindly promised me his photograph'. This was duly passed on and three photographs in silver frames were produced. With an unmistakable twinkle in his eye, Lloyd George said: 'I have a lot of photographs at Churt and have considerable difficulty in arranging them. Would you object if I were to place your photograph next to those of

Clemenceau and Foch?' Hitler replied, slowly at first, that he would have no objection, since they were both patriots who had fought for their country, but he would never tolerate his photograph's being placed next to those of any of the German generals, who so basely surrendered in 1918. He then blew up about the future of Germany and ranted on for the next half hour.

Fuller recollected that he was on the reviewing stand at Nuremberg and watched the tanks go by. Hitler asked him: 'What do you make of your children?' 'I am not worried about my children', replied Fuller: 'What concerns me is the use to which they will be put by their guardians'.

Megan raised with Slim the question of U Saw of Burma. U Saw was a controversial character, having formed the Myochit Party and Galon Tat, which was a private army, in 1938. He was regarded as having strong sympathies with the Japanese cause. He was Prime Minister from 1940–42 and visited the UK and the USA in 1941, at which point he was thought to be sympathetic to the Western Allies. However, he contacted the Japanese Ambassador in Lisbon, indicating another switch of loyalties. He was arrested by the British in Cairo and kept in internment in Uganda from 1942–45. On returning to Burma after the war he reformed the Myochit Party and was wounded by a hireling suspected to be acting on behalf of Uang San, a prominent member of the government. However, in 1947 he travelled to London with Uang San and reached an agreement providing for the independence of Burma. On his return to Burma, he repudiated the agreement.

Megan asked Slim how he could be certain that U Saw wouldn't rat again. Slim's jaw tightened like a vice and he said: 'I told U Saw that if he defected again I would hunt him with the entire British army, and with his family present, in a clearing in the forest, would hang him upside down. He knew I meant it, as indeed I did.'

U Saw was heavily involved in the murder of a group of Burmese cabinet ministers. He was arrested in 1947 and charged with murder, and was hanged in May 1948.

The last time I saw Lloyd George was in 1944 at Bron-y-de at Churt, where I had tea with him. He was anxious to listen to the German news in English being broadcast from Germany and was obviously still incredibly well informed. I told him I had ambitions to become a Liberal MP, and he said: 'Always lean on your constituency'. By this he meant that before you took a highly unpopular line, as for example his own stance on behalf of the Boers in the South African War, your constituents should be taken into your confidence and made familiar with the arguments on an issue to which they may initially be strongly opposed. You should always ensure that your constituents know the reason you support a cause, which may at the time be unpopular. After tea we toured the orchards, with Lloyd George in a flowing cloak and with a shepherd's crook, looking every inch the Old Testament prophet.

David Lloyd George

Lord Hankey had been in both war cabinets and lived in our village, Limpsfield. On the strength of his experiences, I asked him which of the two was the greater war leader, Lloyd George or Churchill. He replied that only fifty years after their deaths would a balanced objective view be possible. He, himself, had had a row with Churchill and therefore could be said to be prejudiced. They were both Olympian figures, but that in his opinion, Lloyd George would lead by a photo-finish. In support of Hankey's view, it must be remembered that it was Lloyd George's inspiration and drive which placed the country on a war-time footing, against the hostility from the generals, and not without criticism from the House of Commons, as indeed was the case with Churchill. He transformed the output of munitions, created a general headquarters to coordinate the Allies and set up a war machine which had not existed before. It does not detract from Churchill's superb leadership in the Second World War to point out that he adopted and adapted many of Lloyd George's blueprints. Some time a book should be written comparing the methods and achievements of both war leaders.

I was privileged to give the address in Westminster Abbey on the occasion of the unveiling of Lloyd George's memorial stone by the Prince of Wales in July 1970. The original plan was that Harold Wilson, as Prime Minister, would give the address, and that Ted Heath, as Leader of the Opposition, and I, as Leader of the Liberal Party, would each read a lesson. However, the June election brought about a change of government, and Heath was Prime Minister. Dingle Foot, coming from a radical background, coordinated the service. He said to me: 'I'm damned if I am going to have a Tory Prime Minister delivering the tribute. You must do it, Jeremy.' It was a matter of days after my wife Caroline's fatal accident and although it was a colossal responsibility I saw merit in throwing myself into work; in any event Lloyd George has always been one of my heroes, so it was a labour of love.

The Rt Hon. Jeremy Thorpe, speaking at Westminster Abbey at 12 noon on Monday, 27 July 1970, on the occasion of the unveiling of a memorial stone to:
David Lloyd George
by his Royal Highness the Prince of Wales

Those of us who were present twenty-five years ago in this Abbey at Lloyd George's memorial service will feel that this recognition has not come a moment too soon.

Lloyd George had none of the advantages of birth or fortune. His father died before he was two years of age, and one can never over-estimate the debt which he owed to his uncle, Richard Lloyd, the shoemaker at Llanystumdwy, whose cottage became a home for Lloyd George, his widowed mother and brother. Uncle Lloyd determined that Lloyd George should become an advocate, and finding that the examinations required a knowledge of Latin and French, the cobbler, at fifty years of age, taught himself these languages so that he could in turn instruct David, who was then fifteen years old. Lloyd George duly qualified and, like Abraham Lincoln, of whose career he was a very close student, he started as an advocate; went on to establish a reputation as a superb orator; and as with Lincoln, eventually held the highest office, in which, without any military training, he proved himself to be a supremely successful war leader. Throughout Richard Lloyd's life, uncle and nephew would regularly correspond with each other on all the great issues of the day. And on one memorable occasion Richard Lloyd, by then an old man, was persuaded to leave Criccieth to make his first visit ever to London to hear a debate in the

The Prince of Wales unveiling the Lloyd George Memorial, Westminster Abbey, 27 July 1970

House of Commons and to spend the night at No. 11 Downing Street, where his nephew was ensconced as Chancellor of the Exchequer.

Lloyd George was a single-minded warrior. Before the First World War he was dedicated, in his own words, 'To wage implacable warfare against poverty'. With his colleagues, led by Asquith, and in the face of bitter opposition, he was the chief advocate of old age pensions and the main architect of unemployment benefit and national insurance. He thereby helped to lay the foundations of the welfare state. The fact that this involved the introduction of the 1909 Budget and a massive constitutional struggle with the House of Lords, was, if anything, something which he relished. Had his career ended in 1914 he would still rank with Shaftesbury and Wilberforce as one of the great social reformers of this country.

But from 1914–18 he was *literally* at war with those who threatened the very existence of this country. As Minister of Munitions, as Chancellor of the Exchequer and finally as Prime Minister, he placed this country on a total war footing. The story is told how Kitchener, as Secretary of State for War, advised the Minister of Munitions that four machine guns per battalion was sufficient for the army. Lloyd George's reaction was typical: 'Take Kitchener's maximum: square it; multiply that by two; and when you are in sight of that, double it again for good luck.' Accordingly, the British Army was provided with 250,000 machine guns. He overruled the First Sea Lord and introduced the convoy system; he created the concept of a War Cabinet and Allied Supreme Headquarters.

It is therefore particularly appropriate that his stone in the Abbey should lie near to the tomb of the Unknown Warrior. He was Prime Minister when the tomb was unveiled by King George V, and as Prime Minister was one of those responsible for its conception. Likewise it is right that his stone should lie hard by that of his friend and colleague of a lifetime, Winston Churchill. For these two men, as war leaders in the First and Second World Wars respectively, inspired this nation to resist the greatest dangers that it had faced since the days of Napoleon. Indeed, Churchill, Lloyd George and Chatham may be accounted the three greatest war leaders that this country has ever produced.

Churchill and Lloyd George were cabinet colleagues over sixty years ago. For Churchill their relationship must have been an unusual one. When Church-

The three party leaders — Edward Heath, Jeremy Thorpe and Harold Wilson — at the Lloyd George Memorial, Westminster Abbey, 27 July 1970

ill, who had rejoined the Conservative Party, became Chancellor of the Exchequer in 1924, the two men had already drifted apart. But Churchill soon after wanted to consult Lloyd George about a passage in the last volume of the *World Crisis.*Lord Boothby was requested to bring about a meeting. After Lloyd George had gone, Lord Boothby waited for a summons; none came; he went into the Chancellor's room to find Churchill brooding before the fire. 'How did it go?' he asked. 'It couldn't have gone better', Churchill replied. 'It is a remarkable thing that within a few minutes the old relationship was completely re-established.' He then looked up with a twinkle in his eye and added: 'The relationship of master and servant — and I was the servant.'

Both men had intense courage; both were the subject of bitter attacks throughout most of their careers. But their backgrounds could not differ more. Churchill was laid to rest at Bladon, within sight of Blenheim Palace, which for him must have symbolised the tradition and sense of history that inspired his life. Lloyd George was buried on the banks of the River Dwyfor, where he played as a child within sight of Snowdon: in the heart of the Welsh countryside from which he had drawn his strength and inspiration. Today the memory of both is intertwined in Westminster Abbey.

After the war Lloyd George was to leave office, never to return. But from 1928–36 he waged his third war, this time against unemployment. He had a genius for gathering around him men of the calibre of Maynard Keynes, Philip Kerr, William Beveridge and Walter Layton — and although his schemes for curing unemployment were never accepted by his own fellow countrymen, they were successfully adopted by Franklin Roosevelt and formed the basis of the 'New Deal'.

Lloyd George sat in Parliament for fifty-five years; a span in which he could count as colleagues his fellow Liberal, William Ewart Gladstone and fellow Celt, Aneurin Bevan.

As an orator he was without parallel. As a debater he was devastating. He was a brilliant conversationalist but equally a receptive listener. One of his most famous perorations is to be found in the speech which he made at the beginning of the war in which he described a valley in North Wales between the mountain and the sea and how the boys were in the habit of climbing the hill above the village. It was to be one of his first rallying cries to the nation: 'We have been living in a sheltered valley for generations. We have been too comfortable and too indulgent — many, perhaps, too selfish — and the stern hand of fate has scourged us to an elevation where we can see the everlasting things that matter for a nation — the high peaks we had forgotten of honour, duty, patriotism, and, clad in glittering white, the great pinnacle of sacrifice, pointing like a rugged finger to heaven.'

'We shall descend into the valleys again; but as long as the men and women of this generation last, they will carry in their hearts the image of those great mountain peaks whose foundations are not shaken, though Europe rock and sway in the convulsions of a great war.'

To me Lloyd George was 'taid', or grandfather. He loved children and I have memories of his white hair and flowing cloak, making a tour of his fruit trees at Churt or pointing out the names of the wild flowers in the hedgerows around Brynawelon at Criccieth. At his home there was laughter, brilliant conversation and he had an amazing ability, not always to be found with the great, to draw out each person there and make them feel they had something vital to contribute. Perhaps one of his greatest joys was when two of his children, Megan and Gwylim, joined him as Members of the House of Commons.

Baldwin said it would take ten men to write his life. But let Churchill's tribute suffice. 'He was the greatest Welshman which that unconquerable race has produced since the age of the Tudors.' Today he could be granted no greater national recognition than that his memorial stone, fashioned by two of Wales' greatest craftsmen, is to be unveiled by his Royal Highness the Prince of Wales here in the Abbey. Indeed Lloyd George, as a former Constable of Caernarvon Castle, was pre-eminent in recognising the historic significance of the Prince of Wales in the life of the Principality. But today we salute Lloyd George not only as a great Welshman but as a great statesman of Britain.

It was Churchill again who said: 'When the British history of the first quarter of the twentieth century is written, it will be seen that the greater part of our fortunes in peace and in war were shaped by this one man'.

Asquith's and Lloyd George's daughters

The Red Queen and the White Queen
[Article written for *Business and Professional Woman*, Spring 1970]

Two women have exercised a profound influence on my political life. Both were brilliant orators; both were a living link with the most exciting and turbulent periods in the life of this country; both were fearless in defence of great causes; both were daughters of dynamic Liberal Prime Ministers and in their loyalty to the memory of their respective fathers each became the symbol of the bitter dynastic struggles which split the Liberal Party.

For historical reasons neither liked the other. I adored both!

I refer of course to Lady Violet Bonham Carter, latterly Lady Asquith, and Lady Megan Lloyd George.

Had neither possessed qualities in their own right, the experiences which each had enjoyed during the political careers of their famous fathers would in themselves have been totally absorbing.

As a child of six, Violet Asquith was taken to No. 10 Downing Street to meet the formidable William Gladstone. Winston Churchill was one of her father's junior ministers, and her life-long friendship with him is contained in her brilliant and penetrating book, *Churchill as I Knew Him*.

For her the triumphs of the 1906 Government; the battle of the suffragettes; the bitter debates on House of Lords reform and the 1909 Budget were vivid memories. Indeed, she was in the Lords Gallery for most of the debates during the clash between the two Houses.

Lady Megan, like Lady Violet, spent part of her youth at No. 10. In 1916 Asquith fell from power and was succeeded by Lloyd George, so as a young girl Megan accompanied her father to the Peace Conference at Versailles and there met Woodrow Wilson, Clemenceau, Briand — in fact all the leading statesmen of Europe. In the '30s, with her father and brother Gwilym, she met Hitler at Berchtesgaden. Like Violet, she had met and usually knew every leading political figure of the past fifty years!

Both of these remarkable women were politicians to their fingertips. Megan sat in the Commons for over thirty years. Violet twice fought unsuccessfully to gain a seat in the Commons, and in 1964, after inexcusable pettiness had prevented her from becoming a life peeress, the present Prime Minister [Harold Wilson] on taking office immediately recommended her for a life peerage.

In appearance and in character they were totally different, but both drew much of their strength from their immediate family.

Megan I knew from childhood, since she had been my mother's bridesmaid. She was minute, with tiny but beautiful little hands and feet, and eyes that at once revealed her vivacity. She was a fierce Welsh patriot and was

Jeremy Thorpe and Megan Lloyd George at Criccieth

happiest in her garden in Criccieth which, in itself, was testimony to her good taste and extravagance! Her sense of fun was irrepressible.

Like Violet she was extraordinarily well read, an excellent broadcaster and a polished French speaker. Like Violet she would defend a colleague with whom she *agreed* like a tigress. In debate she could be formidable and would tear into her opponents with her left index finger crooked, jabbing the air — an identical gesture to that of her father.

Despite their antipathy, Violet and Megan agreed on countless radical issues — from opposition to appeasement in the '30s to the implementation of the Beveridge Report.

Violet in many ways was more intense. Once roused by an issue she would 'bear down' (her own phrase) on those whom she generally admired but who on a particular issue she felt misguided. One of the last to receive this treatment was the present Archbishop of Canterbury, over abortion reform, which Violet supported! I doubt if she ever compromised on any major principle in her life.

Her profile, her lucidity, her wit and courage are still a recent memory to millions of television viewers. What is not so well known is her service to the arts: Glyndebourne, the Old Vic, the BBC.

In debate her tongue could lacerate. As a relentless politician, within weeks of her death she was leading a deputation to the Prime Minister on Biafra and attending a European conference in The Hague.

In such a brief summary I can do justice to neither of these dynamic women. Both gave me their affection and their loyalty, which was returned in full measure.

Alas, both of them have now left the battlefield.

Platform gems: Lady Violet Bonham Carter (Lady Asquith of Yarnbury)
Violet Bonham Carter, the formidable daughter of Prime Minister Herbert Henry Asquith had, in common with Megan Lloyd George, a facility for

worshipping her father on a Chinese scale, which led Philip Guedalla to comment: 'In her youth, Violet Asquith over-indulged in mental incest'. In 1916, Lloyd George, then Chancellor of the Exchequer, displaced Asquith as Prime Minister. This created bitterness, the traces of which are still to be found.

One example of the Lloyd George/Asquith feud: in the 1951 general election, Violet, largely at the behest of Churchill, was not opposed by a Conservative candidate in the Colne Valley constituency, and actually had Churchill to speak in her support. Many Liberals felt that the straight fight was digestible, but the appearance of the Leader of the Conservative Party was not. At the meeting of the Liberal Party Council following the election, Frank Byers complained that Violet had made the task of Liberals fighting Conservatives more difficult and this was to be deplored. As far as Megan was concerned, she had been asked for messages of support for Labour candidates where no Liberal was standing. She steadfastly declined, and this was to be commended. Violet rose to reply: 'If', she said, 'having the greatest European and architect of victory in the Second World War on my platform was a sin, then I glory in my sin'. This was too much for Megan, who rose: 'Well, Colonel Byers, you are correct to say that certain Labour candidates did indeed ask me for messages of support, which I declined. If that be a virtue, then for my part, I glory in my virtue.'

I remember in particular two of Violet's speeches. The first was at the Torrington by-election in 1958, when the local MP, sitting as a National Liberal Conservative succeeded to his father's viscountcy, thereby causing a vacancy. Violet's son, Mark Bonham Carter, who had already fought the Bideford end of the seat when he had contested the old Barnstaple constituency in 1945, was invited to stand as Liberal candidate for the Torrington by-election. There has been some suggestion that Ambrose Fulford, the then current prospective Liberal candidate, was pushed aside to make way for Mark. This is far from the truth. The previous year at his home, Ambrose took Jo Grimond and me aside to say that he would fight a general election, but a by-election should have a national figure, and that in any event he was suffering from diabetes and was fully aware of the additional strains involved in a by-election as opposed to a general election.

Violet had deliberately been kept back to enable Mark to establish himself on his own account. When she did arrive, I drove her in my pocket-size

Austin A30 to a meeting in the Pannier Market at Okehampton. Violet was in sparkling form. Addressing the meeting, she said:

> I have been straining at the leash and am delighted to be here. Not surprisingly I have known the Liberal candidate longer and better than any of you, and I shall say a word about him in a moment. But first, what is the line-up? There is a Mr Leonard Lamb, appropriately named for the slaughter. We have yet to discover whether his socialism is of the palest pink or flaming crimson. Then there is Mr Royle, standing — please correct me if I have it wrong — as a National Liberal Conservative. I have never seen an animal to compare with a National Liberal Conservative, except once, with a horse in a pantomime. The man playing the front legs had a wonderful time — he could actually see where he was going. The man playing the hind legs was crouched up and had to go where the front legs told him. In the Torrington Stakes on Thursday next you can vote for my son, a real live Derby winner, or you can vote for the hind legs of a Tory pantomime horse.

This was devastating ridicule and the reaction of the audience was like the parting of the Red Sea. Liberals, who had been the under-dogs, rocked with laughter, whilst the Tories present looked alternately sheepish and infuriated. In the end, the Liberals won by a majority of 219, only alas to lose the seat in 1959, but the Liberal Democrats regained it in 1997.

The second speech of Violet's marking the Torrington by-election, and delivered at the National Liberal Club, lasted for a few moments, but moved many of its hearers to tears. She remarked that she had celebrated her father's by-election victory in Paisley, and now celebrated that of her son with equal pride and joy. Then she turned to the attack: 'When I went to Torrington, I had a strange feeling that I was a member of an army of liberation, setting out to free territory which had been held by Quislings and collaborators [this refers to the Liberal Nationals (subsequently re-named National Liberals) whom I deal with elsewhere], whose day was at an end. There are still thousands of Liberals living in occupied territory, whom we have yet to liberate. The message which goes out to them today is: "Hold on, hold out, we are coming, and we are!"'

Encounter at the National Liberal Club
In 1968 the National Liberal Club organised a dinner to mark the centenary of the formation of Mr Gladstone's first administration. The speakers

were Roger Fulford, who placed Gladstone in historical perspective; the Archbishop of Canterbury, Michael Ramsey, who spoke on his theological beliefs and the appointment of bishops; Violet Asquith, who had actually called on Gladstone at No. 10 Downing Street for tea, aged six, and described this; and I myself, who spoke of him *qua* his role as a politician. It was a glittering occasion.

Lady Violet told an engaging story about Mr Gladstone and his liability to sea-sickness. On one occasion prior to his crossing the Channel he consulted his physician who advised him that he should concentrate his mind totally on some great issue. In Mr Gladstone's case this involved finding a suitable book to occupy his mind. He repaired to his library and took down a slim volume entitled *Pickering on Adult Baptism*.

I had already arranged to take Lady Olwen Carey Evans, Lloyd George's elder daughter, back to where she was staying and found no provision had been made for taking Lady Violet home — she accepted my invitation that I should do so. I realised at this point that I was about to transport Lloyd George's and Asquith's daughters whose families had been engaged in a feud since 1916, when Asquith was deposed as Prime Minister and was succeeded by Lloyd George, who had been Chancellor of the Exchequer. I said to Violet: 'I believe you know my Aunt Olwen'. 'Yes', came the reply, 'slightly'. It was a decidedly chilly beginning. After we had dropped Violet, Olwen turned to me and said: 'I cannot think why Violet is always beastly to me. We were, after all, neighbours once.' 'Yes', I replied. 'But the addresses involved were No. 11 and No. 10 Downing Street, and the tenants of No. 11 evicted the tenants of No. 10 and moved in themselves. For that they have never been forgiven.'

Churchill

In the autumn of 1961 I was with an ITV camera crew in Jamaica. We were assessing the likely economic effects of the new United Kingdom immigration laws on Jamaica. In the course of our enquiries we visited the Royal Jamaican cigar factory and there we saw the largest cigars I had ever seen — nearly eight inches long, taking approximately 1 hour 45 minutes to smoke. It was decided that if he would accept them, we would give Churchill a box of these tobacco zeppelins.

The Liberal front bench of 1910, by Max Beerbohm; from left: Burns, Birrell, Harcourt, Haldane, Churchill, Asquith, Lloyd George

On returning home I asked Christopher Soames (Churchill's son-in-law and himself a minister) whether he could make the necessary arrangements for a presentation. I could call on Churchill in his room in the House of Commons, his London home or Chartwell, where my mother lived a few miles away. Christopher suggested Hyde Park Gate, and on arrival at the appointed hour, before I could ring the doorbell, the door swung open and I was ushered into the hall. There, laid out, were what I could only describe as the great man's props: the ebony cane with its silver top, the round/square bowler and the overcoat with its fur collar. Looking through the doorway I saw the old man sitting, brooding by the fire. He warmly welcomed me and gestured for me to sit in the chair next to him. He accepted the cigars and even he expressed surprise at their size. 'They are vast', he said and proceeded to offer me one of his cigars to smoke. I politely declined as I did not want him to feel under any obligation. 'Very well', he said, 'You must take one of your own cigars as a souvenir.' This I gladly agreed to do, and the cigar and a charming letter from him are both framed and hang in my study.

The second occasion on which I spoke to him was in the smoking room at the House of Commons. I had previously called in at Agnews, the picture dealers in Bond Street. Geoffrey Agnew asked me whether I was interested in Max Beerbohm's work. He had a cartoon of the Liberal front bench in 1910, which included Asquith as Prime Minister, Lloyd George as Chancellor and Churchill as Home Secretary. Geoffrey expected that each of the three daughters of these men might want to buy the cartoon, thereby arousing the anger of the two unsuccessful ones. What should he do? I replied that he should sell it to me. It would be rather like the Peace of Amiens, of which no-one was proud but everyone was relieved.

The picture was duly delivered to me at the Liberal Whips' Room. As luck would have it, Willie Whitelaw was passing the door and I showed him the cartoon. I said that I had just seen Churchill making for the smoking room and I wondered whether he would be amused by the cartoon of himself and his colleagues. 'He would be fascinated', said Willie. 'That is, if we got through to him.' Churchill was seated surrounded by half a dozen Tory MPs, who were acting as his acolytes. We propped the picture up in front of him and at first there was no reaction from him. Then suddenly he lit up and pointed to the first figure, and said: 'It's David'. 'Yes sir. It is Lloyd

George in 1910.' 'And it is HH.' 'Yes sir, Asquith. And that's you, sir.' Churchill looked up and said: 'Fine team, great team, none finer — ever'. Needless to say, I agreed, but I doubt whether his Tory entourage approved of these views! I felt that it was a pity that Campbell Bannerman had died before the cartoon was drawn, since the 1906 cabinet had produced four Prime Ministers, of whom he was one. As luck would have it, Beerbohm had previously drawn a cartoon of Campbell Bannerman, which I discovered and bought a week later.

Lying in state: Gladstone and Churchill
After the tributes were paid in the House of Commons to Winston Churchill on 25 January 1965, I returned to my flat and went down for dinner in the restaurant. In the corner was a distinguished elderly man. I asked him whether I was right in thinking that he was Sir Albert Gladstone, to which he assented. I told him I had just returned from the House of Commons from the Churchill tributes and that the lying-in-state plans for Churchill were based on those for his grandfather, who was the last commoner to lie in state. Did he have a picture from his parents describing the scene? 'Oh', he said, 'I was there as a very young child'. I asked him if he had been to Churchill's lying-in-state and he said he thought he was too old to queue. I told him that with great respect he should be there since he was a living link with history; MPs' guests could reach Westminster Hall by a side door and that I would like to escort him there tomorrow. He could be in and out in fifteen minutes. I remember noting the shape of his head was like Gladstone's! We duly arrived at Westminster Hall and he appeared wrapped in thought. I asked him how different Churchill's lying-in-state was from that of his grandfather. He said that the atmosphere was the same but there were virtually no children, fewer women and for the most part the men were wearing frock coats or morning coats and took off their top hats as they went past the catafalque. He said: 'There is something different. Yes, it's the coffin. Mr Churchill's is draped with the Union Jack. My grandfather's coffin was draped with a grey silk pall given to the family by the Armenian community. It was a token of their gratitude to him for the way in which he had denounced the atrocities perpetrated by the Turks against the Armenian people. We still use the pall for family funerals.'

I had with me my nephew, then aged ten, and thought what an amazing link he will be in later years, having been to Churchill's lying-in-state with Gladstone's grandson, who in his turn had been to Gladstone's lying-in-state.

Isaac Foot

One of the most dramatic occasions that I have experienced at a political meeting was provided by Isaac Foot, former Liberal MP for S.E. Cornwall and the venerable father of Dingle, Michael, John, Hugh and Christopher. Isaac was to be the main supporting speaker at a 1955 election meeting in the town hall in Liskeard. A leaflet had been given out by some freelance Tories in which the Sixth Earl of Rosebery advised Liberals in Devon and Cornwall to vote Conservative in the general election. This advice followed the pattern in which Conservative candidates called themselves Liberal Conservatives, Conservative Liberals, National Liberal and Conservatives and every other possible variant.

'Leave Lord Rosebery to me', said Isaac before the meeting. 'I understand', he told a packed meeting, 'that Lord Rosebery has ventured to give advice to Liberals in Devon and Cornwall. I thought he was only a specialist of the Turf, but possibly he claims authority from the fact that his father was a minister in one of Mr Gladstone's administrations.' 'Silence', said Isaac, 'I hear voices coming from over here'. He advanced towards an upright piano at the back of the platform, lifted the lid and the top of his head disappeared into the piano. 'Yes, it's Isaac Foot, good evening, sir, I am very well, thank you. I hope you are too. It is difficult to hear you, since there is background noise. Hush', said Isaac, waving his hand towards the audience. Total silence ensued. 'Yes, that's very clear, thank you very much. I'll certainly tell them that. Good day to you, sir.'

With that he extracted himself from the piano, closed the lid and advanced to the front of the platform. 'I've just been talking to Mr Gladstone', said Isaac, 'and his advice is that all Liberals in Devon and Cornwall should vote Liberal. So much for Lord Rosebery.'

The audience was captivated. My reckoning was that 80 per cent regarded his intervention as a *tour de force*, 10 per cent thought it might possibly have happened, the other 10 per cent weren't sure what to think.

Isaac Foot was a West Country institution. His house, Pencrebar in Callington, was bursting at the seams with books. He was unquestionably the best-read man I've ever known. The distillation of his reading was to be found in Commonplace Books: on the spine of each was the name of a statesman, historian, poet or author whose works or writings about them he had absorbed. Thus, for example, the Commonplace Book on Edmund Burke represented the cullings of twenty books or more. He took particular delight in getting telephone calls from his sons: Dingle, checking a quote for an article in the *Observer,* or a similar enquiry from Michael for *Tribune* or from John and Hugh, checking an historical allusion for a future speech. When his wife protested that there was no further space in the house for more books, he had some of his future purchases delivered to the gardener's cottage, and smuggled them into the house in a wheelbarrow, covered in logs. He was almost always discovered.

A passionate orator and local preacher, he was a formidable campaigner for Liberalism and Methodism, which were the driving forces of his life.

Viscount Samuel

By the time I Joined the Liberal Party in 1948, Lord Samuel was already the elder statesman of the party and sole surviving member of the Asquith Government. As he got older, his quips become crisper and more effective. Seeking to maintain an equidistant position as between the Conservative and Labour Parties, he told the story of a bathing beauty competition at Brighton. The judges were unable to decide between two finalists and happened to see a Chinaman who had just got off the train. Here was a guarantee of an impartial judge! The Chinaman looked from one to the other, shook his head and said: 'Both are worse!'

In the same context Lord Samuel said that when he was asked to vote Conservative in order to dislodge the Socialists, he was being asked 'to jump out of the frying pan into the refrigerator!'

Liberals always regarded the National Liberals (previously known as Liberal Nationals) as anathema. They were formed to fight the 1931 general election, having broken away from the Liberal Party on the issue of tariff reform, pledging their total support to the Conservative Party, from whom they become indistinguishable. They thereby confused the electorate, until they were ultimately wound up as a party. It was not before the Conservative Party had postured as Liberal Nationals and Conservative Liberals, and every other variation, that the hybrid party ceased to exist in 1966.

As Sir Archibald Sinclair said: 'The National Liberals are like a mule, in that they have no pride of ancestry and no hope of posterity'. Lord Samuel was to deal with them in a different way, but one that was equally devastating. When speaking in the House of Lords, he commended a measure which had the support of the three major parties. Listening intently, Lord Teviot, who had signed the post-war Teviot–Woolton agreement formalising the relationship between the National Liberals and the Conservative Party, rose to interrupt and said: 'Surely the noble Viscount means that there are four major parties involved — the Conservatives, the Socialists, the Liberals and the National Liberals?' Samuel eyed him quizzically and then replied: 'I am grateful to the noble Lord for his interesting and useful observation, of which no doubt the House will take note. For my part, I shall endeavour to tie a knot in my handkerchief.'

On the eve of Parliament in 1960, the Liberals in the Commons had a joint dinner with the Lords for the first time. There was some doubt as to who should read out the Queen's Speech — Jo Grimond as Leader of the Parliamentary Party, or Lord Rea, the Liberal Leader in the Lords. With considerable finesse, Lord Samuel, who had been Liberal Leader in both houses, was asked to read the speech. At the discussions which followed the dinner, Lord Samuel said that whilst he was flattered to read the Queen's Speech, and with the Suez fiasco (which I deal with later) clearly in mind, he said: 'When I was reading the gracious speech I was tempted to interpolate comment, and then thought it might be disrespectful to the monarch. When I came across the claim that: "My Government will continue to support the United Nations", I was tempted to say: 'says you!'

Lord Beveridge

I was privileged to come into contact with Lord Beveridge as a result of the founding of a charity, with one or two colleagues in 1957, known as the National Benevolent Fund for the Aged. The purpose of the charity is to provide holidays for elderly people from inner cities who have never been away on holiday, or have not been away for decades. The charity started in a small bottom drawer of my desk in my chambers, when the holidays cost £7 per person. Lord Beveridge was invited to become the first president. Beveridge had always maintained that however advanced the welfare state, there would always be a role for voluntary action. This was one reason why he was disappointed at the minor role which was envisaged for Friendly Societies. He would have been delighted at the way in which this charity has developed. 37,000 elderly people have been provided with a week's holiday in a number of seaside resorts. The cost today is £100 per head, or £200 if special care is needed. The financial turnover is on average a quarter of a million pounds per annum. The charity also provides tens machines which relieve pain, to over 300 individuals and 400 hospitals.

Lord Beveridge had some very distinguished successors as presidents: Lady Spencer Churchill, Mary Soames (as Patron), the former Speaker of the House of Commons, Lord Tonypandy, and the current Speaker, Betty Boothroyd.

Working breakfasts are my idea of purgatory, but there are always exceptions. One of these was breakfasting with Lord Beveridge at the Reform Club, where we not infrequently stayed.

He was at the time heavily involved in writing a history of prices. He would, for example, refer to the terms and conditions of employment of a mason in the fourteenth century, or a cabinet-maker in the fifteenth century, and he would then draw fascinating conclusions as to their social status and economic significance.

He came into active party politics late in life, but as a senior civil servant he drafted the Labour Exchange Act in 1909. He also helped draft part of the National Insurance Act of 1911 in support of Asquith and Lloyd George. Beveridge then became, in 1919, the Director of the London School of Economics, and thereafter Vice Chancellor of London University. But he will be most remembered for the Beveridge Report, which was adopted by Attlee and the post-war Labour government and earned Beveridge the title of Father of the Welfare State.

In 1944, he was adopted as Liberal candidate for the Berwick-upon-Tweed by-election. The constituency had been represented by the young George Grey (son of the late General W.H. Grey, one-time Liberal Party Treasurer). George Grey was killed in the Second World War and under the terms of the party truce during the war, any by-election would permit the party holding the seat to provide the replacement MP. Under these circumstances Beveridge became the MP for Berwick. The supreme irony of the 1945 election was that the campaign was fought by all parties on the basis of the Beveridge Report, and yet he himself was defeated at the polls. Thereafter he was created a peer. In the 1959 election he came to speak in support of my candidature in North Devon and drew large crowds.

Beveridge had a formidable wife. On one occasion Donald Wade (Liberal MP for Huddersfield West) arranged for the mayor to receive Beveridge. Beveridge had barely arrived in the mayor's parlour when the telephone rang. It was Lady Beveridge wishing to speak to the mayor. Having established that she was talking to the mayor she said: 'I want you to be personally responsible for seeing that my husband has a hot water bottle in his bed tonight!'

Aneurin Bevan at his most sparkling

I only met Bevan when he, Megan Lloyd George and myself had tea on the terrace of the House of Commons. The two Celts sparked each other off and it wasn't long before Bevan switched to a subject which always seemed to fascinate politicians, namely rubbishing some of their parliamentary colleagues. For some reason I cannot recall, the discussion involved Chuter Ede, the Home Secretary. 'Chuter is a frightful bore', said Nye. 'He is suburban, which accounts for it. His speeches are a series of generalisations. They are rather like branches of a tree in that they sprout from a wizened trunk, spread in all directions and very seldom touch ground.' On Morrison: 'Herbert has a way of taking over other people's brilliant plans, storing them up in perpetuity in case they should ever become useful'. Nye asked the name of a Tory backbencher who he was eyeing quizzically. He was told the identity of the Member and Nye noticed that his head was connected to his shoulders without an apparent neck. 'Ah', said Nye, 'a hangman's puzzle!'

Herbert Morrison — the wrong speech

My own prize recollection of Herbert Morrison occurred when I was an undergraduate. Morrison was to make two speeches, one the day after the other. The first was to the Oxford University Labour Club and the second to the Ladies' Co-operative Guild at High Wycombe. When he rose to address the audience he discovered that his press secretary had given as a press release the High Wycombe speech which he had in front of him and in view of the press release he felt honour-bound to deliver the address meant for the Ladies' Guild! It was not a felicitous occasion. When he said: 'Mr and Mrs Consumer, I want to discuss your weekly shopping pattern', he was greeted with mock cheers and guffaws, both of which steadily increased in volume until finally Morrison was reduced to saying: 'Either my sense of humour is rum, or yours is'. Ever since, for my part, I have always religiously checked any handout before it is distributed.

Harold Wilson's haymaking

One of the more civilised customs of the House of Commons is the practice whereby one MP informs another — whether of his party or not — of his intention to visit the constituency of the MP concerned. This is based on the fact that the MP to be visited is the representative of all the electorate in the constituency.

One day, standing at the Bar of the House, Iain Macleod turned to me and said: 'I've just come back from your constituency'. 'So I noticed', I replied, 'having read it in the press'. 'Surely you are not suggesting', he replied, 'that one gives notice to MPs of a different persuasion?' Attempting to and succeeding in sounding my most pompous, I rejoined: 'When my father and grandfather took the Tory whip in the House, it was always done, and I am sorry to see that standards have deteriorated since my family left the Tory Party'.

Harold Wilson, observing the custom, and also as a friend, in the spring of 1962 gave me notice that he intended to visit the North Devon Labour Party. He said that he would not be dealing with the Liberals, but concentrating on the record of the Tory government. Having learnt the date, I told him that I, too, was going to North Devon that weekend and would be happy to give him a lift across Exmoor from the station at Taunton, where I kept the car. I would thereby save him between an hour and an hour and a half on his journey. 'Do you mind?' said Harold, to which I replied: 'Of course I don't mind. You are going down in any event, and I will have the pleasure of your company.' 'Will your supporters object?' asked Harold. 'I doubt it', I replied, 'but if they do, I shall tell them that an opponent should not be treated as a mortal enemy'. 'Will the Labour Party mind?' he asked, to which I said: 'That concerns me even less!'

On the journey I filled him in as to what to expect: the North Devon Labour Party consisted of pockets in three places; at the next election the local party would be lucky to save their deposit; he would get an attend- ance of between fifteen and twenty; the chairman would be Dick Acland's former Liberal agent, now a convert; and no arrangements would be made to feed him, so that I would expect him to come back for a late supper.

All went merrily along, until we rounded a corner in remotest Exmoor to find a haywagon fully laden with bales of hay sideways on, blocking the lane. 'I suppose this has been laid on', said Harold jocularly. 'Yes', I said, 'this is an ambush by the North Devon savages.' It became clear that the shaft of the haywagon had broken and the farmer was frantically moving hay bales into the neighbouring field. I became slightly worried and turned to Harold and said: 'It is a point of honour for me to get you to your meeting on time. We must get out and help carry bales of hay, but please leave your pipe behind.' Harold rolled up his sleeves and obliged. The farmer said: 'Good evening, Mr Thorpe, I am sorry to delay you'. He kept looking quizzically at Harold, as if to ask: 'Where did I last meet you?' 'Oh', I said, 'Let me introduce you. This is Mr Harold Wilson who has very kindly come down to help us with the hay harvest!' 'Very kind, I'm sure', said the farmer.

We got to the Labour meeting on time. The Labour faithful were aston- ished to see their speaker driven to the door by the local Liberal MP. Harold got out, with wisps of hay clinging to him, and with total aplomb, went into the meeting.

Later that evening a Labour supporter brought Harold to the country hotel where I was living. Harold told me that the meeting was as proph- esied, likewise the chairman, likewise the likely outcome in the next gen- eral election and most importantly, likewise the absence of supper. This was soon repaired.

Harold Wilson: a tribute at the time of his death
When Harold Wilson died I paid him this short tribute:

Harold Wilson was a good friend and a formidable opponent. He was a great

Parliamentarian and a dedicated democrat. His belief in democracy was not limited to fine phrases but led to positive action. When in government he was convinced that opposition parties were not sufficiently well equipped to oppose the government in power. He therefore initiated the so-called 'Short Money' to finance the parliamentary activities of the opposition parties. Although at the time attacked, it is now a generally accepted part of parliamentary life. He considered that the job of the Opposition Chief Whip was full time and therefore should be salaried. He also took the view that the Chief Opposition Whip and the leader of the third party should be Privy Councillors, which had been by no means automatic in the past.

Harold Lever

Harold Lever, who was Financial Secretary to the Treasury, was one of the great humorists in the House of Commons, and I particularly enjoyed his remark: 'I am a fair-minded man and I would never accuse this government of dishonesty when a simple explanation of stupidity would suffice'. I wrongly attributed this dictum to his brother, Leslie Lever, who was the MP for the Ardwick Division of Manchester. Leslie had many qualities but these did not include a ready wit. I am delighted to have this opportunity, albeit posthumously, to correct the record in Harold's favour.

Pierre Trudeau

There are Liberal parties and Liberal parties. In Australia and Japan the Liberal parties are the equivalent of the Conservatives. In the Republic of Korea the Democratic Liberal Party is also Conservative. In Russia the Liberal Democrat Party is an anti-reform neo-fascist party. Canada stands out as having a liberal Liberal party in a three-party system, which certainly corresponds to the UK Liberal Party. We were loosely bound together by the Liberal International and I was determined to strengthen the links between the UK and Canada.

Trudeau made his first appearance as Prime Minister of Canada at the Commonwealth Conference in London in January 1969. I wrote to the High Commissioner of Canada asking whether it would be possible for him to fix up a meeting with Trudeau and was told that it was impossible. I therefore telephoned Trudeau's private secretary to say that I understood he was dining at No. 10 that night and so was I; and he would be leaving Claridges for No. 10 and so was I; how would it be if my driver dropped me off at Claridges and I travelled to Downing Street in his car? It worked! I looked forward to our encounter.

By way of introduction I told Trudeau that the UK Liberal Party had a two-million vote behind it and regarded Liberal Canada as the political equivalent of Mecca. The two parties were linked by the Liberal International but it was a very tenuous connection.

Pierre Trudeau and Jeremy Thorpe arriving for a dinner at 10 Downing Street, January 1969

Lester Pearson had in fact taken part in a UK party political broadcast for the Liberals shortly after giving up the premiership. John Turner — one-time Minister of Justice and Attorney General, Minister of Finance and subsequently Prime Minister in the Canadian Liberal government, had been a college secretary of the Oxford University Liberal Club, of which at the time I was president. Trudeau might be warned by his advisers that some of the European Liberal parties were anti-clerical in nature. This could endanger the Roman Catholic vote in Quebec. Whilst this criticism was justified before the war, it no longer applied. I felt that getting to know people like Walter Scheel and Hans-Dietrich Genscher of Germany, and Gaston Thorn of Luxembourg, as fellow Liberals, could be invaluable.

Secondly, Trudeau might have started his premiership with reservations about the utility of the Commonwealth. In fact he would find within its ranks people of the intellectual ability of Lee Kuan Yew of Singapore, Julius Nyerere of Tanzania and Indira Gandhi of India. It was not without significance that Canada had played a major part in preventing the break-up of the Commonwealth on the issues of Suez and Rhodesia. For my part, I felt that one of the most important factors of the Commonwealth was that it was about the only organisation in which men and women of all colours, creeds and ideologies sat down with complete equality and relative trust, based on shared history. Finally, he might have regarded the monarchy as something outdated. But he could well find the Queen, with her many years of experience, an invaluable source of knowledge and wisdom.

I felt we had established a rapport and so it was to prove to be. At this stage we reached Downing Street.

Canada under his leadership was to play a vital part in defusing the crisis over the shipment of arms by the UK to South Africa, which I deal with elsewhere. On two occasions Canada, on the issue of Rhodesia, probably averted the break-up of the Commonwealth. I have always thought that Canada felt over-shadowed by her neighbour to the south. It was part of Trudeau's success that Canadians recognised Canada as the world power which she had a right to claim to be.

Charisma is an overworked word, but it certainly applies to Trudeau: a man of infinite charm and negotiating skills which, allied to the fact that he is trilingual (English, French and French-Canadian), were all to play an invaluable part in dealing with the crisis of Quebec. The fundamental amendments which were made to the Canadian constitution during his premiership owed much of its success to the skills of the monarch and the Prime Minister of Canada. The Canadian Liberal Party has played a vital part in the recent history of the Liberal International, meeting on occasion in Ottawa. Now no Liberal International Congress is complete without the participation of Canadian Liberals.

Golda Meir

One of my favourite stories involved Golda Meir, Prime Minister of Israel and President Nixon. Henry Kissinger was the American Secretary of State, whilst Abba Eban, Cambridge-educated, was the Israeli Foreign Minister. Nixon remarked: 'We both have a vital factor in common in our two

Jeremy Thorpe and Golda Meir, November 1972

administrations'. 'My God', said Golda, 'What is it?' to which Nixon replied: 'We both have Jewish foreign Foreign Secretaries!' 'Oh, yes', replied Golda, 'But mine speaks better English than yours!'

On one occasion in November 1972 I called on Golda in the Prime Minister's office in Jerusalem. It was at the time when there had been several cases of hijacking of aeroplanes. She was anxious to make clear that Israel would never give in to the hijackers. And yet, she said, 'We are vulnerable. I am a grandmother. Suppose my grandchildren, along with other children, were flying abroad and were hijacked. I hope I would be strong enough to resist the terrorists' claims. And then again, one is only human, and the temptation would be very great to act in a way which might spare the lives of innocent children.'

Roy Thomson

Roy Thomson was an eminently approachable man, but was very close when it came to cash. At one Guildhall banquet which was part of a state visit, Roy approached me and said: 'Have you got your car here?' I replied: 'Yes, are you in difficulties? Has yours broken down?' 'No', replied Roy. 'I just don't pay overtime and sent the car away'. I duly gave him a lift home on this and several occasions. But the most dramatic manifestation of his economy was the 125th anniversary dinner at Claridges for the *Illustrated London News.* Prince Philip was the chief guest and I would guess that even Roy would have certain inhibitions about asking him for a lift. However, Harold Wilson, then Prime Minister, could be and was asked. I heard Roy say: 'You just drive to Downing Street and I'll tell your driver where to take me afterwards'. On the journey back, Harold Wilson apparently said: 'I hear *The Times* is in difficulties'. 'Is that so?' said Roy. 'What do they need to do?' Wilson: 'They need a first-class business brain, a man of wide experience in owning and administering newspapers. In fact, Roy, you would be the ideal man. Why don't you take it over and thereby be a national benefactor?' 'Oh', said Roy, rising to the challenge, 'I'll ring them up tomorrow'. This was precisely what he did and took over *The Times* into which he pumped millions. I always wonder whether, had he paid his chauffeur overtime, he might not have taken over *The Times.* As it was, he *was* a benefactor and I like to feel that the experience of losing so much money was good for his soul.

One abortive exchange between us took place in October 1960 in connection with the *News Chronicle.* This was a national newspaper which spoke for the liberal conscience in Britain. Rumours were rife that it was about to go out of business; the *Manchester Guardian,* then printed in Manchester, was more a provincial than a national paper, and there was a need for a radical version, of the quality of the *Daily Telegraph.* I told Roy that I thought £2 million would be needed to buy the *News Chronicle.* Broken down, this figure provided for £½ million for pensions; £1 million for losses in the first two years and £½ million for promotion. I made strenuous efforts to contact Lawrence Cadbury, the owner of the *News Chronicle,* but he was 'not available', having already sold out to the *Daily Mail.* In the debate in the House of Commons I referred to him as the Butcher of Bouverie Street, where the *News Chronicle* was situated. As predicted at the time, the liberal influence of the *Chronicle* was submerged and obliterated.

Max Beerbohm

After the war I visited Max in his spiritual home, Villino Chiaro, Rapallo. It was on the side of a hill overlooking the Mediterranean. Unfortunately 'progress' had cut a road at the foot of the property which was the main coastal road to the south. He was slightly protected against the noise by the fact that he lived on three levels. At the road level they had a reception room where they received their guests. Further up the garden path was Max's studio-cum-study which opened on to a verandah giving a superb view of the sea without vision of the road. In his study he had a small, thin waist-high shelf on which he kept a fabulous collection of cartoons by himself and others. Higher still was a small house where they entertained. When Lady Beerbohm wished to go from level one to level three, as it were, she would clap her hands and two retainers would appear to carry her up the garden to save her heart from being strained. It seemed a rather sensible arrangement. At tea-time she apologised for the fact that the cake had been bought. 'No need to apologise', said Max. 'You always get that little something extra from shop cake that you don't get with homemade cakes.'

Max Beerbohm, Jeremy Thorpe and sister Camilla at Rapallo

'For Mr and Mrs Ralph Wood from their very grateful friend Max Beerbohm, June 1943. This was my formula for Lytton Strachey.'

We had driven through Viareggio the day before, down the coast from Rapallo. It was there that Shelley had drowned. I asked Max whether there was any permanent memorial to Shelley. The reply was unexpected: 'Florence and I have never been to Viareggio.' In spite of the fact that they had lived up the coast for many years, they had obviously regarded Viareggio as a vulgar seaside resort and given it a wide berth.

One delight of being with Max was that he would often indulge in drawing an instant cartoon. He had given a lecture on Lytton Strachey, and my great uncle asked him what Strachey really looked like. 'Oh', said Max, 'I'll show you'.

I mention the Beerbohms' sojourn with my Wood relations elsewhere.

Noel Coward

My friendship with Noel (:a
with him in Switzerland ;   is
writings were at their best.   '-
land. 'Not very much', h(n
window each morning, I s

Perhaps his best-known   e
Coronation. Anxious not t(t
it was raining, this huge n   r
carriage down so that she c   Ə
she reached Westminster A   Ə
her in the carriage was an u   Ə
Sultan of Kelantan from M   -
monia. Somebody asked N.... who is the little man in Queen Salote's carriage?' 'That', said Noel, 'is her lunch!'

On another occasion, Megan Lloyd George visited Noel in his house in Jamaica. Noticing a rather splendid picture over the chimney piece, she asked who painted it. 'I did', said Noel. 'Is there any limit to your genius?' she asked. 'None', replied Noel, 'I call this picture Touch and Gaugin!'

Almost the last time I saw Noel, we had supper at the Grill at the Savoy. Unfortunately our table was quite near the door and countless people would come up and say good evening to me, hoping it would lead to an introduction to Noel there and then. I found that this was slightly embarrassing and apologised. 'Don't apologise, dear boy', was the reply. 'I always wondered what it was like to be the station-master at Clapham Junction!'

Noel at his most Rabelaisian produced a classic on the occasion when his god-daughter came to have tea with him. To his dismay he saw two dogs copulating on the lawn. He was anxious to deflect the attention of the little girl from this basic scene and of course the inevitable happened. She saw the dogs and asked what was going on. Noel was only temporarily stumped, then replied: 'The dog in the front is blind and the one behind is pushing her all the way to St Dunstan's!'

Edward Boyle

It is difficult to sum up Edward Boyle. But I think I would say that he was the most knowledgeable man I have ever met. His knowledge was not only encyclopaedic but covered the widest possible spectrum of interests: race relations; education; literature; music, and the arts generally. When one was locked in conversation with him, he flattered one by assuming one's knowledge was as great as his.

My first recollection of him as a speaker was at the Oxford Union, when he was defending the Conservative government in a no-confidence debate. His protagonist was George Brown, who made a rip-roaring, swash-buckling speech. Edward followed and with his usual courtesy thanked George Brown for his thoughtful speech which he proposed to answer. With breathtaking coolness, Edward said that he had heard what George had had to say in regard to the government's general economic strategy but was bound to say that he, George, would come to a very different view if he had read the latest work of Professor K. R. Popper. 'Christ,' said George, and that was the end of the matter.

I remember seeing Edward shortly after a new gramophone record release of some slightly esoteric conductor's interpretation of a new work. Edward was not only aware of three previous recordings but pointed out that in this new recording the conductor had taken liberties with the tempo of the piece half a dozen bars before the end of the third movement, which had spoilt the lead into the fourth movement!

He was deeply shocked by the state of race relations in Birmingham, where he was the Member of Parliament for Perry Bar. Suez had been the reason for his resignation as a minister, and his deep unhappiness over the trend of racial intolerance within the Tory party, as he saw it, accounted for his retirement from membership of the House of Commons. He was to become totally fulfilled in his job as Vice-Chancellor of Leeds University and could often be found seated in the cafeteria surrounded by a posse of undergraduates engaged in lively discussion. He was the humane face of Conservatism. His death from cancer prematurely removed from the scene one of the civilising influences in our society.

Chapter Four
National Politics

How I joined the Liberal Party

When I was at school in America during the war, the presidential elections took place, when Franklin Roosevelt, uniquely, sought a third term of office. He was opposed by Wendell Wilkie on the basis of 'no third term'. Roosevelt, who in my judgement was the outstanding president of this century, in the midst of a deep depression in the United States, used his presidential powers to commission large projects of public works to get America back to work. The Tennessee Valley Authority is but one example. He formed two public corporations to carry out the works — the WPA (Works Project Association) and the CCC (Civilian Conservation Corps). This was partly the basis for the New Deal. Interestingly enough, his ideas were inspired by the British Liberal Party's report on *Britain's Industrial Future,* known as the 'Yellow Book'. This formed the basis of the party's 1929 election campaign slogan: 'We can conquer unemployment'. A colleague told me that there is a copy of the Yellow Book in Roosevelt's private library at Hyde Park, with annotations in the margin as to how the proposals contained in the report could be applied to America. The Republican opposition reacted very much as the Tory party in Britain did after the war in opposing virtually all state intervention.

The post-war Liberal programme based on industrial partnership, profit-sharing and worker representation on company boards, with a massive extension of the Lloyd George/Asquith welfare state and with an overall insistence on personal liberty, all added up to the philosophy and policies with which I wholeheartedly agreed. This was a practical expression of Roosevelt's policies of the New Deal, which inspired me as a child.

I found the Britain of 1945 politically class conscious. The Parliamentary Conservative Party was dominated by the knights of the shires; although they could proudly produce two trade unionist MPs (the MPs for Bath and

Totnes) as evidence of their classlessness. They were passionately opposed to all nationalisation, were frankly hostile towards Europe and insufficiently aware of the need to bring colonial territories towards their independence. The Labour Party was still predominantly under the influence of the trade union movement, both for its philosophy and sources of finance.

For me, the Liberal Party offered a chance of a more enlightened Britain. I decided I would join the University Liberal Club when I went up to Oxford, and called in at the Liberal Party Headquarters, then in Gayfere Street, to ascertain whom I should approach in the university. I felt that the best contribution I could make to the fortunes of the Liberal Party was a build-up of the membership of Oxford University Liberal Club. I hit the target of 1,000 members. To achieve this required the efforts of individual college secretaries, one of the most colourful of whom was John Turner, who was briefly to become Liberal Prime Minister of Canada.

I also organised undergraduate tours during vacation time, in which half a dozen undergraduates would visit a key seat to do a week's canvassing and loud-speaking throughout the constituency. The effect was to galvanise local activity and also to show that the Liberal Party was rich in young talent. One of my early tours, and certainly the first in Devon and Cornwall, was in the Bodmin district in support of John Foot (now Lord Foot, brother of Dingle, Michael and Hugh). I am staggered to realise that this was fifty years ago. I also welcomed a tour in North Devon, during which the date of the 1959 election was announced. The team included a young Martin Bell, and some of them stayed on to help the campaign.

At an early stage in my membership, I was elected to the Liberal Party Council and the Party Executive, which met quarterly and monthly respectively. Although there were some stalwart members on both bodies, I felt too much time was devoted to debating lengthy resolutions, which were seldom if ever reported. An inordinate amount of time was devoted to amendments to the constitution of the party. I took the view that it would be far more valuable to leave the two bodies referred to and concentrate on the North Devon constituency, where I had agreed to become prospective parliamentary candidate in 1952. I was convinced that the seat could be won but that two attempts would be necessary.

During this period my guru was Megan Lloyd George, who was the Liberal MP for Anglesey, one-time Deputy Leader of the Liberal Party and, in a family connection, had been one of my mother's bridesmaids. To my deep distress, she later defected to the Labour Party. She had all the sparkle and vitality of her father and inherited his radical views. I would go into the Central Lobby of the House of Commons and, whilst waiting for her, would survey the scene and identify Members who passed through. On one of these occasions in St Stephen's Hall, I saw Megan's brother, Gwilym Lloyd-George, by then a Tory MP, talking to Harold Macmillan, whom I had as yet not met. Harold Macmillan was somewhat surprised when he heard a cry of 'Uncle Gwilym!' Gwilym asked whether it was true that I intended to stand for Parliament. 'Yes', I replied, 'but as a Liberal'. 'But', said Gwilym, 'there is no need, since all the best policies of the old Liberal Party have been taken over by the Tory party'. I replied: 'I never thought that I, as a son and grandson of Conservative MPs, would tell the son of a Liberal Prime Minister in the Palace of Westminster how profoundly wrong he was'.

The Oxford Union

I have always maintained that the ideal way of learning to handle hecklers is to debate at the Oxford Union. I certainly found it a wonderful experience in preparing for a political career. Two debates in particular come to mind. The first was during the Suez crisis in 1956. Aneurin Bevan and David Maxwell-Fyfe had both accepted invitations to speak on the Suez debate at the Union. Both had to cancel because of a three-line whip in the House of Commons. It was therefore decided to invite four dogsbodies, who had just gone down from Oxford, of whom I was one, to fill their place. William Rees-Mogg and Peter Tapsell were to lead for the government and the two speakers in opposition were Bryan Magee and myself. The house was packed. It was barely a week since Sir Edward Boyle had successfully fought off a no confidence motion tabled against the government in the Union. Clearly the government was not going to have an easy run in the Suez debate and they were ill-prepared for the body blow that was to hit them. In the course of my speech I said: 'Mr Anthony Nutting has resigned from the government and there will be others whose consciences will prick then, to the point of resignation'. This was greeted by jeers from the government side and cries of: 'Name them, name them'. I

Oxford Union Standing Committee, Hilary Term 1951;
from left, front row: Robin Day (ex-President), Canon Claud Jenkins (Senior Librarian), Dingle
Foot (ex-President), Jeremy Thorpe (President), Michael Stewart MP (ex-President), Asa Briggs
(Senior Treasurer), U. Kitzinger (ex-President), G. Smith (ex-President);
back row: H.E. Shuman (Secretary), M. Summerskill, I. Yates, O. Kerensky, J. Lucas, W. Rees-
Mogg (ex-Librarian), M. Barrington-Ward, G.N.L. Dalzell-Payne (Librarian),
Hon. D. Wedgwood Benn, H.H. Dubber (Steward)

replied: 'We shall not have to wait long before we see who will be next. They will have an honoured place'. The time was 9.05 P.M. and at that moment a piece of paper was handed to the secretary of the Union, Brian Walden. He handed me the piece of paper, on the strength of which I said: 'I have news for the House. News relating to an old friend of mine, who is the youngest minister to have attended a cabinet meeting since William Pitt; a man who was elected to the presidency of the Oxford Union with one of the largest majorities of the century. And the news that I have for the house is that on the issue of Suez, Sir Edward Boyle has resigned from the government.' The effect was electric; and since the news had been first broadcast on the 9 P.M. news, nobody in the hall had been forewarned. There were wild scenes of enthusiasm on the opposition benches and during the uproar I pointed a finger at the main heckler and waited for complete silence before turning to him and saying: 'I hope that goes some way to answering the Honourable gentleman's question'. Poor Rees-Mogg had to follow immediately afterwards and since Edward was a personal friend of his as well as being a political colleague, William couldn't have asked for a more unhelpful lead into his speech.

The second debate which comes to mind was on the European Community on 3 June 1975, in the middle of the referendum campaign. The debate was carried live on television: Ted Heath and I spoke for the 'yes' lobby and Barbara Castle and Peter Shore for the 'no' lobby. Barbara Castle was not very much at home in the Union and during her speech I asked her if she would give way, which she was graciously pleased to do. I asked: 'Since the Rt Hon. Lady's opposition to the Common Market is sincere, deep, and some might think pathological, and since the referendum seems likely to produce a 'yes' majority, what will she do? Stay on in government implementing policies to which she is diametrically opposed, or will she surrender the seals of office?' She retorted: 'If the vote goes 'yes', my country will need me'. It was a gallant come-back but didn't carry the house, which passed by a large majority the motion 'That this House says "Yes" to Europe'.

Each term a group photograph was taken of the Standing Committee and the officers. One term the photographers were late in delivering prints and were very coy about providing the reason. Ultimately the truth came out: the Senior Treasurer and Regius Professor of Ecclesiastical History, Canon Claud Jenkins, had been wearing copper fly buttons on his trousers, but had omitted to do them up. Under the influence of the flashbulb they made a glistening appearance on the prints and had to be individually

Oxford Union: EEC debate, 3 June 1975; speakers include: (front row, from left) Jeremy Thorpe (third), Edward Heath (fifth), Barbara Castle (seventh) and Peter Shore (ninth)

etched out of the picture! Although they did a superb job, one can still just make out the offending buttons! However, I am not going to say under whose presidency this occurred!

A closing note about our venerable Canon, Claud Jenkins. Mr Dubber, the steward at the Oxford Union, had completed fifty years' service. Viscount Simon, the senior ex-president, had been asked to present him with a clock, and had been invited to take the presidential choir. The Canon, as senior librarian, was also asked to say a few words. None of us knew what — if any — were the Canon's political beliefs. We were soon to learn that he had been embittered by Lord Simon's defection from the Liberal Party and his founding of the National Liberal Party. He began by welcoming Lord Simon and remarked that he was one of the most distinguished lawyers of the century. As to Lord Simon's politics, he was originally a Liberal — at least, he believed in 'Liberalism' as he chose to interpret it. In 1931, he broke away from the Liberal Party to form the National Liberals, who became, in due course, indistinguishable from the Conservatives. He was present at what he regarded as the last obsequies paid to the Liberal Party. The Canon continued to say that he could only hope that with the foresight which the noble Lord had shown in directing his own political career, he took care to see that there were holes in the coffin, as it appeared that the burial was somewhat premature. These withering remarks must have brought back to Lord Simon memories of Lloyd George's attack in the House of Commons: 'Many Honourable and Right Honourable gentlemen have crossed the floor of the House, and done so out of conviction, but never has an Hon. or Rt Hon. gentleman crossed the floor and left behind him such a slimy trail of hypocrisy'. And again: 'The Rt Hon. gentleman has sat for so long on the fence that the iron has entered into his soul'.

The North Devon constituency

Following the near rout of the Liberal Party in the 1950 general election, when out of 475 Liberal candidates fielded, 319 lost their deposits, the 1951 election which followed was an exercise in survival. To give one example: the Devon & Cornwall Federation consisted of fifteen Parliamentary seats. In the 1951 general election six of these were not fought by the Liberals —

including Torrington and Truro, both of which were subsequently to return Liberal MPs. Of the remaining nine constituencies, three Liberal candidates were in second place, thousands away from winning, whilst six others were in third place — including North Devon. It would take a great act of faith in the '50s to prophesy that in the '90s there would be seven Liberal Democrat MPs in the area. It was against that background that the Liberal headquarters in London launched a project known as 'Operation Basic' to assess the position of the party throughout the country and plan for a recovery.

When the team came to Devon and Cornwall, the North Devon representatives asked if they could see the team privately after the public discussions were completed. It transpired that their reason for asking for this procedure was that they were disappointed in their Liberal candidate in the last election, when they had sunk to third place. However, the candidate's brother was an officer of the Devon & Cornwall Federation and would have found it rather embarrassing if the North Devonians had made their complaints public. A private meeting took place and for some unknown reason the agent for North Cornwall, Frank Tyrell, attended it. North Devon indicated that if they could find a young candidate who was prepared to work, he would have every chance of winning the seat back. Frank Tyrell chipped in to say that he had just the man for North Devon — a young graduate who had campaigned with Dingle Foot in the North Cornwall constituency in the 1950 and 1951 elections.

After this, things moved fast. I received a telephone call from the chairman of the North Devon Liberals, Tom Friend, who asked whether I could come up from Cornwall, where I was ostensibly studying for my Bar finals, to meet the four divisional officers. I had only just heard from Frank Tyrell that he had recommended me as Liberal candidate for North Devon. I told Frank, as I was to tell the North Devon officers, that I was not interested in taking on a constituency until such time as I had built up a practice at the Bar. However, I agreed to meet them and said that although I was not planning to become a candidate, I would gladly give them a hand in building up the organisation. At the end of the meeting the president, Tom Dunn, who was widely loved and deeply respected, asked me whether I would give them a promise that if I changed my mind about becoming a candidate I would give North Devon the first option. I had known and loved the area as a child on

Jeremy Thorpe and his grandmother, Lady Norton-Griffths, on his first election for North Devon, 1959

holiday and gladly gave such an undertaking. I remember the old boy looking at me and saying: 'May we treat that as a firm promise?'

When I got back to North Cornwall I rang Dingle Foot at his London number to tell him the news. He seemed horrified, and went on to explain his reaction: I had campaigned in his support throughout his constituency of North Cornwall; he had now regretfully decided to stand down as candidate, owing to pressure of work; he had refrained from doing so until such time as he could contact me and obtain my agreement to become his successor. He had not as yet discussed this with Frank Tyrell or the constituency. I told Dingle that I had given a firm promise to North Devon and could not give them the chop. 'They are bound to understand and release you from your undertaking.' I replied that I could not let them down. Had I not given my word I would have given very serious consideration to taking on the candidature of North Cornwall: the Liberals had a full-time agent; we were in second place, and I believe I could have won the seat in the 1955 election.

The following week I received a letter from the Torrington Liberal Association asking me whether I would consider being their candidate.

The smell of battle became too strong and I decided that if I was going to win any Liberal seat in the West Country, I would probably need to fight two elections and put in five or six years' hard work. I relented and agreed to be prospective parliamentary candidate for North Devon in April 1952, thereby establishing a partnership which continues to this day.

During that period I have come to rely on the loyalty and affection of my supporters in the constituency. This was put to the test in 1979. My trial was due to start at the Old Bailey on 8 May, and polling day was on 3 May. I was exposed to the full glare of publicity. Nevertheless I was reselected by the North Devon Liberal Association to fight the seat. Although we did not hold it, 23,000 people voted for me — a wonderful assertion of solidarity. I have no bitterness about the result. My great regret was that I would no longer be able to look after my constituents' interests. I can now derive immense satisfaction from the vigorous representation which the constituency enjoys in Nick Harvey, our Liberal Democrat MP. I am privileged to serve him as President of the North Devon Liberal Democrats.

Two wonderful ladies

There are two wonderful ladies, each of whom has played a vital part in my political life. I refer to Lilian Prowse, MBE, and Judy Young, MBE.

Lilian became my agent in North Devon in 1956 and remained so until and including the election of 1979. Our partnership lasted for twenty-three years, our friendship for over forty. In 1956 the divisional officers, who included the Hon. Divisional Secretary, Jack Prowse (Lilian's husband), were wrestling with the setback which had relegated the Liberals in the 1955 election for the first time to third place. Someone asked if there was anyone who would keep the minute books, deal with correspondence and send out the odd circular. Jack said: 'I think my wife might be able to fit the bill'. She was duly appointed and no-one at the time could have imagined that she would provide organising skills for which she was to become famous. Perhaps the greatest compliment paid her was that the Tories used to refer to her as 'that woman'! She must take a very large share of the credit for the growth of membership, the birth of local branches in almost every part of the constituency and the increase in income to the North Devon Liberal Association.

Just after the polls closed in the 1959 election, I called in at the office, not only to find everything beautifully tidied, which is rare at the end of a hectic campaign, but two duplicator stencils laid out for immediate use, one assuming we had won, the other on the basis of defeat. Happily the first draft was used, and my majority was 362.

Torchlight procession celebrating Jeremy Thorpe's victory in North Devon in 1959; on his left, Lilian Prowse and Ursula Thorpe. (The banner, made in the 1930s, had last been used in Sir Richard Acland's victory in the Barnstaple seat in 1935. It was given to Jeremy Thorpe by the man who made it, on the basis that he was sure it would come in useful one day.)

The most closely fought election was that of 1970. The Conservative candidate had been virtually full time, visiting house to house for the four years preceding the election. The Tory and Liberal machines were evenly matched, and each was a formidable army. At the end of the day, neither side could have done more. We had 1,000 people working on polling day. The total postal vote was 2,500, of which 1,200 were Tory, 1,200 were Liberal and 100 were Labour. The majority was 369. Lilian kept superbly calm during the rather hair-raising count.

I always used to be amused watching Lilian appealing for help on the telephone: first the left earring would come off, and was stripped for action; she would usually start off to the effect: 'I don't expect you can help me', and then went on to describe what job of work she wanted her listener to take on. Her powers of persuasion were almost always successful. It is difficult to imagine that she is now a great-grandmother, although not immune from tackling challenges, such as raising £100,000 for the organ appeal for Barnstaple Parish Church. She and Jack must be very proud of the fact that in one way or another all of their four children have followed in the tradition of giving public service.

In 1965 I was elected Treasurer of the Liberal Party. Judy Young was working in the Finance Department of the Liberal Headquarters in Smith Square. When I became Leader of the Party in 1967, I had to give up the Treasurership and I asked Judy whether she would like to come over to the House of Commons and join Marilyn Moon and the team in my office, which I am delighted to say she agreed to do. I was immensely fortunate in having in the office, in addition to Judy and Marilyn, Tom Dale, who dealt with organisational matters, such as Leader's tours, and Richard Moore, who carried out research and gave invaluable assistance, not only in the drafting of speeches and articles, but also in response to requests for information on our position regarding political matters in the UK and abroad. Between us we succeeded in moving a mountain of correspondence. Judy accumulated detailed knowledge of North Devon constituents' cases, and liaised with the Barnstaple office. The two offices would very often decide what was the appropriate action to take in regard to an outstanding case — for example, was a particular National Insurance claim to be handled by the local NI manager, or was it a case which I ought to raise with the minister in London? She continues to take an intense interest in the fortunes of North Devon, where she has many friends and is always warmly welcomed.

She can always be relied upon, particularly in a crisis, which could sometimes involve working into the small hours. I remember writing and re-writing my first Leader's speech to the Liberal Assembly, calling it a day at 3.30 in the morning, which then needed to be typed. Apart from the continuing benefit of Judy's invaluable assistance — in view of the fact that she still looks after my affairs — she has kept in immaculate order all the papers relating to my political career.

Amongst her other gifts, Judy is also a skilled gardener, and plants flourish under her 'green fingers'. Our garden in Devon is well stocked with birthday and Christmas presents from her of plants, shrubs and trees, which are known as 'Judy's children'. It is a growing horticultural family.

Judy has organised many personal events in my life, and has supported me in happy and less happy circumstances. It has been a partnership and friendship of over thirty years.

Liberal fortunes

At various times between 1950 and 1970, the Liberal Party came close to extinction. In planning the 1950 general election, the party strategists, comprising Frank Byers, Philip Fothergill and Edward Martell, decided to fight on a broad front. We had often been told that by fighting on a narrow front we would not have enough MPs to form a government. It was worth the attempt, but the result was slaughter! As I have already mentioned, 475 candidates stood, of whom 319 lost their deposits. The organisation simply was not there. We polled a total vote of 2,621,548 and returned nine MPs. It was clear that the party had been kept alive by a handful of dedicated Liberals who, like Horatius, had bravely held the bridge but, alas, this was not enough. It was a replay of the Charge of the Light Brigade. The only redeeming feature of that election was that Lloyds' Insurers must have thought it unlikely in the extreme for any national party to lose so many deposits, and we were fully insured!

Somehow we managed to regroup and face the 1951 election, but we only had 109 candidates, and polled 730,556 votes and returned six MPs. The party's fortunes had reached rock bottom.

In retrospect I don't think any of us realised how near we were to disaster in the 1959 general election. The Conservative Party had used the name 'Liberal' in a whole variety of situations, which was bound to confuse the electorate. Thus, standing as Conservative candidates were six calling themselves Conservative and National Liberal; one National Liberal; four National Liberal and Conservatives; six Liberal and Conservatives; but the most debilitating argument was that of the 'wasted vote' for the Liberals. However, we fielded only 216 candidates and returned six MPs. Of these, two were the subject of the Bolton and Huddersfield pacts, as the result of which the Liberal Party gave the Tories a straight run against Labour in Huddersfield East and Bolton East, in return for a similar dispensation in Bolton West and Huddersfield West. The arrangements were highly vulnerable and easily revocable. The Tories decided not to fight Cardigan, which was Liberal-held although we would have held it had the Tories stood. However, the fact remains that only three of the six MPs were re-turned in a three-cornered fight: Clement Davies, the former Liberal Leader, Jo Grimond and myself (with a majority of 362). With Clem's death, we were temporarily reduced to five Liberal MPs, as was the case after the Carmarthen by-election in 1957. How much smaller could we get before we were no longer recognised as one of the parties in the House? In the event there was only one Liberal gain in the entire country, namely North Devon, and one loss, which was the neighbouring division of Torrington.

The next crisis was in 1965, when the Liberal Party seemed to be una-ware, or at least unconcerned, that it had an overdraft of £70,000, which for a small party at that time was enormous. Sir Andrew Murray was the incum-bent Treasurer, and I was approached at the Liberal conference that year and asked whether I would stand against him, to which I agreed and won. My first step was a visit to Coutts Bank, where the party had its account. I was courteously received by the directors, wearing their traditional frock coats. I indicated that I had been elected Treasurer and that I would clear off the overdraft at the earliest possible moment. There was, however, one

'Dear Santa' (*Daily Mail*, December 1970)

thing they could do to assist the process, and that was to increase the overdraft to £100,000! They agreed. I realised that I had a formidable task ahead of me, and took the view that unless we could turn the figures round in six months the party would have to go out of business. Tremendous efforts were made by Liberals throughout the country. When I first became Leader in 1967 I resigned as Treasurer, but for the first few years of my leadership I had to devote a great deal of energy towards raising funds. This had not been regarded as part of the Leader's job in the past.

In the general election of 1970, the Liberal Party lost seven MPs, including Eric Lubbock. The combined majority obtained by John Pardoe in North Cornwall, David Steel in Roxburgh, Selkirk & Peebles, and me was 1,600. If 800 Liberals had voted Tory we three would have been out and the Parliamentary Party would have consisted of one Welsh MP and two Scottish MPs. It was clear that we had not yet then turned the party round.

By-elections

By-elections are always of crucial importance to a third party. They can launch a campaign on equal terms as the two other major parties, expressed in terms of funds, organisation and outside help. Also very important is that the media, certainly in recent years, has given almost equal coverage to the three main parties. A successful by-election can do wonders for morale, but one always has to ask the question: is any one result a false start, or is it a harbinger of spring?

The first successful by-election in my lifetime was the Torrington by-election in March 1958. The campaign was fought on the condition of the area in terms of low wages, lack of industrial jobs and the very restricted incomes of local farmers. I led an army of North Devon volunteers day after day, and finally Mark Bonham Carter cracked the Tory vote, and won by a majority of 219. It was a dress rehearsal for North Devon the following year, when I won the seat.

The next earth-shaking by-election was at Orpington in March 1962. This constituency, in the stockbroker belt, had at one time as MP Sir Waldron Smithers, who was so right-wing that he was regarded in Parliament as a bit of light relief. The sitting Tory, Donald Sumner, caused a by-election when he was appointed to the county court bench. When the Orpington

Liberal executive met to plan the by-election campiagn, they were informed by Jack Galloway, the very attractive prospective candidate, that there was an unusual complication. Jack had not fully understood the technical terms 'nisi' and 'absolute', and in good faith had married his present wife before his first marriage had been dissolved. This would not have mattered, but the first wife threatened to attend all Jack's meetings and denounce him as a bigamist. All agreed that Jack was not to blame but these vindictive wrecking tactics led them to agree reluctantly that he was wise not to fight.

The Chief Whip, Donald Wade, was telephoned immediately and asked if he could suggest a prominent Liberal, such as Mark Bonham Carter, to step in as candidate. Donald warned them that the writ might be moved at any time and that the Association should find someone local who would not need time to get known in the constituency. After discussion,

'Take no notice, children' — Harold Wilson and Denis Healey reassure Labour front-benchers after Cyril Smith's by-election victory in Rochdale (October 1972)

the agent, Christine Parker, who had made the telephone call, turned to Eric Lubbock, a local councillor, and said: 'What about you doing it, Eric?' Eric replied that his employers, Charterhouse, were already long-suffering about his absences on council business and he didn't like to ask them for more time off to fight a by-election. The members of the executive pressed him to reconsider his position and he agreed to put it to his boss the next day.

He marched into the office of the managing director, Bill Warnock, and said that he had been asked to stand in the by-election. Warnock asked what the figures had been at the last election, and having heard them, laughed and said: 'Do have three weeks off at the company's expense.' The figures requested were 24,303 Conservative, 9,543 Labour and 9,092 Liberal. Eric Lubbock, now Lord Avebury, fought a splendid campaign and won a majority of 7,855. The news was given to Jo Grimond, then Leader, live on television — he gasped almost in disbelief. Eric held the seat until 1970, when I, then Leader, received the news of his defeat live on TV, and felt shattered.

His first constituency case was initiated by a telephone call at 2 A.M. His wife, Kina, said that he was asleep but that she would give him a message: 'Tell the MP', said the constituent, 'that my neighbour has thrown a dead

Sutton & Cheam by-election (*Guardian*, December 1972) — picture © *Guardian*

badger into my garden, and I want Mr Lubbock to arrange with the council to have it removed!' Such is the variety of tasks facing an MP.

When Eric took his seat, the Tories in the chamber greeted him with utter silence. The only Tory MP who shook him by the hand was Bob Boothby. For Liberals it was a memorable occasion. Watching from the Peers' Gallery in the Commons was the Liberal Party's elder statesman, Viscount Samuel. He came into the Whips' Office to congratulate him: 'This gives me particular pleasure, since I sat in Parliament with both your grandfathers'.

David Steel won a splendid victory at the 1965 by-election at Roxburgh, Selkirk & Peebles, followed by Wallace Lawler in 1969 at Birmingham Ladywood. These contests were not enough to turn round the fortunes of the party in time for the 1970 general election. However, in 1972 and 1973 there were five successful by-elections: Rochdale, covering a Labour industrial area, returned Cyril Smith; Sutton & Cheam, a home counties commuter base, returned Graham Tope; the Isle of Ely, in the agricultural Fenlands, elected Clement Freud; Ripon, in rural Yorkshire, returned David Austick, and Berwick-upon-Tweed returned Alan Beith.

In the spring of 1973 Liberals won 1,500 council seats and proceeded to practise community politics, which resulted in some first-class electoral organisations. For my part, I campaigned in all the by-elections, devoting as much time as I could to help ensure that each contest had adequate organisation, enough outside help, funds and sufficient publicity. Things were beginning to turn round, and the five by-elections already mentioned were the launch pad for the February 1974 election. In an interview I gave to Kenneth Harris prior to the 1973 Liberal conference I said that while Jo Grimond had built up the intellectual credibility of the Liberal Party, my task had been to build its political credibility.

The result of the February 1974 general election is well known, but bears repetition. Starting from a baseline of two million votes the Liberal strength shot up to six million. It was a bitter fact that those four million additional votes gave us only three more MPs. Under any fair voting system, this should have been a breakthrough.

Winnable seats

Having often experienced Liberal failure to win a winnable seat, whether at a by-election or general election, I determined in the 1960s to set up a Winnable Seats Committee, to concentrate on enough seats to give us a proper foothold in the House of Commons. We decided to keep the Committee to three in number — namely Ted Wheeler, who was also Chief Agent, and Dominic le Foe, a brilliant publicist and speaker. We decided to keep our activities as free from publicity as possible as we didn't want the other parties to know which constituencies we were targeting nor to incur the hostility of those Liberal Associations we could not help through lack of resources.

Ted would go to the selected constituency well in advance and would prepare a highly detailed report which itemised the strengths and weaknesses of each particular constituency. The three of us would then meet the constituency officers for two or three hours. In every case we set targets for membership, income, publicity campaigns and the formation of new branches, the achievement of which was the condition of continuing help from our Committee. Money was always tight — sometimes I would get an individual to sponsor a constituency and on several occasions the candidate himself chipped in.

The stimulus of £1,000 channelled by our Committee to a local Association would be more likely to hit the targets than relying on the candidate to raise the money, or part of it, himself.

Each constituency was a different case. One particular example was in the Inverness constituency, which was eminently winnable. For the candidate, travelling distances from his place of work to the constituency were so vast that by the time he arrived it was almost time to return. I suggested that the candidate should give up his teaching post; that we should set up a Scottish Research Centre in Inverness; and that the candidate should become its Director, with a modest honorarium. As far as I was concerned he could pack the work of the Centre into four days a fortnight, provided the remaining ten days were used in nursing the seat. David Russell Johnston, as he was then known, the candidate in question, agreed and the distinguished parliamentary career that followed is evidence that our strategy paid off.

JEREMY THORPE

LEADER OF
YOUTH AND ENERGY
LEADER OF THE LIBERALS

Election leaflet, 1970 general election

I visited the constituencies of all my parliamentary colleagues to help reinforce their tenure. I also included another group of constituencies which were considered winnable by us. When I became Leader I carried on this work, which I believed was absolutely vital.

Critical timing

A critical aspect of campaigning lies in timing, whether nationally or locally. If the campaign peaks too early it will begin to run out of steam and may run down very fast. If it fails to reach a peak at all, the campaign clearly will not get off the ground. Ideally the contest should be on a rising market up to and including polling day. This was particularly true in the Torrington by-election in 1958, which was the Liberals' first gain in a by-election since before the war. If the vote had been taken a week earlier we would have won by a majority of 1200–1500 votes. As it was, we reached our peak too early and won by 219 votes. Had polling been, say, two days later, the Conservatives' counter-offensive would have had an effect and we should probably have been out by 1200–1500 votes.

In the February 1974 general election I was shown a private opinion poll which showed the Liberals could poll 7½ million votes. My reaction was to conclude that the other parties had also seen this poll and would sense the appalling dangers which the figures represented to them, namely that with a further half a million votes we could make the breakthrough under our present electoral system. In the remaining days of the election they would turn their fire on us. Any votes over 5 million for us would be a bonus.

To give one example of the power of the big brigades: the government in office take the eve of the eve of poll for their last political broadcast in the series; the official opposition take theirs the day before that, namely the Monday before polling day; the Liberals are relegated to the previous Saturday — five days before polling day. The pressure on us was tremendous but we still ended up with 6 million votes.

The miners' strike 1974

By January 1974 it was clear that the government and the miners were on a collision course. To conserve coal stocks, industry was working on a three-day week and there were power cuts nationwide. The government was insistent that any settlement should be made within the framework of Phase 3 of the government's anti-inflation policy. The miners took the view that events in the Middle East, with the price of oil soaring, made them a special case in which Phase 3 had become outdated.

The TUC offered not to use the miners' settlement, when and if achieved, as an excuse for demands for other industries. On 31 January 1974 I asked the Prime Minister in the House of Commons: 'Does he regard the TUC's initiative and the Relativities Report on the Pay Board at least as giving some scope for hope? Is not the general acceptance by the government of the Relativities Report at least a recognition by the government that greater flexibility is required under Phase 3?

'Could the Secretary of State under paragraph 61 regard the case of the miners as one of special national interest for immediate consideration and to be referred to an examining body? Is the Pay Board's suggestion that the pay code may have to be amended if the recommendations go beyond Phase 3 something the government would accept? Since we are in a situation in which we are heading for a head-on collision, if the miners regard the £44 million as an interim offer awaiting the outcome of the examination, and the government regard it as an immediate settlement under Phase 3, honour could be settled on both sides.'

Mr Heath replied: '... when we operated the freeze and then Stage 2, we recognised that anomalies had arisen and asked the Pay Board to report on how this should be dealt with. We immediately accepted the Anomalies Report, and this came into effect with Stage 3. As a result, over 90 per cent of the anomalies have already been peacefully settled and worked out through the Pay Board as a result of the Report. I believe that relativities can be dealt with in exactly the same way ... the question of relativities can be dealt with as soon as this machinery is set up. I am right in inviting the TUC and CBI to help us set it up as soon as possible.'

I was convinced that there was scope for compromise that could lead to a settlement. Accordingly, Cyril Smith MP, our industrial spokesman, who knew Joe Gormley, President of the NUM, through his Lancashire and previous Labour connections, arranged a visit to the National Union of Mineworkers' headquarters on 7 February 1974. Our delegation consisted of Cyril Smith, John Pardoe MP and myself. Joe Gormley and two of his colleagues, Mr McGahey and Mr Daly, represented the union. I suggested that the £44 million on offer should be regarded as an interim settlement, pending examination of the whole pay structure of the miners as a special case. The government should be asked to make it clear that whilst they could not go beyond the £44 million at this stage, the offer should cover the present situation. The existing pay deal was due for renewal by 1 March, by which time the Pay Board should be asked to produce its report.

Although the government could not accept any Pay Board recommendations without seeing them first, nonetheless it should indicate that it would accept any reasonable suggestion, and that in any event £44 million was money on the table which the union was entitled to take up without prejudice to their right to argue their claim for special recognition. In my view, if the union turned down £44 million and therefore turned down further opportunities for negotiations, Mr Heath on that basis could go to a general election and, in my view, be returned with a majority of 20–30 MPs. If, on the other hand, the government, having conceded the £44 million, accepted the Pay Board's recommendations, and on the strength of this made an additional offer, a refusal by the union would strengthen Mr Heath's position, and in my view he would get back with a majority of nearer fifty.

We had a fruitful hour's discussion, and whilst Mr Gormley very properly indicated that all decisions on these issues would have to be decided by his Executive, he was grateful for our interest. He said that we had raised some valuable points and were clearly working for a constructive compromise.

After leaving the miners, more than ever convinced that there could be a compromise, we contacted Derek Ezra, Chairman of the National Coal Board, and raised the issues which had come up at our meeting with the miners. I was delighted to learn that his mind was moving in a direction similar to our own. That morning he had a meeting with Campbell Adamson, Director-General of the CBI, and Len Murray, General Secretary of the TUC, at which they agreed that they ought to see the Prime Minister informally to try to find a solution to the miners' problem, with a suggested compromise not dissimilar from our own.

We called on Michael Clapham, President of the CBI, with whom we had a constructive session. From his office, I decided to telephone Willie Whitelaw, then Employment Secretary, to tell him what progress we had made. We asked for an urgent meeting. He replied that whilst he had taken careful note of what we said, an announcement had been made minutes before by the Prime Minister on the 1 o'clock news that the Queen had granted his request for an immediate dissolution of Parliament, so that a general election would be held on Thursday 28 February 1974.

Any further hopes of a settlement, at least before an election, were swept away.

1974 general elections

The Liberals went into the February 1974 general election in good heart. The Liberal Party's financial crisis was resolved; its policies had been brought up to date at the Southport Assembly in September 1973 and five by-elections had been won. Taking the batch of eight by-elections, our total vote was higher than that of the other two parties.

As I said at that conference:

The electorate are obviously prepared to give us a chance, for which we are grateful; they are anxious to listen to our policies, to which we must respond. We are witnessing nothing less than the renaissance of the Liberal Party. But before I touch on our policies, may I be allowed at the outset to offer to the Conservative and Labour Parties, and for that matter one or two political commentators as well, a few home truths, which I suspect the electorate are more ready to accept than they are.

First, there is no God-given or man-made right for the Conservative and Labour Parties to rule this country for ever — much as they may dislike to hear it.

Second, they most certainly do *not* between them represent the sum total of human and political wisdom — however surprised they may be to learn that.

Third, in the mind of the electorate they have both failed in office: failed to keep inflation under control; failed to maintain the value of our currency; failed to modernise industrial relations; failed to end class divisions in our society; failed to give Britain the democratic institutions she deserves; failed to stem the growing sense of disillusionment with them and their leaders. Above all, failed to give this country a sense of national purpose. The brutal fact is that the electors are bored to death with both of them. And one final

Election poster, February 1974 general election

piece of advice: the Tory and Labour Parties won't dispel this unpopularity by abusing the Liberal Party.

TV press conferences

I went into the February 1974 general election defending a majority of 369. It would have been fatal in my view if I had taken the daily press conference in London, either absenting myself from North Devon for most of the campaign or flying back to North Devon late in the morning, re-turning to London by car through the night. I therefore decided to explore the possibility of setting up a television land link between my office in Barnstaple and the National Liberal Club in London, where the daily press conferences were held. I was told it was practicable and so I pressed ahead. I understand that Conservative Central Office took legal advice as to whether this development infringed the Representation of the People Act and/or whether the cost of transmitting from North Devon should be counted against the constituency expenses. I suspect they received the same advice as I did — namely that provided the background was not recognis-able as being any place in particular it was perfectly legitimate.

This new procedure worked like a charm. It had the added advantage that questions had to be asked through the medium of a hand-held mike passed round by the press officer. Therefore we had one question at a time with suitable time given for reply. I think this calmer atmosphere helped us to pitch our campaign more reasonably than the usual dogfight.

Although I went into the October 1974 election with a majority of 11,000, I repeated the land link to London, which resulted in my having more time to tour round the rest of the country rather than being stuck in London.

The campaigns

The nation was bitterly divided; we were experiencing the miners' strike, which produced some very ugly incidents, and the three-day week. I was determined to see the Liberal Party acting as the voice of moderation. The pattern of the opinion polls, although differing in their final figures, all showed a steadily increasing volume of support for the party.

I set out in the *Daily Mirror* on 27 February 1974 why I thought electors should vote Liberal:

Your vote at this election could help to make history. The Liberal Party stands poised on the verge of a major breakthrough, and for the first time in fifty years you have the alternative of three parties from which to choose the next government.

The Liberal Party offers you a new choice, because it offers a fresh approach to our problems — and no easy solutions.

A new approach which is not based on any class or sectional interest, and which recognises that if this country is to recover it must first be united.

We must break down the artificial barriers that divide us. We should begin in the factories and offices by ending suspicion between management and workers, giving workers an equal share in the running of their company — including a share in the profits.

We must tackle rising prices, because inflation always hits hardest at the weak and the poor.

To tackle it effectively, we must first introduce greater fairness in our society.

We must have guaranteed minimum earnings for the lowest paid.

We must extend family allowances to the first child and eliminate the means-test society by guaranteeing every family an adequate minimum income through the tax-credit system.

Equally vital, we must protect our pensioners. Pensions should be linked to national average earnings. As earnings rise, so should pensions,

For single persons, the pension should be fixed at one-third of average earnings. For a couple it should be half.

When we have made provision for the most needy, we can reasonably ask some restraint from those who can afford to tighten their belts.

The Liberal policy for prices and incomes is to control both equally. We would act on prices by tackling monopolies and price-fixing to get genuinely competitive prices.

We must decide every year how much as a nation we can afford to pay ourselves and how much we can allow prices to rise. Those that exceed these limits would be taxed.

But our first task must be to unite this country. So before you vote, please consider one point: which party do you think has the best chance of uniting us?

A party which represents big business and gets a large amount of its funds from that source?

A party almost wholly financed by the trade unions?

Or a Liberal Party dependent on no vested interest and therefore free to work for the country as a whole?

This time you must vote Liberal.

The headlines indicated that things were really moving in our favour. The *Daily Express* on 27 February 1974 carried the banner heading:

'HERE COMES JEREMY. HAROLD, TED ARE WORRIED'

Again another headline read:

'SENSATIONAL POLL RESULT. LIBERALS ARE GAINING FAST'

and:

'TED, JEREMY NECK AND NECK'

Evening Standard:

'HEATH, WILSON FIGHT TO WIN OVER THE NEW LIBS. THE BATTLE FOR JEREMY'S ARMY'

The Sun, 25 February 1974:

'THE JEREMY JITTERS'

'HEATH FEARS HE WON'T GET OUTRIGHT WIN'

'Suddenly Liberal Leader Jeremy Thorpe was public enemy number one with the Tories.'

Evening News, 27 February 1974:

'TED AHEAD'

'RACE TO LIBS FALTERS'

'Mr Jeremy Thorpe has achieved a staggering 38% in personal popularity in the London and South-East area which contains many marginal constituencies. National opinion poll in the *Evening News* today shows the Liberal Leader with an impressive lead over his two main opponents as the campaign deadline looms. Mr Heath's popularity rating in London and the South-East is 24% and Mr Wilson's 15%.'

In the event, Harold Wilson formed a minority government and it was clear that he would seek to increase his majority, probably by calling a second election at the earliest opportunity. I felt that October was a real possibility and launched our campaign with the hovercraft tours in the summer, to which I refer elsewhere.

The big issue for the Liberal Party that autumn was to establish the party's position in the event of no party having an absolute majority. At the Conference in Brighton on 11 September 1974, I said:

Daily Mail

MONDAY, FEBRUARY 18, 1974   4p

Polls give Thorpe's men a mid-campaign shot in the arm

LIBERAL GAINS SHAKE BIG 2

By ANTHONY SHRIMSLEY, Political Editor

WORRIED Tory and Labour chiefs last night debated the growing threat of a Liberal revival.

For Jeremy Thorpe's hopefuls, shown by a series of opinion polls yesterday to be gaining support rapidly, could drastically upset the chances of the two main parties.

As the polls serve this, the Tories are ahead.

Two as b... col... in

Mr Thorpe says party is 'out for jackpot'

From Martin Harkerby
Barnstaple, Feb 24

Mr Jeremy Thorpe, the Liberal leader, said Tory today "We are out for Tory today."

Liberal lead up another 5 per cent.—and Thorpe tops the popularity stakes

By DAVID COSS, Political Reporter

THE GREAT Liberal revival c o n t i n u e s its spectacular progress. Today's National Opinion Poll shows yet another 5 per cent. gain for Mr Jeremy Thorpe's party in just one week.

Tories, Socialists, even a few Nationalists — as well as the crucial floating voters — are leaping onto the accelerating Liberal bandwagon, NOP shows.

And Mr Thorpe himself is now the most popular political leader in the country, having swept 8 per cent. ahead of Mr Heath from level-pegging last week.

NOP estimates that today's Liberal share of the vote would give them around 20 MPs. Above 25 per cent. they would really 'lift off' and seats would come thick and fast for

Here is the sensational new political popularity chart. NOP asked: *How do you think you will vote at the General Election on February 28?*

	Election 1970 per cent.	Feb. 21 1974 per cent.	NOW per cent.
Conservative	46.2	43.4	40.5
Labour	43.8	37.8	35.5
Liberal	7.6	18.9	22
Others	2.4	1.9	2
Conservative lead	2.4	5.6	5

comfort that at least he

JEREMY'S JOY

JEREMY THORPE'S Liberals were jubilant yesterday as, with only three campaigning days to go, the still appeared to be gaining ground.

Four polls show Libs are gaining

By VICTOR KNIGHT Parliamentary Editor

The battle is on for Jeremy's new army

By ROBERT CARVEL

AN INDECISIVE result in Thursday's General Election could mean another before long.

This warning came from Mr Heath today coupled automatically with the statement of his confidence that the Tories are heading for a clear victory.

The Prime Minister said his daily news conference: "If there was to be an indecisive situation I would think it quite invidious to everybody that another or later there would have to be another election fairly shortly to resolve the position."

Polls 'encouraging'

He added that an indecisive result would obviously mean another contest sooner than a decisive one.

Lord Carrington, the Tory chairman, then chipped in to say he found the opinion polls 'pretty encouraging'. Almost without exception these were showing the Tories in the lead from the start of the campaign.

Mr Heath fiercely attacked the Liberals whose poll ratings have been rising in spectacular style. He commended Mr Thorpe for talking too much about himself and only about how well he can claim the Liberals are doing.

On a bandwagon

The Tory leader continued: "He is trying to persuade the electorate he is set on to a bandwagon in

All the election news

We will save London—Wilson
Page 6

Why I shall vote Liberal
—by George Malcolm Thorpe
Page 13

Heath shrugs off Powell's speech
Page 4

Harold on the jet-set campaign
News of Centre—Page 5

JEREMY THORPE—being the bandwagon, says Heath

Daily Mail

MONDAY, FEBRUARY 25, 1974 4p

LEEDS STARS IN TROUBLE —Back Page

Three days to go—and another boost for Liberals

NOW 'STOP THORPE' IS THE ORDER

By ANTHONY SHRIMSLEY, Political Editor

A DESPERATE battle for the

LOOK ON THE

£1m

By ANTHONY SHRIMSLEY, Political Editor

A DESPERATE battle for the centre vote is now raging as the election accelerates into the last three vital days.

The opinion polls are now showing a surge in Liberal support so remarkable that even Mr Thorpe's men can hardly believe it.

Yesterday the leaders of both major parties adjusted their campaigns to deal with this threat.

Ship on rocks is saved at last

By JON RYAN

ONE of the richest prizes in sea salvage history was being wrung up the Channel last night.

Suffer

London: Wednesday February 20 1974

Tories surge ahead—six per cent in the lead

SENSATIONAL POLL RESULT

Liberals are gaining fast

Noll's £680,000—

Election outcome hangs in balance as Liberals keep up pressure

Neither of the main parties can be sure of the outcome as Britain's electors cast their votes today, because of the unknown quantity represented by the Liberal challenge, our Political Editor writes.

However, four opinion polls published today report the Conservatives maintaining or increasing their lead over Labour. The Opinion Research Centre survey has the Liberal support slipping by 2.5 per cent, but the others show the Liberal Party still making advances.

Mr Heath gave a warning yesterday that Britain needed a government with experience. Mr Wilson promised a "clear" to recovery" under Labour and Mr Thorpe said there was no reason why Britain could not have a Liberal Government if his supporters stood firm.

All party organizers hope for a full turnout

By David Wood
Political Editor

THE Sun

Bikini bottom

THE JEREMY JITTERS

WHAT THE SUN SAYS ABOUT VOTING LIBERAL:

Heath fears for his ruling majority in polls shock

MAYOR IN JAIL STORM

We now face the supreme test of our conviction and courage.

Our unity of purpose and our strength of character will be tested as never before. This time there will be no honeymoon period before the other two parties, hitherto contemptuous of our influence, turn their wrath on us simultaneously. This time the warning lights are already on.

Liberals entered the contest as free agents owing no favours to paymasters and with no pacts or promises hedging their position.

Dealing with the controversial coalition issue, I said:

I do not and never have believed there is under present conditions a sufficient basis of agreement for a Tory–Liberal or Labour–Liberal coalition.

But that does not mean that we have ever suggested that government should be made impossible, nor in such a situation that we would opt out of our parliamentary responsibilities.

If this country was faced with a catastrophic economic crisis, then we would be prepared, for a limited period on an agreed programme, to join an all-party government of national unity. Is it really thought to be in the interest of the nation to say less?

I asked:

Are you going to say: 'There may be 4,000,000 unemployed, there may be a collapse of the currency, and there may be bankruptcy. We have no responsibility. We wish to play no part in the rescue of the nation, we are pure'? Of course we are not going to opt out of the responsibilities facing this nation.

Liberals offer the electorate a unique combination of reasons for giving the party their support. Only the Liberals can unite the country in a common fight against inflation.

It is only the people of Great Britain who can insist that men and women of common sense, high talent and goodwill should come together to rescue the country from desperate economic peril.

If I am right in thinking that the supreme need is for unity, let me ask any Conservative this question: do they really believe that the return of a Conservative government will gain the support, trust, and enthusiasm of the trade union movement, and has Mr Heath really proved to be the key to industrial peace?

And to any Labour voter: do they in all conscience think that a majority Labour government will engender the confidence and enterprise of industry to invest, to expand and create new jobs? Is Mr Benn really the answer to economic prosperity? Don't we as a nation need to gain the trust of both?

At the last election, 6,000,000 Liberal voters formed an alliance for unity and struck a mortal blow against a discredited two-party system.

The politics of this country can now be totally changed.

I had some fears that our vote might not hold up as the result of the electoral system, which had disfranchised millions of voters in February. Happily we were within 1 per cent of our previous total. The outcome was just as disappointing as it was in February and followed the same pattern, namely:

February: Conservatives 12 million votes — 300 MPs; Labour 12 million votes — 300 MPs; Liberals 6 million votes — 14 MPs.

October: Conservatives 10½ million votes — 276 MPs; Labour 11½ million votes — 319 MPs; Liberals 5¼ million votes — 13 MPs.

The supreme irony is that the Liberals polled, in October 1974, 5,231,477 votes, winning 13 seats. The Liberal Democrats in May 1997 polled 5,243,440 votes and won 46 seats. In almost every Western European democracy a vote of five to six million would have produced a minimum of 100 MPs!

Will we join a coalition?

In February 1974 the Conservative Prime Minister, Edward Heath, against the background of the miners' strike and the three-day week, had called a general election on the basis of: 'Who governs Britain, the miners or the elected government?' The result of the poll was indecisive: the Conservative Party had a larger number of votes than Labour, whilst the Labour Party had a larger number of MPs than the Conservatives. So much for our electoral system!

In his autobiography, *The Course of my Life,* Edward Heath says: 'I tried to contact the Liberal Leader, Jeremy Thorpe, who was in the West Country celebrating his party's improved showing. On the Saturday afternoon when all the votes had been counted, he turned up at Downing Street for talks.' This rather bland statement suggests that I was carrying out a sort of cold canvass of Downing Street looking for work!

The position is quite clear: on the Friday evening following polling day — 1 March 1974 — Number Ten rang me at my home in North Devon. I was still in Barnstaple leading a torchlight victory procession. It was suggested to Number Ten that I would be back in my cottage by 10.30 P.M. and they indicated that they would call back. I arrived back in time, but by midnight no call had come through, so I decided to ring Number Ten myself to be told by the Prime Minister that they had been unable to get through. Once again the local Chittlehamholt exchange had broken down at a crucial moment!

The Prime Minister indicated that our two parties appeared to have similar views on Europe and the statutory incomes policy — when would I be able to meet him? I agreed to come up to London the next morning.

The Prime Minister suggested that we keep the fact that we were meeting private. I agreed, and in so doing, recognise now that I made a mistake. When the news broke that a meeting was to take place, many Liberals panicked and thought that I, as Leader of the Liberal Party, was about to sacrifice the very independence of the party which I had spent the last twenty-five years working to preserve. However, I felt that if the Prime Minister of the day requested a meeting, one had an obligation to go. Although I had always been opposed to joining a Tory coalition, at least I had a duty to find out what was proposed so that, with my colleagues, we could make an informed judgement.

Jeremy Thorpe arrives at 10 Downing Street, 2 March 1974

The meeting consisted of the Prime Minister, myself and Robert Armstrong, Secretary to the Cabinet. The Prime Minister opened by saying that the Conservative Party had obtained the largest national vote at the general election and therefore had a right to try to form an admin-

istration. His offer was a complete coalition with th
seat in the Cabinet. I can state with utter conviction
istry was mentioned or suggested. Mr Heath sugg
expressed the preference for the job of Home Secr'
The statement he made to the Press Association of
had absolutely no intention of offering Jeremy Thorpe the Home
in a coalition government, nor did I ever mention it to him'. If in fact I had
raised the matter twice, it is odd that I should have drawn no response from
him at all. I later learnt from a reliable source that what he had in mind was
a Foreign Office job with specific responsibility for Europe.

I conceded his constitutional right to form an administration but pointed
out that as we sat there I had the equivalent of almost half his popular vote
behind me — six million people had obtained fourteen MPs. Or to express it in another way, four million extra votes had yielded three more
MPs. 'Does this mean that you are asking for electoral reform?' the Prime
Minister asked, to which I replied: 'Yes'. He went on to say: 'We have no set
policy on this'. I remember reflecting at that moment that it was high time
they did! In fact insofar as they did have views, the Conservative Party had
favoured the status quo or first-past-the-post. The term proportional representation was never used, as is wrongly suggested in his book.

Apart from general considerations I made two specific points. First, we
did not know who had won the election, but we did know who had lost it.
Secondly, apart from the likely views of my colleagues, who were frankly
hostile to the idea of a coalition, we had many grave reservations about
him leading a coalition. I had been highly critical of his handling of the
miners' dispute before the election.

Another important point was the mathematics of the situation: 296 Conservative MPs plus 14 Liberal MPs, making a total of 310, which was a
figure of less than half the total of the House of Commons. The Prime
Minister confirmed that he had not approached the Scottish or Welsh
Nationalists, nor the Ulster MPs. I predicted that his suggested coalition
government would be brought down on the first critical vote on the Queen's
Speech. With this he disagreed.

I said I would, however, report our discussion to my parliamentary colleagues. I don't think I left him very sanguine about the chances of success.

Our second meeting took place on the following day (the Sunday). At

meeting the Prime Minister opened the discussion by saying that he
d discussed the matters raised by me with his Cabinet colleagues and
they were adamant that they wished to continue to serve under his leadership. There was therefore no question of a change being made. On the
question of electoral reform he would offer a Speaker's Conference. (This
is an established procedure, presided over by the Speaker, for dealing with
such electoral matters.) The Prime Minister said that there would be a free
vote on the recommendations made. I made it clear that unless the Cabinet took a collective view in favour of reform and made it a vote of confidence in the government, no reform would have any chance of going
through Parliament whilst the Conservative Party continued to favour the
present first-past-the-post system.

In the meantime I sounded out my colleagues informally on the Sunday, and arranged a meeting of the Parliamentary Party for Monday morning, by which time I would know the outcome of my second meeting
with the Prime Minister on the Sunday evening.

In my letter of Monday 4 March to the Prime Minister I referred to
the second meeting, to which his letter to me of the same date, strangely
enough, did not allude. I continued: 'I made it clear that in my view, after
preliminary soundings, there was no possibility of a Liberal–Conservative coalition proving acceptable, but that we might give consideration
to offering support from the opposition benches to any minority government on an agreed but limited programme. This you have now ex-
plicitly rejected.'

My Parliamentary Party met on Monday and confirmed my reservations on the question of coalition and the following statement was issued:

> The outcome of the election clearly shows that the electorate is not prepared
> to give either a Conservative or Labour administration a mandate to pursue
> their conventional policies. The six million people whom we represent voted
> for policies of moderation. In the present situation we are convinced that
> such policies can only be carried out effectively by a government of national
> unity consisting of members of all parties, committed to a limited programme
> for an agreed period. This would give overriding priority to those policies
> required to be implemented in the national interest. The gravity of the coun-
> try's economic plight is such that party conflict must be subordinated to the
> country's need.
>
> It is now the duty of the other parties to enter into immediate discussion

with a view to achieving this. To this end we have urged the Prime Minister to convene an immediate meeting of the party leaders.

Mr Heath's book makes the extraordinary claim that I (JT) 'was very keen to enter a coalition, as were many of his colleagues'. As the Duke of Wellington replied to the lady who said: 'Mr Smith, I believe' — 'Madam if you believe that you'll believe anything!' The suggested arrangement for general support for the government from the opposition benches for agreed measures in the national interest, short of coalition, was taken up by Jim Callaghan, when he was Prime Minister, and David Steel, and was the basis of the Lib–Lab Pact some years later. Mr Heath, for his part, felt unable to accept such an arrangement.

Hovercraft

By June 1974 it became clear that there was a real possibility of an autumn election. I was determined to get the Liberal campaign off the ground before the other two parties. This again was a question of timing. I was told, however, that it was no good, as everyone would be on the beaches. 'Very well', I said. 'Let's go to the beaches and do a beach-storming campaign by hovercraft'. On Wednesday 28 August at 9 A.M. we set off from North Devon in perfect weather. The hovercraft jumped some twenty feet off the RAF Chivenor runway on to the mud flats of the Taw river below, spattering us with mud! This was rapidly washed off by the spray. My real concern in making the leap had been that we might turn a somersault, with the hovercraft landing upside down in the mud. We crossed the bar where the rivers Taw and Torridge meet and flow out to sea, arriving at Ilfracombe at 9.15 for an open-air meeting by the quay, which was attended by 1,500 people.

The next two days were spent travelling around the Devon and Cornish coastline, accompanied by two West Country neighbouring MPs, John Pardoe (North Cornwall) and Paul Tyler (Bodmin). We called on sixteen different seaside places. Wherever we landed, a large, enthusiastic crowd turned out. One or two scenes have particularly stuck in my mind: the picturesque harbour at St Ives was filled at the quayside with a mass of people, dressed in bright holiday colours; the stretch of the Barbican in Plymouth, lined with some 10,000 people; and perhaps the most memora-

The Liberal hovercraft tour
(*Punch* front page, August 1974)

ble of all — our arrival at Kingsbridge, as we came up the river Dart, accompanied by a flotilla of small boats.

The only human casualty was a lady journalist who was given a brandy to steel her for the journey; at this point the hovercraft bucked and the brandy went up her nose, an experience which, I am told, is very painful!

Our last stop for this part of the tour was Sidmouth, after which we were to resume on the Monday, calling at Bournemouth, Brighton and Eastbourne along the south coast. However, no sooner had we all disembarked on to the beach than a rogue wave hit a window of the hovercraft and pushed it in, rapidly filling it with water. Subsequently it transpired that that particular hovercraft had been on duty in the desert in the Middle East and had been involved in several sandstorms. The effect of this was that sand had settled in the rubber sealing around the window, causing the rubber to perish. In fact I now know that this could have happened at any time while we were at sea. We must be thankful it didn't.

I arranged a further hovercraft to be made available to us from the Isle of Wight on the Monday. Unfortunately the weather had turned and there were gale warnings. It would have been too dangerous to put to sea. As we learnt later, it was in fact also the day of the Fastnet Race during which Ted Heath's boat, *Morning Cloud,* sank. Our cancellation was an inevitable decision, though a disappointing one. I am certain that had we gone to the remaining seaside resorts, people would have turned out in even greater numbers, not only to hear the word, but to see whether we were likely to sink! In spite of these setbacks, we carried on by car and reckoned to have addressed over 60,000 people during the course of the tour. It was well worth the effort.

Helicopters

'Have we scalped a woman?' — general election 1970
Although Jo Grimond made the occasional hop by helicopter, I believe I was the first party Leader to use the helicopter on prolonged regional tours. During the 1970 election and the two 1974 elections, I travelled thousands of miles, which enabled me to visit scores of targeted seats.

One major disaster was averted in 1970. Caroline and I had left North Devon and had called on five Welsh constituencies in South, Mid and North Wales, proceeding to Liverpool for a meeting with candidates of the region, and thereafter on to Cheadle in support of Michael Winstanley, before going on to Yorkshire. At Cheadle we landed in a field which was surrounded by a housing estate. A large crowd of people were waiting and dangerously some of them lunged towards the machine, whose rotor blade was still turning. One of these was an over-enthusiastic Tory lady, who held aloft a banner which was sliced in two by the blade. At that moment Caroline shouted: 'Look!' and there on the ground was unmistakably a tuft of hair which looked as though it belonged to a woman. 'My God', I thought, 'We've scalped a woman!' My mind shot back to Wild West films, when Native Americans scalped palefaces — was this always fatal? I concluded that it was. A series of thoughts flooded through my mind: should I cancel electioneering for the rest of the day as a mark of respect to the deceased? should I call on the next of kin? would the inquest take place during the election campaign? presumably the press, to whom bad news is often good news, will carry banner headlines: 'Thorpe kills woman!'

Caroline and I climbed out of the helicopter looking ashen, only to discover to our immense relief that a young lady had indeed lost her hair, but it was a wig which had blown off in the whirlwind of the rotor blade, and was trampled underfoot!

Jeremy and Caroline Thorpe on helicopter tour, 1970 (Edinburgh Airport)

I met the young lady months later at a Liberal meeting and was relieved to hear that she was none the worse for wear, though not wearing a wig.

To give another example of the amount of ground one was able to cover in a short space of time, I recall particularly a two-day tour during one of the 1974 elections. Starting in North Devon where I took the 10 A.M. national press conference by a special TV link between Barnstaple and the National Liberal Club in London, I set off by helicopter for an open-air meeting in Hereford, followed by North Hereford and four other constituencies, ending in Birmingham, and returning to London that night.

Day two: I took the daily press conference in London, before flying to Chelmsford, Orpington, Richmond, the Isle of Wight, North Dorset and back to North Devon for four meetings in the constituency. Not surprisingly, we were running late, and as it was getting dark, the pilot insisted that we should land at Exeter, where there would be appropriate lighting for the landing. He reckoned that it would be impracticable to land in my neighbour's field in North Devon, which was the usual landing and take-off place during the campaign. From Exeter, I could not have got to the meetings in time and therefore I suggested that four tractors should be positioned in the four corners of the field, with headlights full on. This was successfully requested by radio from the helicopter and we duly landed in a blaze of lights to fulfil the evening engagements. My neighbour had already started the first meeting and was surprised and relieved to see me.

Electoral reform

I have been fully committed to the cause of electoral reform for many years. One of my earliest recollections is of taking part of a deputation to the then Home Secretary, Gwilym Lloyd-George, led by the Independent MP for Oxford University, humorist and writer Sir Alan Herbert, in 1955. We urged the case for a Royal Commission on voting systems. At that time HMG was drafting constitutions for colonial territories about to receive independence. Quite apart from the distortions which our present system of first-past-the-post produces, nothing could be more dangerous than giving our own electoral system to a colonial territory where a group, either ethnic or religious, might be under- or over-represented in the en-suing election. We have been very careful to avoid this danger. I was Hon-orary Secretary of the committee seeking the Royal Commission, and our support covered a widespread cross-section of political opinion from Tony Benn and Michael Foot on the left to Douglas Savory, the MP for the university seat of Belfast University.

The Orme Square meeting
Reference should be made to the Orme Square meeting which took place on 24 March 1974. I had decided to invite the leaders of the busi-ness community for a meeting in my home. I organised six of my parlia-mentary colleagues to deliver the invitations personally. Each was to be assured that we were not going to ask them for money, but might raise matters which would be of possible interest to their shareholders. Almost every invitee accepted and turned up, twenty-four in number. A further four indicated that they were unable to be there but expressed interest.

They included: Sir Marcus Sieff (Marks & Spencer); Sir Val Duncan

(Rio Tinto); John King (Babcock & Wilcox); Sir Mark Turner (British Home Stores); Jim Slater (Slater Walker Securities); Ralph Bateman (Turner & Newall); Sir John Clark (Plessey Company);Viscount Caldecote (Delta Metal Co.); The Earl of Inchcape (P & O); Sir Kenneth Keith (Hill Samuel Group); Maxwell Joseph (Grand Metropolitan Hotels); Hon. David Montagu (Orion Bank); Ronald Grierson (GEC); John Hargreaves (IBM); Maldwyn Thomas (Rank Xerox); Edmund de Rothschild (N.M. Rothschild & Sons); Sir Ian Morrow (Hambros Industrial Management Ltd); Nigel Broackes (Trafalgar House Investments); Lord Stokes (British Leyland Motor Corporation); Sir John Partridge (Imperial Group); Mr John Pile (Imperial Group); Mr R.A. Garrett (Imperial Tobacco); Sir Alex Alexander (Imperial Foods); Mr Bruno Schroder (Schroder Wagg J. Henry Co.); Mr A. Macdonald (General Accident); J.R.M. Whitehorn (CBI); and Anthony Wigram (CAER).

The Hon. John Sainsbury, Sir Paul Chambers, Sir Arnold Weinstock and Professor Sir Ronald Edwards expressed interest, but were unable to be present.

In thanking them for their presence I said that the one thing they all had in common was that in one way or another they subscribed to Conservative Party funds. Whilst I was able to recommend a wider scattering of bread upon the waters, this was not the purpose of the meeting. I wanted to make it perfectly clear that I applauded the fact that their companies were contributing financially to the cost of keeping democracy alive, but I suggested that their motive was not because Mr Heath was the soul of flexibility nor Mr Anthony Barber the greatest Chancellor of our time. I suggested that what they wanted was a degree of continuity without bouts of nationalisation, de-nationalisation and re-nationalisation. What they needed was the strengthening of the middle ground in politics.

As far as the recent election was concerned (February 1974) they had not had very good value for money. With a turnout of 78.8 per cent, which was high, a Labour government had been returned with only 37.2 per cent of the electorate voting for them — 222,000 votes less than the Conservatives. In fact Labour with fewer votes was returned with five more MPs than the Conservatives. The Labour Party had formed a government with no less than 60 per cent of the votes opposed to them. The Liberal Party vote had gone up by four million to a total of six million which resulted in an increase of three MPs. One may ask why the Liberal Party declined the invitation to join a coalition with Edward Heath in February 1974. Although I did not wish to embroil them in a party-political discussion, I would like to make two points which I had raised with the Prime Minister:

First — simple arithmetic: 296 Conservative MPs plus 14 Liberal MPs makes a total of 310 out of a House of 635. A coalition, in the absence of a majority, would have fallen on the first vote — probably on the Queen's Speech.

Second, and far more fundamental, we did not know who had won the election, but we knew who had lost it. My colleagues and I had been very critical about Mr Heath's handling of the miners' dispute, which I believe could have been honourably settled. I did, however, offer him a formula of giving general support from the opposition benches for agreed measures. Mr Heath felt unable to accept this (although years later the formula was accepted by Mr Callaghan).

My suggestion to those present was that in order to get value for money, they should press the Conservative Party to give serious consideration to the whole question of electoral reform. In fact, the Conservative government had reintroduced proportional representation for Stormont in order to avoid a distortion of the respective strengths of the religious communities in the province of Northern Ireland.

The case for PR was simple. Taking the number of MPs returned, say, from the City of Leeds as being a total of six, PR would ensure two things. First, that each party would be represented in direct proportion to their vote in a multi-member constituency. Therefore a party gaining one sixth of the vote would get one seat, and so on. Second, since the voter could vote for up to six candidates of his or her own party, thus representing a wider choice between varying shades of opinion, this usually strengthened the hand of the moderates.

Sir Val Duncan (Rio Tinto) immediately reacted by saying: 'No more money for the Conservative Party until they come out for electoral reform'.

I want to state clearly that acceptance of the invitation to the gathering did not of itself imply acceptance of the case for electoral reform.

However, since then support for electoral reform has been growing in all quarters, including the business community, as expressed by the CBI.

The Jenkins Commission

In December 1997, the Prime Minister, Tony Blair, appointed Lord Jenkins of Hillhead to chair an independent commission on the voting system, charged with making its report in the autumn of 1998, after which the government was committed to a referendum.

The Commission's terms of reference were:

> The Commission shall be free to consider and recommend any appropriate system or combination of systems in recommending an alternative to the present system for parliamentary elections to be put before the people in the government's referendum.

> The Commission shall observe the requirement for broad proportionality, the need for stable government, an extension of voter choice and the maintenance of a link between MPs and geographical constituencies.

I include my memorandum, which I submitted to the Commission.

Memorandum by The Rt Hon. Jeremy Thorpe, submitted to the Independent Commission on the Voting System

This memorandum seeks to establish a voting procedure which reconciles the almost irreconcilable objectives of combining numerical accuracy with the retention of a strong connection between an MP and his or her constituents. This involves running two different systems in harness, namely: proportional representation by the single transferable vote in the larger cities of the United Kingdom, complemented by the alternative vote in the remaining constituencies.

One extraordinary factor which arises from the 1997 general election is the fact that there is no Conservative MP in Birmingham, Bradford, Bristol, Cardiff, Leeds, Liverpool, Manchester, Sheffield, Glasgow or Edinburgh. This cannot be healthy in a democracy. Taking approximately sixty city constituencies, there is set out in the accompanying table the collective total gained by each party; the percentage that this represents in the individual constituency; what seats were actually won; and what the probable outcome would be if those constituencies had run the elections collectively on a PR basis. It is fair to say that this latter figure is only an estimate, since the electorate might have voted slightly differently given the absence of what I might vulgarly call the squeeze factor. Cities very often have a corporate view of their problems which brings about a degree of cooperation between local MPs, often of differing political persuasions.

I do not believe that a three- or four-member constituency in, say, Manchester or Birmingham would make the individual voter feel remote from his MP. On the contrary, it might be the first occasion where a significant minority, at present deprived of representation, would have a chance of getting their voice heard. The great joy of PR is not only that it accurately reflects the support enjoyed by each party, but enables the electors to make a choice not only of party, but of individual candidates within their party. The enlarged parliamentary constituencies would be created by bunching together existing single-member parliamentary constituencies, and could safely be left to the Boundary Commissioners, who would decide the number of parliamentary constituencies to be bunched and any routine amendments to existing constituency boundaries.

It is an extraordinary thought that the official opposition, by reason of the eccentric voting system under which we labour at present, should be totally without representation in many of the major cities in the United Kingdom. It used to be said that the first-past-the-post system was excellent in a two-party situation and produced 'strong government'. My dual comments are that we no longer have a two-party situation — we have three UK parties, the two nationalist parties in Scotland and Wales, and no less than four parties in Northern Ireland. I do not know what is meant by 'strong government' unless it means arming one party with an overall majority, disregarding the extent to which it might be in a minority nationally, and producing an unrepresentative result for the rest of the political field. To give one flagrant example: in the February 1974 general election the Liberal vote increased from two million to six million. The effect of adding four million to the total result produced only three more MPs.

The first-past-the-post system does not ensure a fair outcome, even with a contest involving only two candidates. In 1948, using the first-past-the-post system, the United Party of South Africa polled more votes than the Nationalist Party, but the Nationalists won a majority of the seats and claimed that this gave them a mandate to extend and formalise the system of apartheid. It is interesting to reflect that that outcome did not represent the majority view of the South African electorate. For this they paid a heavy price. To have brought this about is attributable to the system whereby one has only one MP returned whether he and his party have polled say 80 per cent or 20 per cent — the majority or minority of votes.

Although sixty constituencies have been considered for amalgamation, there are other cities which think corporately, such as Coventry, with three MPs at present, which could suitably become a three-member seat. Other cities could be considered by the Commissioners. The whole process could be completed before the next election.

In order to maintain a close link between the MP and his or her constituency outside the big towns, I would recommend the use of the alternative vote. It does away with two weaknesses of the present first-past-the-post system. It is a fact that over 300 MPs, or almost half the House of Commons, were elected on a minority vote in the 1997 general election — that is, a majority of their constituents were opposed to their return. In the general election of February 1974, the number was 405! Once these results are aggregated it becomes more likely than not that the government returned will also be in a minority nationally.

The second great defect of the present electoral system is that where the likely outcome is closely contested between any two political parties in an individual seat, the parties in third place are crucified and their supporters advised that they must in no way vote in accordance with their convictions, but must vote for one of the two leading contenders as the only way to prevent their least favourite party candidate being returned. No vote should be regarded as wasted if people vote according to their convictions. There is something highly civilised in saying to the electorate: 'As a result of the poll to date no one party has a clear majority, your party is clearly defeated, but we would like you to express your second preference, which you have conveniently marked on your ballot paper'. The present situation is rather like a man who goes to buy twenty Benson & Hedges cigarettes, only to find that his brand is not in stock and his money is put in the till. Good commercial practice would suggest that the customer should be asked what was his second preference. Equally he could play his part in the election of his Member of Parliament. The need for tactical voting is proof of the shortcomings of the first-past-the-post system. The alternative vote is to be preferred to the second ballot system used in France, which unnecessarily prolongs the contest and takes place in two stages and leads to unseemly bargaining. The additional seat formula linked to AV runs the risk of party listing and is a very blunt way of trying to introduce a proportional result.

There will be criticism that the proposed arrangements will involve using two different systems in the same election. With the advent of the new Scottish Parliament, the Welsh Assembly and the European Parliament, we will all be using proportional systems of voting (some better than others!) whilst Westminster is still saddled with the old-fashioned first-past-the-post system. When a Conservative government sought to increase the numbers of Euro MPs in Northern Ireland from two to three so that the Catholic minority would be fairly represented, our European colleagues made it clear that the first-past-the-post system would in all probability result in three Protestant Euro MPs being returned. They insisted that if there were to be a third Euro

MP, the use of PR for a three-member constituency would be the only guarantee that the Catholic minority would be fairly represented. This, of course, would be on the assumption that they had one-third of the vote, which was highly probable.

Different electoral systems involving the same principles operate for local government in Northern Ireland and there is no move afoot to revert to the first-past-the-post system operating in the rest of the UK. When David Lloyd George partitioned Ireland he was determined that the Catholics in the north and the Protestants in the south should be fairly represented. He therefore provided PR for the elections north and south. He also hoped that the system would make it less likely that polarisation on a religious basis would occur. It is not a mere accident that in the south, where PR has never been abolished, the Protestant community have produced distinguished state presidents and Cabinet ministers. What is enormously significant, to me at least, is that there are two cathedrals in Dublin, both of which are Protestant, and in the absence of a Catholic cathedral a Protestant one is loaned out when needed for great state occasions!

Another minor example of dual electoral systems being used in an election was the university seats: nine MPs were elected by STV and three by first-past-the-post. I suppose it could be said that the German electoral system is a blend of first-past-the-post topped up with a proportionate formula, which incidentally was the invention of Asten Albu, the Labour MP for Edmonton, and member of the Control Commission.

I enclose by way of postscript certain county oddities produced at the last election. With regard to the 1948 South African election result, 547,000 votes for Smuts produced sixty seats, while 442,000 votes for Malan produced seventy-eight seats. Every contest was a straight fight.

The dual system which I have suggested was recommended by the Speaker's Conference of 1917. They recommended that PR with the transferable vote should be used in constituencies returning three to five members, and the alternative vote in single-member constituencies with more than two candidates. While the coalition government of 1916 was in office, a scheme was prepared, in pursuance of the Representation of the People Act 1918 for the election of 100 Members by PR. But the Liberal motion to carry it into effect was defeated on a free vote by fifty-six votes.

At the 1930 Speaker's Conference, the Conservative Party voted in favour of electoral reform by means of the single transferable vote, whilst the Labour Party supported the alternative vote. In 1931 a bill making provision for the introduction of the alternative vote was actually passed by the House of Commons but was rejected by the House of Lords.

13 March 1998

Analysis of 1997 general election results for some cities

City (no. of seats)	Lab	Con	Lib Dem	Ref	Others
Birmingham (11)					
(Including Sutton Coldfield)					
Votes %	54.6	28.4	12.7	2.8	1.5
Actual votes	256,687	133,315	59,961	13,086	7,003
Actual seats	10	1	–	–	–
PR seats	7	3	1	–	–
(Excluding Sutton Coldfield)					
Votes %	58.5	25.3	11.9	2.6	1.7
Actual votes	244,100	105,942	49,833	10,685	7,003
Actual seats	10	–	–	–	–
PR seats	6	3	1	–	–
Bradford (5)					
Votes %	49.4	32.6	13.1	3.3	1.6
Actual votes	116,984	77,273	30,961	7,790	3,865
Actual seats	5	–	–	–	–
PR seats	3	2	–	–	–
Bristol (4) *					
Votes %	49.6	27.1	17.9	2.7	2.7
Actual votes	106,951	58,689	38,626	5,878	5,902
Actual seats	4	–	–	–	–
PR seats	2	1	1	–	–
Leeds (8)					
Votes %	55.3	28.0	12.9	2.6	1.2
Actual votes	199,352	100,887	46,635	9,459	4,296
Actual seats	8	–	–	–	–
PR seats	5	2	1	–	–
Liverpool (5)					
Votes %	68.8	10.3	15.0	1.6	4.3
Actual votes	144,635	21,605	31,483	3,272	8,904**
Actual seats	5	–	–	–	–
PR seats	4	–	1	–	–
Manchester (5)					
Votes %	64.6	17.2	13.4	2.6	2.2
Actual votes	126,100	33,618	26,059	5,016	4,371
Actual seats	5	–	–	–	–
PR seats	4	1	–	–	–

City (no. of seats)	Lab	Con	Lib Dem	Ref	Others
Sheffield (6)					
Votes %	54.5	17.1	25.1	2.4	0.9
Actual votes	139,588	43,858	64,433	6,061	2,431
Actual seats	5	–	1	–	–
PR seats	4	1	1	–	–

City (no. of seats)	Lab	Con	Lib Dem	Ref	PC/SNP	Others
Cardiff (4)						
Votes %	51.8	24.4	13.9	2.4	3.5	4.0
Actual votes	89,868	42,239	24,165	4,166	6,010	6,970
Actual seats	4	–	–	–	–	–
PR seats	2	1	1	–	–	–
Edinburgh (6)						
Votes %	42.2	22.9	18.4	1.0	14.8	0.7
Actual votes	111,514	60,529	48,515	2,665	38,968	1,808
Actual seats	5	–	1	–	–	–
PR seats	3	1	1	–	–	1
Glasgow (10)						
Votes %	60.2	8.5	7.3	0.6	19.4	4.0
Actual votes	193,427	27,366	23,349	1,815	62,326	12,862
Actual seats	10	–	–	–	–	–
PR seats	6	1	1	–	–	2

* Bristol East and Bristol North West extend outside the city boundaries, including small parts of the unitary district of South Gloucestershire.

** Includes 6,040 votes cast for *Liberal* candidates.

Note: There is a difference of opinion as to whether Sutton Coldfield is included or excluded as part of the City of Birmingham. Both figures have been given to cover both situations.

Analysis of 1997 general election results — county oddities

	Lab	Con	Lib Dem	Others
Avon (10)				
Second party with fewest seats				
Votes %	36.5	32.7	26.3	4.5
Seats	6	1	3	–
Cornwall (5)				
Third party has a seat — second party has none				
Votes %	17.1	30.4	44.0	8.6
Seats	1	–	4	–
Dorset (8)				
Largest party has all seats for 41.8%				
Votes %	18.8	41.8	34.1	5.3
Seats	–	8	–	–
Surrey (11)				
Largest party has all seats for less than half the vote				
Votes %	22.2	46.2	24.5	7.0
Seats	–	11	–	–
Suffolk (7)				
Largest party with fewer seats than second largest				
Votes %	40.2	37.6	17.6	4.6
Seats	2	5	–	–
Sussex East (8)				
Largest party with fewer seats than second largest				
Votes %	29.2	39.4	24.0	7.4
Seats	4	3	1	–

1979 election: application to the courts

In the course of the 1979 general election, I was provided with an advance copy of a leaflet which was to be distributed in North Devon by Mr Auberon Waugh, a fringe candidate in the constituency. The leaflet was scurrilous and libellous, and I decided that we should issue a writ for libel and an injunction in the High Court restraining the circulation of the leaflet. The importance of an injunction was that without it, by the time the libel action came to court, the damage would have been done. Accordingly we decided to ask immediately for an injunction from a judge in chambers, who happened to be the Lord Chief Justice, Lord Widgery.

During that morning I was canvassing in a remote area on the North Devon–North Cornwall border at Woolfardisworthy, known as Woolsery, when a black cloud emerged on the horizon, and the entire press corps arrived. 'What was my reaction to the fact that the Lord Chief Justice had refused to grant me a injunction, on the grounds that the matter should be left until the hearing of the libel action?' It was pretty depressing news. I said that I would not comment until I had been briefed by my lawyers. How right I was!

I made for the next village, where there was a telephone box in the square, and managed to track down Christopher Murray, one of my solicitors, to find out what had happened. He replied: 'You are not up to date — understandably.' It transpired that my legal team had left the Lord Chief Justice and proceeded immediately down the corridor leading to the Court of Appeal, presided over by Lord Denning, the Master of the Rolls. At a suitable moment they had broken into the proceedings in hand and asked, as a matter of urgency, for an appeal to be heard from a decision just made by the Lord Chief Justice. They had asked that pending the appeal a restraining interm injunction be granted. Lord Denning had recognised the urgency of the matter in view of its relevance to the election. Within two hours he had heard the appeal and determined in my favour, reversing Lord Widgery's decision, and had issued an injunction. The law is capable of acting with speed in an emergency!

I returned to Woolsery and found the press corps still there. I told them that they were inadequately informed and had themselves been scooped.

Leadership

In 1966 Jo Grimond let me know that he intended to relinquish the party leadership. I urged him strongly to stay on to continue to make his undoubted contribution to the party and the nation. Frank Byers, at a private meeting, asked Jo whether he had enjoyed being Leader, to which Jo replied: 'Yes'. 'In that case,' said Byers, 'you can disenjoy the job for a bit longer'. Jo stayed on, but did not tell me when he finally decided to retire, as he felt that in all probability I would try to persuade him to stay on.

The Parliamentary Party of twelve were the total electorate at the time. We all knew how everyone was thought likely to vote. We subsequently discovered that Peter Bessell, the MP for Bodmin, had pledged his support to two of the three candidates! The one commitment was that Eric Lubbock and I agreed that if either of us were elected the other would give him whole-hearted support. Against that pattern, he continued as my Chief Whip when I became Leader. The twelve votes were counted by Donald Wade, a Liberal life peer and former Chief Whip in the Commons. The votes were taken out of a champagne cooler on the Chief Whip's desk. The result was Thorpe six, Lubbock three, Hooson three. The latter two withdrew and moved that I should now be elected unopposed.

The Liberal Party has its fair share of internal criticism. Apart from the hamfisted attempt to depose me while I was on my honeymoon in 1968, I received much help from the party in the House and in the country. One cause for unrest was the relationship between different sections of the party. In the '40s and '50s there was very little contact between the Liberal MPs and the party in the country. There was also profound disagreement in the Parliamentary Party itself. Sir Rhys Hopkin Morris (MP for Carmarthen) was a proponent of nineteenth-century *laissez-faire;* whilst Megan Lloyd George, along with Emrys Roberts (MP for Merioneth) stood for the radical, reforming wing. To the horror of loyal Liberals in the country, the Parliamentary Party was known to split and vote in two different lobbies, some for the 'ayes', some for the 'noes', which justifiably earned the derision of the rest of the House. Despite the fact that the House of Lords contained considerable talent in Viscount Samuel, Lord Beveridge, Lord Franks and Lord Layton, the Liberal Lords had equally weak links with the MPs in the Commons. On her peerage, Lady Violet Bonham Carter, now

Baroness Asquith, asked the Liberal Leader in the Lords, Lord Rea, how often the Liberal peers met. 'Never', came the reply. 'Never?' said Violet. 'We must meet regularly once a week.' 'And this', said Violet to me, 'we now do'.

Political development at local level was taking place by the time I became Leader. Local councils which had had no Liberal representation for three decades woke up to find them being elected in twos and threes. This was attributable to the practice of community politics, in which the activist relates to the problems of individuals and fights hard to find solutions. It was suggested that the leadership was hostile to community politics, but far from it; Liberal MPs attributed much of their electoral success to their campaigning in their constituencies on a local and personal basis.

It was about the time when I became Leader that the so-called 'Red Guards' were spawned. Originally enthusiastic young Liberals, many of them campaigned for policies which had little to do with the philosophy of Liberalism, and they were becoming an electoral liability. Their criticism of the leadership was intense, not all of it fairly placed.

Young Liberal national leaders came and went, Peter Hain, now a Labour minister, being one. A number joined the Conservative Party. A point was reached where it appeared that the youth movement and the party were on a serious collision course. I asked their newly elected leader, Steve Atack, to come and see me and told him of my concerns about the situation. I was anxious to face criticism where it was merited, but expected the Young Liberals to provide chapter and verse where it was not. I suggested as an experiment that I would be available for an hour a week for the foreseeable future for meeting him and some of his colleagues. This proved beneficial and was continued on a less formalised basis. The irony of the situation is that those who at the time were most critical of the leadership have gone on to join the other two parties and may now be regarded as birds of passage. It was a further irony that in the closing period of my leadership I received very loyal support indeed from Atack's Young Liberals.

Our local government base continues to expand, and the activity involved strengthens constituency organisations, which has helped lead to striking advances at parliamentary level.

In May 1976, with extreme reluctance, I resigned as Leader. I felt that the intense publicity on the subject of the so-called Scott affair was crowding out Liberal coverage of the real issues of the day. North Devon was a different issue, and I felt, as did my local Association, that it was just and reasonable that I should contest the seat at the next election.

I was asked recently what I was most proud of and what I most regretted during the course of my political career. For the former: first, to have played a major part in the evolution of a united Europe. Second, that I was involved in the introduction of legal reforms, including being a sponsor of the abolition of capital punishment. Third, the devolution of power from the centre, including Parliaments for Scotland and Wales. Fourth, partnership in industry. Fifth, that I can claim to have fought for the principles of human rights, which include opposition to racialism everywhere, and in particular opposition to the apartheid system in South Africa.

Three party leaders at the Banqueting Hall, Whitehall, for the Churchill Centenary — Harold Wilson, the Prime Minister, had to bail out Edward Heath, Leader of the Opposition, by lending him £1 (2 April 1974)

Above all, I played my part in taking the Liberal vote, which had got stuck in a rut, from two million to six million votes. And although this led to almost no increase in representation in Parliament, it broke the mould in that it was recognised at last that we had a three-party political set-up, operating under a two-party electoral system. The electorate at the last general election in 1997 exercised their own electoral reform by tactical voting, and it was the turn of the Conservative Party to be punished by the system. They were denied representation in almost every major city in the country.

One essential for a third party is to keep in the public eye, to ensure its voice is heard. It was particularly important to be part of the inter-party negotiations (for example on the allocation of party political broadcasts) and also to be involved in three-party discussions on arrangements for general elections. It was also important to ensure that the Liberal voice was

Vaulting fence, February 1974 election

heard in debates in the House. I recall on one occasion when there was a two-day debate on an important issue and not a single Liberal was called. As a result of strenuous efforts, which did not please the other two parties, time was granted on what was called Supply Days, which is debating time for the subject chosen by the opposition. When Harold Wilson was Prime Minister he took the view that the opposition was insufficiently funded and in consequence state grants were provided for opposition parties to finance their parliamentary offices — before this, when I became Leader I received financial support from party headquarters for one secretary, the other secretary being paid out of my own salary of £3,250 per annum. This new grant was known as the 'Short' money after Edward Short, the then Leader of the House.

When it was mooted that the government alone should lay a wreath at the Cenotaph on Armistice Day, Liberal reaction was expressed with devastating force by David Steel, then Leader, that the Liberal Party had provided two Prime Ministers who were in charge during World War One, and we wished to join in the tribute to the fallen.

On the question of life peerages, Macmillan steadfastly refused to consider the appointment of Liberal life peers, despite the fact that they had supported the Life Peerage Act on the basis that it would make for a more effective balance in the House of Lords. When Harold Wilson became Prime Minister in 1964, he offered Jo Grimond two life peerages and asked who they might be. Grimond replied that a strong case could be made for the nomination of two former Liberal Chief Whips in the House of Commons — Frank Byers and Donald Wade. However, he had some difficulty in deciding, as there was a strong case for including Lady Violet Bonham Carter, as she merited membership of the House of Lords. However, she had had a minor stroke and could not be guaranteed to give full-time service, and not least, she was Grimond's own mother-in-law. 'I see the difficulty', said Wilson. 'I'll give you three peerages, provided Lady Bonham Carter is the third, and to save you embarrassment, I'll put

Speech at Liberal Assembly

her on my list as opposed to yours'. In 1967, as Leader, I asked Wilson whether we could expect further creations. Wilson replied: 'Yes, you can have two', to which I replied: 'I have known certain generous Prime Ministers who have agreed to three recruits'. I got the Prime Minister's agreement to nominate three.

As for regrets, having actively campaigned when Liberal fortunes were at their lowest; having seen them revive in the '60s and '70s, until the present breakthrough with forty-six MPs, I regret that I am no longer on the front line of the battlefield, although I continue to be involved in the encouraging Liberal Democrat advance. Tactical voting is a very fragile plant. Given the next election, with by then a possibly unpopular Labour government and/or a possibly revived and united Conservative Party (which I think unlikely), the Liberal Democrats will need resolutely to campaign to hold, reinforce and improve upon their six million supporters. I hope I may claim that my leadership achieved, as I intended it to achieve, the three political Rs — relevance, reliability and radicalism.

Chapter Five

The Commonwealth and Africa

My interest in the Commonwealth started back in the 1940s when I was at Oxford. This was a time when colonial territories were struggling for their independence. India, Pakistan and Sri Lanka had already attained their independence within the Commonwealth in 1947, but African nations, led by charismatic figures like Nkrumah in Ghana, Kenyatta in Kenya, Seretse Khama in Botswana, Kaunda in Zambia, Nyerere in Tanzania, Nkomo in Southern Rhodesia, and a whole raft of countries in the Caribbean and the Far East such as Jamaica, Fiji and Malaysia were all campaigning for their independence. Britain at this period was by no means wholly committed to a multi-racial Commonwealth, and faced problems of racial tension within the UK itself. As a result of my commitment to decolonisation, I have been privileged to count many of the Commonwealth leaders as life-long friends.

I had early on taken a great interest in the plans to federate Northern and Southern Rhodesia and Nyasaland, all still under minority white rule. In my first speech as prospective Liberal candidate for North Devon in July 1952, I said that federation, without African support being a condition of acceptance, was doomed to failure. Significantly, talks on Southern Rhodesia's position in a future federation took place at the Victoria Falls Conference in 1952 with no African present. In practice, the Labour government laid out the plans for a Central African Federation, and the subsequent Tory government gave it legislative effect — in short one loaded the gun, and the other squeezed the trigger. However, I deal with Rhodesia in the next chapter.

One of my commitments was in regard to the Rivonia Trial in South Africa, where there was a very real possibility that if found guilty, Mandela, who was one of the accused, and at least some of his co-defendants would have been hanged. In May 1964 Judge De Wit adjourned the case for three weeks in order to consider his verdict and sentence. In those precious weeks the world was galvanised into action. All-night vigils were held outside St Paul's Cathedral in London and I myself became Hon. Secretary of the world campaign for the release of South African political prisoners — specifically calling for an amnesty for all political prisoners, the ending of the Rivonia Trial and the abolition of the death penalty. We lobbied scores of governments and although I can only claim that we played a small part, the UN Security Council, with four abstentions that shamefully included the UK and USA, urged the South African government to end the trial and grant amnesty to the defendants. This was backed by the UN as a whole. In the event the accused were sentenced to life imprisonment.

It is a chilling thought as to what might have happened had the majority view of the whites been allowed to prevail and the death sentences had been carried out. The history of South Africa might have been very different today. Notwithstanding twenty-seven years in prison, Mandela has shown tremendous magnanimity and a total lack of bitterness. This attitude and that of de Klerk, the last white president of South Africa, brought about a measure of reconciliation in South Africa, which is nothing short of a miracle. Mandela's address to both Houses of Parliament in Westminster Hall in July 1996 was tremendously moving and I leave the last word with him by quoting the wind-up of his speech:

… To close the circle, let our people, the ones formerly poor citizens and the others good patricians — politicians, businesspeople, educators, health workers, scientists, engineers and technicians, sportspeople and entertainers, activists for charitable relief — join hands to build on what we have achieved together and help construct a humane African world, whose emergence will say a new universal order is born in which we are each our brother's keeper.

And so let that outcome, as we close a chapter of two centuries and open a millennium, herald the advent of a glorious summer of a partnership for freedom, peace, prosperity and friendship.

South Africa

Black Sash protest

In 1961 South Africa decided to cut links with the Crown and become a republic. In view of her changed status, it was necessary for her to apply to rejoin the Commonwealth. The Commonwealth Heads of Government were due to meet in London at Lancaster House. A group of MPs, of whom I was one, and who included Fenner Brockway, Barbara Castle and Edith Summerskill, took the view that the racialist policies practised by South Africa, particularly following the 1948 election, which had enshrined apartheid as a social objective, were incompatible with a multi-racial Commonwealth. We therefore decided to protest outside Lancaster House by organising a Black Sash vigil along the lines of the heroic women protesters, outside Parliament buildings in South Africa, wearing black sashes as a mark of protest against apartheid.

We planned that each picket would be four in number and would last two hours. We did not intend to cause any obstruction and, if attacked, would not resist. As a preliminary measure we called on Pandit Nehru, the then Prime Minister of India, to inform him of our intentions and asked for his vote on the question of South Africa's exclusion from the Commonwealth. The answer was a very carefully chosen diplomatic reply, much to the fury of his sister, Mrs Pandit, who was then the Indian High Commissioner in London. 'Of course he will vote on the right side for non-racialism. He should have told you so without equivocation', she said.

I suggested to my colleagues that we should inform the Commissioner of Metropolitan Police at Scotland Yard of our intentions to minimise any difficulties which might arise. We were immediately received by the Commissioner, who thanked us for our courtesy but said that the area in question — around Lancaster House — was not within his jurisdiction since it was the Queen's private property. Would we like to talk to the Lord Chamberlain at St James's Palace? We gratefully accepted this suggestion and a call was duly put through to his office. Lord Scarborough was away in India, but the Deputy Lord Chamberlain, Sir Norman Gwatkin, would be delighted to see us straight away. He likewise thanked us for our courtesy in coming to see him, but said there was some difficulty involved, since the Commonwealth delegates were the Queen's personal guests whilst at Lancaster House and it would be a little embarrassing for her to invite her guests on the one hand and license a protest against them on the other! Why didn't we mount our protest on the steps of Lancaster House, which come under the Ministry of Works and therefore it would be a matter for Lord John Hope who was then Minister of Works. Would we like to see him? We replied that we would, and accordingly a telephone call was put through there and then. He agreed to see us after lunch. He received us very courteously, to which we were becoming accustomed! He said he couldn't allow us to picket the steps of the front door of Lancaster House since he was responsible for the unimpeded entry of delegates and there simply wasn't the space. He said that he could offer us the strip of roadway leading from the Mall to Lancaster House. I replied that there was another point of entry by road from St James's Palace. 'Very well', said the Minister, 'you can have two pickets'. That will mean', said I rather churlishly, 'that we will have to double the number of people required for picket duty.' 'I am afraid that is your problem', said the Minister. 'Right', I said. 'We accept'. 'But you haven't heard the conditions on which I am granting this. One of your pickets will be directly under the Duchess of Gloucester's bedroom and I want firm agreement that there will be no noise after 10 o'clock at night.'

We complied. The pickets went ahead and carried place-names of Sharpeville and Lange, the sites of notorious massacres. Ours was a dignified, and I believe effective, display. South Africa withdrew her application to rejoin the Commonwealth. It was a particular joy to me thirty-three years later to attend the service at Westminster Abbey in July 1994, welcoming a fully democratic South Africa back into the Commonwealth.

One slightly humorous spin-off was the reference to a photograph of a very tall Edith Summerskill and a comparatively diminutive Barbara Castle on picket duty as 'the Elephant and Castle'! It wasn't strictly accurate or original since it had previously been applied to a photograph of Barbara with Sir Andrew Cohen, an immensely tall colonial governor. However, the job of politicians is to keep good jokes in circulation!

I wondered where else in the world it would be possible to organise a protest in such a civilised manner.

Arms to South Africa

During the six months leading up to the Heads of Government meeting in January 1971 in Singapore, the Commonwealth was within an ace of disintegrating, as a result of Edward Heath's Government's decision to resume arms sales to South Africa. There had been a reference in the Conservative Party election manifesto, *A Better Tomorrow,* that Conservatives would lift the non-mandatory embargo on arms sales. The embargo had been approved by the UN Security Council in 1963, and the Wilson Government had honoured it. Within a week of the Conservatives' election victory on 18 June 1970, the South African Foreign Minister, Hilgard Muller, was waiting at the Foreign Office door. As Harold Wilson put it, it was like an alcoholic waiting at the pub door for opening time.

At the Foreign Office meeting, Muller referred to the Simonstown Agreement of 1955, when Britain handed over the naval base near Cape Town, and had agreed to supply anti-submarine frigates as part of South Africa's programme of naval expansion to guard the sea route round South Africa. Some weapons had already been supplied by 1964, and there was continuing agreement to cooperate on the sea route. In 1970 Alec Home, then Foreign Secretary, agreed to honour the pledge to sell arms for this purpose and this was indicated to the press before the matter was discussed in cabinet. Heath wrote directly to the Commonwealth Heads of Government with reference to the Simonstown Agreement, saying that Britain could not 'continue to benefit from these valuable defence facilities without being prepared to consider requests for equipment directly related to the sea routes, which we believe to be implicit in this agreement'. The statement to this effect would be made in ten days. Although Heath stressed that the equipment would be for external defence, and not for internal security, there was no hint of what he was considering supplying — some helicopters, for which frigates had been adapted, or a whole new range of equipment?

The messages from the Commonwealth Heads of Government started to come in. Most were concerned that these weapons could be used for internal security against the African population in South Africa, and in any event would result in the building up of the defence capacities of South Africa. Kaunda sent messages to all Commonwealth Heads of Government; Nyerere said Tanzania would withdraw from the Commonwealth if

Britain went ahead with a definite decision to resume arms sales; Zambia, Uganda, India and Sri Lanka were also likely to withdraw if Nyerere did so. Pierre Trudeau, the Liberal Prime Minister of Canada, sent Heath a letter expressing his own 'serious misgivings', and claiming that many Commonwealth governments were likely to interpret any arms sales as 'an implicit gesture of acquiescence in the policy of the South African government towards the African population'.

At that stage I went to see Arnold Smith, Secretary-General of the Commonwealth, to urge that a compromise be sought, and suggested that since some thirteen Commonwealth countries bordered the South Atlantic and Indian oceans, could they not form a joint study group which might take the heat out of the situation. It would not matter in practice if they never met but it would be a face-saver for all concerned. Arnold indicated that he favoured the idea and suggested that I should write to Pierre Trudeau in the hope that he might raise the matter at the impending Commonwealth Conference. This I did. Heath, after much persuasion, agreed to postpone his decision to sell arms until after the United Kingdom government had had an opportunity to consult the Commonwealth. Some of the heat was already drawn. In the meantime Kaunda was drafting a declaration of Commonwealth principles, to be presented at the Singapore summit. The dangers of a massive split still remained. It is believed that the Queen was advised against going to Singapore to discharge her now traditional role of entertaining Prime Ministers and Presidents at a state banquet and granting an audience to each in turn. She did not in fact attend. The plenary conference in Singapore agreed to set up an eight-nation study group consisting of representatives from Australia, Britain, Canada, India, Jamaica, Kenya, Malaysia and Nigeria plus the Commonwealth Secretariat. After some skilled drafting amendments by Pierre Trudeau, who had already played a significant part in setting up the study group, agreement was reached on the declaration of principles.

Heath was advised by his Law Officers that he was only under a legal obligation under the Simonstown Agreement to supply helicopters, four anti-submarine frigates and some naval spares. A month after Singapore, he announced that Britain would sell South Africa seven Wasp helicopters. He ignored any other request. In practice six helicopters were delivered.

In 1974 Wilson, following his general election victory, scrapped the Simonstown Agreement. Nigeria, India and Malaysia withdrew from the study group on maritime routes. The whole idea of the study group was dropped. It had served its purpose, granting time for second thoughts.

Lecture tours in South Africa
I was invited by the University of Cape Town to give the annual Feetham lecture in the spring of 1972. It was a lecture designed to remind people that there was segregation in the universities which the academic world deplored. It was fully backed and organised by NUSAS (the National Union of South African Students).

I arrived in Johannesburg and spent the first night in a hotel. Whilst I was dining, my suitcase was broken into and an electric razor stolen, which presumably was intended to persuade me that it was a burglary. In fact I could tell that my papers had been examined, but fortunately there was nothing of any consequence in the case.

I flew down to Cape Town where I was met by the group of students, who pointed out to me that the two burly-looking gentlemen sitting in the waiting room had been sent to 'look after' me. I went over to them and said: 'I gather you are keeping an eye on me. This is just to tell you that I shall be going straight to the Vice-Chancellor's house where I am staying and will not be going out this evening. I say this in case you want the evening off.'

I was in fact due at the Vice-Chancellor's to meet other members of the university. The Vice-Chancellor of Cape Town University, Sir Richard Luyt, was a very remarkable man. He was an Afrikaner, an international rugby player and a liberal. At one time in his career he had been in the British colonial service as a political secretary in Kenya and also Governor of Guyana, which after independence asked him to stay on as Governor-General. The Nationalists in South Africa could hardly accuse him of being a dangerous Marxist.

The Chairman of NUSAS, Michael Harris, was anti the South African government and pro almost anything British. During the night the news had come through of the death of the Duke of Windsor, who as Prince of Wales had been Chancellor of Cape Town University. Michael had requested that the portrait of the Prince should be placed in the university auditorium where the lecture was to take place. This was done and the portrait was draped in black crêpe.

There is a university song in Latin of which one line is *'floreat respublica'* (may the republic flourish). Michael changed it to *'pereat respublica'* (may the republic perish). Very few of the distinguished staff knew much Latin and it was a cause of great amusement to many of us to watch them singing lustily the revised version!

I also paid a visit to Witwatersrand University in Johannesburg to deliver a lecture. I said that I was familiar with Sir Robert Birley's (the educationalist and headmaster of Eton) legacy known as Birley's Law. This stated 'That the gentlemen from the Special Branch are to be found in the second row'. However, reassuringly I noted that the second row was occupied by Mr Oppenheimer, who was Chancellor of Cape Town, the Chancellor and Vice-Chancellor of Wits and many other distinguished people. I apologised for the absence of prominent clergy including Trevor Huddleston, Ambrose Reeves, José de Blanc and John Collins, none of whom could be present, and indeed would be most unwelcome to the government had they put in an appearance.

I met some very wonderful people of all races who courageously were carrying on the campaign against apartheid. None of them would have dreamt that it could have ended without bloodshed.

Seretse Khama

Two of my closest friends in Africa were Seretse Khama, the Chief of the Bamangwato tribe in Bechuanaland — now Botswana — and Ruth Williams, his wife. He studied at Fort Hare University in South Africa and went on to Balliol College, Oxford, where he shared rooms with Eric Lubbock, now Lord Avebury. Whilst reading for the Bar at the Inner Temple in 1948, he married Ruth — as a white woman, this breached tribal traditions and convention. Despite the support his marriage received from a gathering of the tribe, successive British governments from 1949 to 1956 barred him from returning to his country. I went on a Liberal delegation as a Young Liberal representative in 1951 to the Secretary of State for Commonwealth Relations, Patrick Gordon-Walker, in the course of which we urged him to end

Seretse's banishment. He returned home, having resigned his chieftainship, as a private citizen with his wife. He joined the Bechuanaland Legislative Council in 1961 and in 1962 formed the multi-racial Democratic Party. In 1965 he became Prime Minister and negotiated independence. In September 1966 he became President of Botswana and received a knighthood from the British Crown which he used throughout his life. His fourteen years in office were a model of racial harmony and tolerance, and firm opposition was shown to the racism of neighbouring Rhodesia and South Africa. Botswana was, and still is, the most democratic country in the continent of Africa.

Seretse Khama, President of Botswana 1966–80

On one occasion when I was dining with Ruth and Seretse in Gaborone, Seretse asked me whether my college, Trinity, Oxford, still shouted abusively at neighbouring Balliol. I said: 'You embarrass me. You tell Ruth of these exchanges.' Seretse replied: 'Trinity men used to shout over the wall and from neighbouring windows, "bring out your black men".' 'Oh,' I replied. 'That's all changed. There are so few white men in Balliol that they now cry out "Bring out your white men!"'

Following one landslide election, the opposition was reduced to three MPs. I said to Seretse that the very measure of his success had almost wiped out his Westminster-model opposition. He replied that one problem which he faced was that a salary was paid to the leader of the opposition. Any one of the three MPs could qualify as leader of the opposition. What should he do about the salary? I suggested that he split it three ways and this he did.

Kenneth Kaunda

During the Rhodesian declaration of independence (see Chapter Six), I made regular visits to Zambia, which borders on the Rhodesian frontier. There was no doubt that sanctions against Rhodesia had a debilitating effect on the Zambian economy, but this was a price the country was prepared to pay.

Kenneth Kaunda, the country's first President, is a close and valued friend. We used to have a working lunch together — just the two of us in the cavernous state dining room at State House. I became increasingly a means of communication between our governments, and used to appear on Zambian television discussing the political situation.

Kenneth Kaunda, President of Zambia 1964–91

When the Commonwealth Heads of Government Conference took place in Zambia in 1979, Kaunda was fulsome in his praise for the part the Queen had played in resolving the Rhodesian crisis. He made an extraordinary gesture when he discovered that the state banquet to be given by the Queen to the presidents and prime ministers was to be held in a hotel. He made State House available to her and removed himself to the State Lodge up-country. Zambian ministers found it a strange experience to go to State House — before independence the residence of the Governor, and thereafter of the

President — to see the Royal Standard, with the Queen in residence, and to be received by royal staff. This was a tribute to both President and Queen. A similar gesture was made by Seretse Khama during the Queen's state visit to Botswana.

The recent move in Zambia to strip Kaunda of his citizenship, on the grounds that although born in northern Zambia (then Northern Rhodesia), he was a citizen of Malawi (formerly Nyasaland) because his parents came from there, effectively declares much of his twenty-seven year rule illegal. This finding is petty, childish, vindictive, and shows a contempt for the initial years of independence.

Nixon and the Commonwealth

Harold Wilson, as a good democrat, attached importance to opposition leaders in this country meeting visiting foreign politicians. In 1969 he suggested that I, as Leader of the Liberal Party, should meet President Nixon on his visit to London. This was arranged, and indeed, since then, these meetings have become established practice. I saw the President at Claridges, where there was a police presence lining the staircase, the hall and the approaching streets even more numerous than the security provided for the Soviet leaders Khrushchev and Bulganin.

Nixon was obviously well-briefed and, referring to Rhodesia's illegal declaration of independence, said to me: 'I know that the Rhodesian situation is important, but tell me why you think so'. I replied that if there were a third world war it would not necessarily be a clash between Marxist and capitalist opponents. Ironically, the two bitterest enemies at that time were China and Russia, both of whom were Marxist. Conflicts would be more likely to arise through the polarisation of the world on the basis of colour. Jacob Malik, the Soviet Ambassador, had told Lord Gladwyn that, in the eyes of the Chinese, the difference between the Americans and the Russians was that the Americans were the white barbarians who came by sea and the Russians were the white barbarians who came by land. Unfortunately, the world was divided into the 'haves' and the 'have-nots' which in general coincided with the division of colours.

I said that the Commonwealth had come into being almost by accident

In discussion with US President Richard Nixon during his visit to London, February 1969

and was the one organisation covering every continent, creed and colour, which met in conditions of complete equality and relative trust. White supremacy claimed by the Rhodesians was a direct challenge to this concept. The vote in the American Congress to break the chrome embargo to Rhodesia was directly assisting the white Smith regime. Given a substantial black vote in the USA it could become a highly sensitive issue. I think he got the message.

At the independence ceremonies in March 1957 of the Gold Coast colony, which then became Ghana, Vice-President Nixon, as he then was, was representing the USA. Determined to be folksy, he approached a tall man, whom he assumed to be a Ghanaian and said: 'I am very privileged to be here for your independence celebrations'. The man made no reply. So Nixon tried again: 'We were under the British yoke ourselves — some time back, it is true — but we know how you guys are feeling today to have got your liberty and freedom'. The man turned and said: 'Say, Mr

Vice-President, I don't know much about liberty and freedom. I am just a visiting journalist from Alabama!'

The Commonwealth and television

My involvement on the ground throughout the Commonwealth was made possible by acting as a roving reporter to the ITV programme, 'This Week'. In almost every case, it involved a report on some aspect of pre-independence developments in the Commonwealth. I went to Jamaica to interview Norman Manley and Sir Alexander Bustamante, respectively Prime Minister and leader of the opposition. This was to assess the effects of the Commonwealth Immigration Act 1962. I interviewed the leaders of Nigeria, namely Azikwe, Chief Awolowo, the Sardauna of Sokoto, J.C. Okpara and Sir Abubakar Tafawa Balewa, who was tragically to be murdered. I went to Malta during the elections when Mintoff, the Labour Leader and Prime Minister, was interdicted by the Catholic Church. Its leader, Cardinal Gonzi, who was as old as time itself, insisted that the church was not interfering in politics but merely defending the inheritance handed down by St Peter!

In Ghana I went to assess the dangers which the Queen would face on her proposed state visit in November 1961, particularly as Nkrumah, the president, had not dared to venture out of State House for several months. He had assumed dictatorial powers and had made many enemies, and it was thought that there might be a risk of exposing the Queen to violence directed at him. My other concern was that the Ghanaian regime would exploit her visit as representing support for Nkrumah's Convention People's Party. They had already printed, as political propaganda, a photograph of the Queen in the Irish state coach waving in a gesture which quite coincidentally accorded with the logo of the CPP, which was an outstretched hand. Nigeria to the south was making a stab at democracy and was anxious that the true constitutional position should be understood, namely that a state visit to a Commonwealth country did not involve support of the current regime.

The Ghanaian Minister of the Interior refused to grant me an interview on TV, but I 'doorstepped' him as he entered Parliament for the opening of the session and asked him how he could justify the growing list of political prisoners detained without trial or charge. He blurted out a few remarks and disappeared inside. Very shortly afterwards I was approached by an official who said that the minister wished to see me. Before going in to see the minister, I told our cameraman to rush to the airport with the film and get it out of the country and that if I didn't appear within ten minutes, to alert the British High Commissioner. I found the minister surrounded by three other ministerial colleagues and he screamed at me: 'Did you record an interview?' I replied that I had. He then said that he had no idea he was being interviewed, to which I replied that it was hardly surprising since at all times he looked away from me. Another minister shouted at me: 'How dare you behave like this?' To which I replied: 'How dare you speak like this to a fellow Commonwealth MP?' It had a sobering effect and I went on to suggest that we would not need to use the film if he would give me a proper interview. To this he agreed and I duly proceeded to the minister's house. He was Kwaku Boateng, whose son Paul became a minister in the Labour government in the UK after the 1997 election.

During my visit, I did what I could to obtain the release of Joe Appiah, the Ghanaian husband of Sir Stafford Cripps' daughter. He was detained by Nkrumah without trial or charge, and his life was in danger. I went to see Joe's wife, Peggy, and ironically, next door to their front gate, lying on the ground, was the signboard of a previous neighbour, 'Dr H.K. Banda, Medical Practitioner'.

I could not resist commenting on the fact that Banda had been detained by the colonial power, the UK, in Nyasaland, whilst Appiah had been detained by an independent African state, Ghana. Which of these two men would find their detention more of a political advantage as far as their prospects of becoming president or prime minister of their respective countries were concerned? Years later, I was to re-visit Ghana on behalf of Amnesty International to report on the condition of the political prisoners then detained. My first visit was to the Christianborg Castle where Joe Appiah had his ministerial office. I told him that the last time I had come to Ghana, I had tried to secure his release from prison. I was now urging him to release those that *he* and his colleagues had detained! I saw about sixty prisoners in all and struck a bargain with the government that I would make recommendations on the whole question of the rights and conditions of political prisoners, and would only publish the report if the Ghanaian government *unreasonably* failed to act on those recommendations. In fairness to them, they acted on most of the major recommendations.

Hastings Banda

Banda and the bishop
The reference to Banda leads logically to Nyasaland, now Malawi, which I visited during the state of emergency in the spring of 1959. Banda was then detained and the Governor, Sir Robert Armitage, had somewhat foolishly and insensitively decreed that the word kwacha, which means dawn, (i.e. independence) was a banned word and its use was a punishable offence. Ironically, it is now the national currency of Zambia, formerly Northern Rhodesia. I wrote to Banda — whom I had yet to meet — in prison and asked him whether he would be interested, when he was released, in visiting London with all expenses paid and a fee of, I believe, £150, to give me a world exclusive TV interview. The British, being model jailers, ensured that he got the letter and that his reply was duly received by me, the content of which in brief said: 'Yes'. I then sold the idea to 'This Week'.

Banda was due to be released, and it was arranged that he and I would meet in the early hours of the morning of 7 April 1960 at Rome airport, where we would switch planes in the hope of bypassing the press. I noticed that Banda, who arrived very bleary-eyed and still slightly shell-shocked, was wearing a black hat with a black felt rose in the front. At that moment a very tall bishop, who I believe was the Bishop of Uganda, hove to and asked Banda whether by mistake he had taken his hat. 'No', said Banda rather abruptly. I pointed out that the hat he was wearing had got a black felt rose on the front — was this in order? Banda removed the hat and said: 'Ah, that fool has taken my hat!' There had indeed been a mix-up. Exchanges of hats were duly made and Banda started the journey in a very bad mood. To humour him I said: 'Kamuzu, this is an historic journey. You come out of a British jail before independence and therefore will become president; you arrive in Rome wearing a bishop's hat and by the time you reach London you will claim to be Sir Roy Welensky's (former Prime Minister of the Central African Federation) private confessor!' He roared with laughter and the ice was broken.

Another incident which I recall involving Banda was at a state banquet at Buckingham Palace in 1969 for presidents and prime ministers of the Commonwealth. The seating was imaginatively set out in tables of ten, with at least one member of the royal family at each table. Princess Margaret headed our table and at one stage said to me: 'You seem to know Dr Banda very well. How did you first meet?' 'You tell her', said Banda. As tactfully as I could, I replied that it was on another occasion when he was the guest of her sister the Queen. 'Where was that?' she said. 'Gwelo Jail', said Banda. 'I hope you were well looked after', she said. 'Oh yes', said Banda. 'So much so that my white jailers complained that they didn't like having to clean a black man's bath!'

It is a cause for profound concern that Banda was so intolerant of opposition. And yet, as far as his enemies from the Central African Federation days are concerned, he granted them total forgiveness, and in fact invited his two principal white jailers from Gwelo to the Malawi independence celebrations. Likewise, when Roy Welensky's wife died, he made available his lakeside house for him. I discovered how intolerant he had become when a couple of perfectly innocent magazines on African affairs were seized from me on my arrival in Malawi. They had apparently been critical of Banda in the past and had ever since been on the banned list. The treatment accorded to Aleke Banda (no relation), a prominent dissident, who was given assurances of immunity on his return to Malawi and then kidnapped and imprisoned, was a shocking example of his intolerance.

Malawi itself is one of the most beautiful countries in the world. It reminds me of the Highlands of Scotland in good weather.

Banda and the saga of the stole

Banda's mix-up with the bishop's hat reminds me of a similar occurrence at Number 10 Downing Street, at a dinner given by the Prime Minister for the Commonwealth Heads of Government. As we were leaving, the unmistakable voice of Dr Banda could be heard calling out to President Kaunda of Zambia: 'Hey, you robber. Put down that mink stole. It belongs to my first lady.' Somewhat surprised, Kenneth Kaunda replied that he was certain that the stole belonged to his wife and Banda must be mistaken. At that moment Mrs Kaunda came into range and when asked by KK what the position was she suddenly remembered that she had left an identical stole in the car. The situation was smoothed over and I said to Banda: 'This seems to be a repetition of the bishop's hat'. 'You keep quiet about the hat', he said in a jocular mood.

East African Asians

I had been concerned for a long time as to the self-imposed vulnerability of the Asian community in East Africa: whether providing goods from the street-corner shop or as traders and partners in commercial concerns, dealing in tea, coffee, agricultural products and iron and steel. I remember going round an Asian-owned strip-mill in Kenya, which was a massive commercial concern, and was asked for my opinion. I replied that I was surprised that there was not a single African employee to be seen. One complaint that was often heard was that the Asian community exported a large amount of their earnings back to India, which they regarded as their ultimate base. It therefore came as no surprise, at the time of Kenyan independence in 1963, that pressure was brought to bear on the Kenyan Asians, which prompted many of them to leave the country and come to live in the UK. It was also no great surprise when Asians in Uganda came under attack by Amin in 1972 — although the action that he proposed was brutal and inexcusable.

The statutory position regarding immigration into the UK occupied much parliamentary time. The British Nationality Act of 1948 confirmed the principle of uncontrolled entry into the UK for all Commonwealth citizens. The increase of immigrants in the late '50s led the Macmillan Government in November 1961 to introduce a bill which required Commonwealth immigrants to possess a 'special skill' or have a job awaiting them. In the course of the debate on the Kenya Independence Bill in 1963, provision was made for citizens wishing to opt to become citizens of the UK and colonies to do so in preference to becoming Kenyan citizens, within the first two years after independence. The burning question was: what was the legal status of these people as far as emigrating during and/or after the two-year option period was concerned?

I asked a Parliamentary Question and received a massive ministerial evasion on 22 November 1963:

Jeremy Thorpe: If a Kenyan is a citizen of the UK and colonies and has not yet decided to opt to become a Kenyan citizen in the interregnum, do I take it that he is subject to the Immigration Act unless his passport has been issued in this country, or is he allowed free access?

Mr Hornby (Under-Secretary of State for Commonwealth Relations for the Colonies): If the Hon. Member will allow me, I shall leave points about immigration and others which might come up at this stage, because otherwise I might get involved in a rather lengthy argument covering other aspects.

In the wind-up of the debate I again asked:

Jeremy Thorpe: Will the Rt Hon. Gentleman deal with the point about immigration? Do I take it that they would still be subject to the operation of the Commonwealth Immigration Act unless their passports had been issued to them from within this country?

The Rt Hon. Duncan Sandys (Secretary of State for the Commonwealth): I should like notice of that question, but, with reservations lest I make a mistake, I would think, once they have acquired Commonwealth citizenship and have given up their UK citizenship, they would be treated as citizens of the Commonwealth countries to which they belong; but they may for a period still have UK citizenship before they opt for Commonwealth citizenship. That is the point I had in mind.

From these statements it will be seen that the question was not answered. In March 1968 the Wilson Government rushed through an Immigration Act creating a voucher system for Kenyan Asians. Again I asked the question, this time to Jim Callaghan on 28 February 1968:

Jeremy Thorpe: As the Rt Hon. Gentleman wishes to remove uncertainty, may I, without breaking the chronological order of his argument, press him firmly to answer the point which has been raised, namely, what is the legal status of these people? If they are UK citizens, what rights have they? What obligations have they? What will happen if they arrive here illegally? Where will they be shipped to? Are they stateless or not?

Callaghan: I prefer not to deal with the question of legal status, because this is a matter better dealt with by lawyers. It is a most complicated subject, and I have not heard it raised as a major question during the discussion. We have been dealing with the more human issues of what happens to these people, and I would like to come to the question later.

One view taken by David Steel in the debate was:

> It was the amendment in 1965 to the 1962 Act which did that — i.e. remove the right of free entry into this country of people of the Asian and African communities in Kenya.

The two front benches had agreed to let the bill be introduced without division. My colleagues and I took a contrary view to the effect that the government was in fact saying that a citizen of the UK and colonies had no entry rights and was virtually stateless. We decided to oppose the bill and forced an all-night sitting in the Commons.

At the end of the day, we attracted an opposition vote of over thirty, including Iain Macleod and Nigel Fisher, together with other Members from the Labour benches. We then took the fight to the House of Lords where the Liberal peers initiated a debate which was to keep the House up all night. I looked in around 3 A.M. and insisted that any Liberal peer over eighty still attending the debate should go home. It was an unhappy period. Many people had relied on the good faith of successive UK governments.

In 1971 the Heath Government changed the whole approach to immigration. The Immigration Act of 1971 imposed a single system of control on Commonwealth and 'alien' immigrants, while allowing free entry to those with parents or grandparents born in the UK.

On 6 August 1972, in a speech in Kampala, General Amin declared that 50,000 Ugandan Asians with British passports were to be expelled to Britain within three months. He declared that they were 'sabotaging the economy'. In fact, the Asian community played a dominant role in the Ugandan economy, but kept themselves very much to themselves and failed to integrate with the Africans.

During a BBC broadcast, in which I was canvassing these views, the interviewer challenged me to put up a Ugandan Asian family in my home. I replied that provided they did not feel too cut off in the depths of North Devon, and realised that employment was difficult to find, I would certainly welcome a family. The UK Resettlement Organisation accepted my offer, and chose a family to come to stay with me. There were three involved: Suzie Patel and her daughter Rajna, and Suzie's brother Subbash. I met them at Umberleigh station, a rural request stop. They had four or five cardboard boxes, which contained all their worldly belongings. They came from a wealthy family, who had directed a large public company — everything had been abandoned.

I took them to their rooms at Higher Chuggaton and to my horror found in Subbash's room that the bedclothes had been chewed by, at best, a squirrel, or possibly a rat. I told him that he would have to tell his relatives that European houses were infested!

Things moved swiftly: almost at once I got Suzie a job in a North Devon factory, Subbash a place in college to complete his studies and Rajna was accepted by the local school, and a neighbour of mine, who commuted between Cobbaton and Barnstaple, gave them a lift every day.

Subbash turned out to be a very fine cricketer and local cricket clubs competed with each other to get him to play for their side. He soon built up a large number of friends. The Patels stayed with me for the best part of nine months, until they found a flat in Barnstaple. They eventually left North Devon when Subbash found a job in London. They became firm friends.

Uganda

Editor's note: Uganda became independent of British colonial rule in 1962 under Milton Obote. After growing ethnic tensions, particularly with the autonomous kingdom of Buganda, Obote imposed increasingly centralised and oppressive government. Relying on the army, he made the mistake of falling out with its commander, Idi Amin, who mounted a coup in January 1971.

An incompetent and brutal ruler, Amin maintained his grip on power through wholesale slaughter of his opponents. Courting public support, he ordered all Asians who had not taken Ugandan nationality (widely seen as exploiters) to leave the country in 1972, a move which helped to destroy the economy. In an attempt to divert attention from domestic problems, Amin launched an attack on Tanzania in October 1978, but was defeated and overthrown by Tanzanian troops and Ugandan exiles in April 1979.

Obote returned to power after elections in December 1980, but was in turn overthrown by Yoweri Museveni's National Resistance Army in 1986.

Denis Hills

In 1975, relations between Idi Amin and the UK government were almost at breaking point. The situation had been inflamed by a British lecturer and author, Denis Hills, who had been found guilty of treason (11 June 1975), for criticising Idi Amin. The exchanges between Kampala and London became more and more strident and there was very real concern that Hills' life might be in peril.

It was against that background that I rang the Uganda High Commissioner in London to say that relations were getting out of control between our two governments and might I, by visiting Uganda, be able to help, at least as far as Denis Hills was concerned? The High Commissioner asked me to come round to his office at once, and there and then put through a call to Amin. Yes, I should come out to Uganda and catch the next available plane, suggested Amin. Instinctively I thought I needed a little more time and said that I would come out in a day or so. In the meantime I wanted to consult Jim Callaghan, the then Foreign Secretary, to ensure that I didn't do anything to endanger a highly delicate situation. I remember asking the High Commissioner whether Amin knew what I had said about him in the past. Apparently he asked: 'Is this the man who described me as a Black Hitler?' 'Yes', said the High Commissioner. Amin laughed and said: 'After all, that's politics!' When I rang Callaghan I was very guarded and indicated that I wanted to consult him as a matter of courtesy. He suggested that as we were both attending a diplomatic dinner that evening we could discuss the matter then. On that occasion he pointed out that Lieutenant General Sir Chandos Blair and Major Iain Grahame were flying out with a personal letter from the Queen to Idi Amin about Hills (21 June 1975), and although he neither could nor would stop me going, I might think it over-egging the pudding if I went out as well. I readily agreed, and rang up a relieved Marion to say: 'Uganda is off. The weekend is free — let's make for Aldeburgh.'

On 1 July 1975 one newspaper reported:

HILLS' HEAD IS OFF THE CHOPPING BLOCK
Uganda's military dictator, Idi Amin, today gave way to international pressure and granted Denis Hills, the sixty-one year old British author and lecturer, an unconditional reprieve from the firing squad. Hills had enraged Amin by describing him as a 'village tyrant' in a manuscript discovered by Ugandan police in Hills' home.

Military intervention

In 1982 I was back in Uganda. Milton Obote had brought to an end the murderous regime of General Amin and had once again become president. He was himself subsequently to be deposed, and his regime was found to be almost as brutal as that of Amin.

I was catching a plane to Nairobi one Friday afternoon and had arranged to call on the Vice-President, Paolo Muwanga, whose office was in the old Buganda Parliament building, on the way to the airport.

To put the building in context: the British had left an extraordinary constitutional mish-mash at the time of independence. Uganda comprised four hereditary kingdoms, one of which, Buganda, was ruled by the Kabaka, known to those close to him as King Freddie. He was a man of infinite charm, and was well disposed to the United Kingdom, having held a commission in the Grenadier Guards and been an undergraduate at Cambridge. There were also other substantial territories outside the kingdoms in Uganda. The whole country was a republic, and the first president was the Kabaka. Therefore, in part of the capital, Kampala, King Freddie was His Highness the Kabaka, with his own parliament, and in other parts of Kampala he was His Excellency the President. The arrangement could not last; Obote, in pre-Amin days, ousted the Kabaka, who was to die in poverty and exile in the UK. One of the few civilised acts performed by Amin was to allow the Kabaka's body to be returned for burial in Kampala some time after, where he lay in state in a glass coffin. I was invited, amongst others, to accompany him on his last journey. I declined, as I had already paid my respects at his first funeral in London and thought it more appropriate that the accompanying party should be predominantly made up of his fellow countrymen. More recently, Yoweri Museveni, president since January 1986, who has done much to stabilise Uganda after years of repression and turmoil, allowed King Freddie's son to return as Kabaka with limited powers.

With regard to the funeral in the UK, the then Labour government was so anxious not to offend Obote during his first administration that it absented itself from the London ceremony, and instead sent a civil servant. I thought this outrageous and contacted the Conservative opposition, suggesting that the opposition parties should at least turn out and show solidarity, and this we did.

The Buganda Parliament building is at one end of a processional way, leading to the Kabaka's old palace. I asked my driver on the way to the airport to drive via the palace, which I wanted to see for nostalgic reasons. My driver pointed out that the palace was now an important military base, and showed some apprehension. I saw no problem, and said we would just drive past. We slowed down momentarily about 100 yards from the main gates and were waved down by two armed guards, who ordered us out of the car. There was little point in arguing. However, the development that I had not bargained for was to be told that I was a spy. 'You come with us'. 'Where are you taking me?' 'To see our officers.' 'That suits me fine.' A little time later: 'Our officers have left for the weekend. You must stay until they return on Monday.' They were singularly unimpressed by my plans to fly to Nairobi that afternoon.

I did not relish a weekend in military detention and addressed the sergeant who had joined the two guards: 'Sergeant, am I right in saying that the Vice-President's office is in the Kabaka's old Parliament Building, since I was there twenty-five minutes ago, talking to the Vice-President. Please telephone his office, and if he will vouch for me, you must release me.' 'We have no telephone.' I did not believe him, but I was not in a strong position to argue with him! I came up with an alternative plan: 'Put me back in the car, with two guards armed with machine guns, one on each side of me, with orders to drive back to the Parliament Building.' When he showed some hesitation, I said: 'Come on, you are risking nothing if you establish the truth. I am risking my life.' To my great relief, he gave the necessary orders and I got back in the car with my two heavily armed companions. As good fortune would have it, we approached the main gates of the Parliament Building, and the same two security men were on duty who had examined my papers on my visit to the Vice-President. They called up the Vice-President's ADC, who welcomed me with some surprise to see me back. I explained what had happened and he asked what he could do to help. 'Tell the two guards to release me and ring the airport, asking the aviation authorities to hold the plane.' He asked how the soldiers had treated me. I said that their behaviour had been exemplary. By now, duly chastened, the two guards asked if I would give them a lift back to the barracks. I was somewhat apprehensive about stopping at the barracks again, in case of a repeat performance. Having driven some of the way, I stopped the car and said that this was as far as I would take them; they could either walk the remaining distance, or we could return to the Vice-President's office. Grudgingly they got out and we parted company. We drove at fantastic speed to the airport, and arrived two minutes before the departure of the Nairobi plane. I determined that in future I would be more cautious in my sightseeing activities!

Rwanda

One of the most curious missions which I was invited to carry out in Africa centres round Rwanda, the scene of the worst atrocities in Africa in recent years. Shortly after the King of Rwanda, a giant of almost seven feet high, was expelled by the Belgians, the Kabaka of Buganda, to whom I was giving trade and investment advice, asked me whether I would see the King of Rwanda. He was then in Uganda, and wanted some advice. I duly met the King at the Kabaka's palace in 1961, and was told that he was interested in asking me to organise an invasion of his own country so that he could re-capture the throne. I replied that this was not really in my line. The King, unperturbed by the show of modesty on my part, asked me what would be required. I said I supposed a portable radio station, a couple of spotter planes, rifles and training facilities for his supporters — possibly in Tanzania. The King remarked that this would be expensive and I concurred. 'How do we raise the money?' he asked. I asked him where the Rwandan pygmies stood in all this. 'Fully supportive', he replied.

Jeremy Thorpe with ex-King Kegalle of Rwanda, 1961

Somewhat incredulously I asked him whether he and his fellow giants would lead the pygmies into battle. 'Certainly', he replied. 'In that case', I said, warming to the theme: 'I think we can sell the exclusive invasion rights to Metro Goldwyn Mayer for half a million dollars'. 'Excellent', replied the King. 'My Prime Minister will be in London next week and will call on you in order to carry matters further.' Sure enough, a week later an even greater giant knocked at my front door, and said: 'I am the Prime Minister. I have come about the invasion.' Realising that the thing was getting out of control, I said: 'The invasion is off'.

Suez and Menzies

I was invited by the Australian High Commissioner, Alec Downer and his wife Mary, to come for lunch in their beautiful Wiltshire home to meet Robert Menzies, one of Australia's most distinguished Prime Ministers. I was surprised but flattered to see that I was the only other guest invited. Clearly the old boy wanted to put me through my paces. 'Well, young man', said Menzies, 'what future is there for your party?' 'Well', I replied, 'here is something where you could be a real help. You should tell your Conservative colleagues in this country that Australia has a far more representative form of democracy by using proportional systems of voting — the alternative vote for the lower house and PR by single transferable vote for the Senate. Given that the UK adopted a fairer system of voting, the answer is that we would be in government sooner rather than later. For this reason you would find it very difficult to overcome their hostility to a more democratic voting system.'

Menzies had been Chairman of the Canal Users' Association comprising 98 per cent of the users of the Suez Canal. It was clear that he wanted to discuss the Suez crisis. This arose with the announcement on 26 July 1956 by President Nasser of Egypt that he had nationalised the Anglo–French Suez Canal Company. He promised compensation but threatened the imprisonment of foreign canal employees if they quit their jobs. Nasser's decision to seize the canal came in the wake of the refusal by Britain and the US to finance the building of the Aswan High Dam on the basis that the Egyptian economy was too weak to carry through the project. Nasser said that if the imperialist powers did not like what he had done, they could 'choke to death on their fury'. Nasser went on to say that he would use the revenues from the canal to finance the building of the Dam. Anthony Eden's reaction was that 'a man with Colonel Nasser's record' cannot be allowed 'to have his thumb on our windpipe'. The first diplomatic approach was by Bob Menzies, as head of a five-nation team. He took with him a plan for international control of the Suez Canal. Foster Dulles, the US Secretary of State, brought to London a not dissimilar plan, which suggested an international board association with the UN. Eden, for his part, made it clear that the use of force could not be ruled out and reservists were called up.

On 31 October 1956, British Canberra bombers took off from Cyprus and made bombing raids over military airfields near Cairo and in the Canal Zone. The bombing followed the expiry of a twelve-hour ultimatum in which Britain and France called on Egypt and Israel, who had invaded the Canal Zone, to pull their forces back. The USA, supported by the USSR, tabled a resolution in the Security Council calling on all UN members to refrain from the use of force and to refrain from giving aid to Israel. Britain and France exercised their veto. By 6 November, Royal Marine Commandos had landed near Port Said, and the airfield on the outskirts of Port Said was soon under British control. Britain and France were subjected to enormous pressure to withdraw their forces and reluctantly agreed to a UN plan that allied troops would be replaced by an international force, 6,000 strong, from Sweden, Denmark, Norway, Colombia, Finland and India.

Menzies asked me what I had advocated at the time. I told him that the arguments were very finely balanced, but it seemed to me more realistic to recognise the right of a country to nationalise its assets, subject always to the payment of adequate compensation. We should therefore have called for a three-man commission, composed of one nominated by the UK and France, one by Egypt and an agreed person nominated by the United Nations. Their job would be to hear and determine the level of compensation payable to the Suez Canal stockholders. Secondly, there should be a technical commission, nominated in the same manner, to discuss and recommend canal dues payable and maintenance standards required.

At this stage Nasser had no idea whether he could carry on running the canal without the skills of foreign pilots. Our offer should be that if he accepted the deliberations of the first two commissions, then for our part, we would use our best endeavours to persuade the pilots to stay on. However, if he felt unable to accept these measures, a token sum of $100 million would be placed in a reserve account in Zurich. This would be used to meet the increased costs of shipowners who would boycott the canal and go the long route round the Cape.

I felt that this was a reasonable offer that Nasser could not risk refusing. Menzies was obviously intrigued and with admirable reserve said: 'That would have been a very different hand of cards for me to have played'. As it was, he was given an almost impossible job.

The prospect of lasting peace in the area came with the advent of President Anwar Sadat of Egypt, who was the most courageous man I have ever met. Certainly his historic visit to Israel, with his address to the Knesset in Jerusalem, was one of the most dramatic events of the century. Alas, along with Rabin and others, his work for peace in the Middle East was to cost him his life.

Jeremy Thorpe in discussion with Anwar Sadat, President of Egypt, in London

Chapter Six

Rhodesia

Editor's note: Southern Rhodesia, a self-governing colony since 1923, was slowly moving towards granting greater political rights to the black population when the ruling United Federal Party was defeated in 1962 by the more conservative Rhodesia Front, whose goal was Rhodesian independence under guaranteed minority rule. After several attempts to persuade Britain to grant independence, the RF government, now led by Ian Smith, announced a Unilateral Declaration of Independence (UDI) on 11 November 1965. Britain declined to respond to UDI with force, instead attempting economic tactics such as ending the link between sterling and the Rhodesian currency and seizing assets. At Britain's request, the UN imposed economic sanctions in 1968, but these were only partly successful.

Nationalist guerilla operations against the regime began in the early 1970s, and escalated after Mozambican independence in 1975 provided a valuable base for operations. Emergency measures adopted by the government to counter the fighting served to increase anti-government feeling. Under growing diplomatic, military and economic pressure, Smith finally accepted the necessity of an 'internal settlement' in 1979. Talks in London led to free elections in February 1980, and independence, under Robert Mugabe, in April 1980.

Wilson at the dinner table

One evening in May 1965 the House of Commons Members' Dining Room was deserted except, unusually, for a number of Liberals having dinner at the Liberals' table. At this point Harold Wilson, the Prime Minister, arrived and rather than eat in solitude he asked if he could join us. It was subsequently said by the cynics that he had only done this to butter up the Liberals to ensure their support in the lobbies. This was unfair and untrue, particularly as the reason he had come into the dining room was that the Downing Street kitchen was undergoing extensive alterations.

167

I myself had just returned from Rhodesia and seized the opportunity of asking whether I might presume to tell him what was likely to happen in Rhodesia and how it might be tackled. He asked me to develop my theme and I told him that in six months' time, i.e. by November 1965, Rhodesia, a Crown Colony since 1923, would make a unilateral declaration of independence from the UK. Once it happened, we would have lost and while at present the population was disorganised, in a year the whites would become a united nation.

Three things needed to be done. First, the Rhodesian government must be assured that we were not asking for African majority rule overnight, but for partnership, based on merit. For example, if there was a public service commission of, say, twelve people, there should be four Africans. Similarly, with a Royal Commission, there should be adequate African representation. A senior Zambian minister had gloomily predicted that there would not be African majority rule for at least ten years to come. Halve the figure and halve it again, and we are still talking about two and a half years, by which time transitional arrangements leading to independence could be discussed and agreed. Secondly, the Rhodesian government should be assured of the importance attached by the UK government to the financial investment made by the European population through the Commonwealth Development Corporation, for a prestige project like the heightening of the Kariba dam, or building a steel mill, as evidence of our commitment. Thirdly — and I had discussed this with the Zambian government — there should be 1,500 British troops on manoeuvres and general training in Zambia, who at an hour's notice, in the event of UDI, would be placed under the control of the Governor in Salisbury. I felt that this would be an effective deterrent. If it failed, the first shot to be fired at a British solider would galvanise world opinion and give the British government complete freedom to act.

The Prime Minister noted the points and said that in the event of UDI the UK government would take over responsibility for the government of Rhodesia and see that the Governor was provided with radio communication. I felt at the time that this was totally inadequate, and so it proved to be. UDI was declared in November 1965 and the illegal Smith regime was completely isolated and sanctions were applied.

In the course of my next visit to Rhodesia in 1966, Her Majesty's Government announced that there would be 'talks about talks'. I obviously had no authority to speak on behalf of the government. However, the Rhodesian Front were anxious to discover how flexible the UK government might be. It was arranged that I should see Clifford du Pont, who had usurped the role of the Governor and was self-styled as 'Officer administering the Government'. I agreed, but made clear that since I did not accept the legality of his office, I would not meet him at his ministry. In fact it was arranged that I should see him at his home. I indicated that Rhodesia had been a self-governing colony since 1923 and that they alone had the power to time the advancement of the African community; not a single government had recognised Rhodesia's declaration of independence, and this included the Republic of South Africa; that sanctions, although admittedly breachable, had slowed up economic growth and investment. What had been gained by UDI? His reply was surprising: 'Certainty.' I commented that it was a certainty that they would be treated as an international pariah. What compromise, if any, was the Rhodesian Front prepared to make? I gathered from our subsequent discussion that very little was on offer. He asked me how flexible Her Majesty's Government was likely to be. Since Harold Wilson had ruled out the use of force, he assumed that this was binding. I reflected to myself that Her Majesty's Government had an unhappy record of changing and/or reversing policies, and found it reasonable to say that they, the Rhodesians, should rule out nothing. The future of the Commonwealth was at stake and with it the future of racial partnership throughout the Commonwealth.

After an hour's discussion it was clear that one would not get very much further. I asked whether we could ring for a taxi. 'Please take my car and driver', said du Pont. This turned out to be an Austin Princess, the property of the Governor, which du Pont had taken for his own use. I replied that I was going to see the Chief Justice, Sir Hugh Beadle. In fact, Beadle had taken up residence in Government House, and was currently backing the Governor, Sir Humphrey Gibbs. I was to dine with both of them that evening. 'Where do you want to be taken?' asked du Pont. 'Government House', I replied. 'There is no Government House', said du Pont. 'That's a matter of opinion', I replied. 'We are both lawyers, and I reckon that my argument would prevail'. 'Tell the driver where you want to go', said du Pont.

'Government House', I replied. 'Yes, bwana', said the beaming driver. We were off.

Gibbs had no security guard, and was reduced to one loyal ADC, who acted as secretary and was charged with the ceremonial duties which remained, such as lowering the Union Jack at sunset, and raising it at sunrise. A group of ladies regularly come to Government House to arrange the flowers and to help with the cleaning. In the mean time, Gibbs had refused to leave his post. I swept in unchallenged to Government House to find Gibbs waiting for me at the main door. He looked somewhat perplexed and said: 'Isn't that my car?' 'Yes', I replied, 'I am returning stolen property. Give me another week and I'll get the Rolls back!'

After the conclusion of dinner, Gibbs rose and, turning to a portrait of the Queen, proposed the loyal toast. He was convinced that the 'talks about talks' would be a success and would lead to an overall settlement, which all reasonable people hoped for. I indicated that I did not think that there was a hope in hell of reaching a settlement, because one was not dealing with reasonable people. I respectfully reminded Sir Humphrey that Ian Smith had asked for a declaration of emergency. It was asked for on the basis that it was not a prelude to declaring unilateral independence. Having obtained the emergency powers, he promptly declared unilateral independence. I intended on my return to give my assessment to the Prime Minister, Harold Wilson, who was, I believed, also over-optimistic about the chances of a settlement.

In a lighter moment, I asked Lady Gibbs whether there was anything she was short of as a consequence of sanctions. 'Elastic', she said. I undertook to get a consignment brought out by the next British negotiator. On my return I told Elwyn Jones, the Attorney General of Her Majesty's Government, that I was tempted to table a question, to ask the Attorney whether he was aware that the Hon. Member for North Devon intended to breach sanctions by supplying elastic to reinforce the underwear of ladies loyal to the Crown!

Beadle was to desert Gibbs and transfer allegiance to the rebel regime. Gibbs was left even more isolated, but his loyalty to the Crown came first. He was one of the few people who came out of this episode with dignity and integrity intact.

Rhodesia 1966: 'Bomber Thorpe'

As a result of a speech I made on Rhodesia at the Liberal Party Assembly on 23 September 1966, I was called 'Bomber Thorpe'. I said, and for the record I quote in full:

It is now more than ten months since Rhodesia illegally declared independence. The purpose of this resolution is to advocate measures which will end that rebellion swiftly, effectively and without bloodshed. Why is it imperative to do so?

Since the war Britain has granted independence to 700 million people. Today, the Commonwealth comprises twenty-four independent nations drawn from every continent in the world. Despite its imperfections, it remains the most hopeful and the most valuable experiment in bringing together people of all races and of widely differing living standards.

For the British people the choice is simple yet stark. Do they want to preserve that Commonwealth or do they want to perpetuate the Smith regime? They cannot have both. In southern Africa, do they want to allow 200,000 Europeans to create a miniature South Africa in Rhodesia or do they want 150,000 Europeans to continue to live in racial partnership in the seven black Commonwealth countries surrounding Rhodesia? I know the answer of a Liberal — I think I know the answer of a socialist. I sometimes wish I could be more confident of the reply of a Conservative.

In fairness to the Conservative record, a former Premier of Rhodesia, Mr Winston Field, was told before UDI that 'the present difficulty arises from the desire of Rhodesia to secure independence on the basis of a franchise which is incomparably more restrictive than that of any other British territory to which independence has hitherto been granted'. The statement was that of Mr Duncan Sandys, when Secretary for Commonwealth Relations.

We are insisting that independence must first be preceded by universal adult suffrage. Mr Smith himself provides the reason. In April 1964 he declared that he did not believe there would be an African government in his lifetime — on 29 October 1965, he told the British Prime Minister that even if a referendum declared against independence on the basis of the 1961 constitution, he would feel free to reject it; and on the same day he made it clear that if he felt majority rule would be realised prematurely he must be free to arrest this process. In short, no constitution would be worth the paper it was written on. Having torn up the constitution he now asks for the exclusive power to amend any other. In the light of Mr Smith's intractable opinions, how can anyone seriously suggest that any honourable or lasting agreement can now be reached through discussions? We would in fact be giving unlim-

Speech at Liberal Assembly

ited power to those who have already used their illegal independence to censor the press; to detain men without trial or charge for up to five years; to interfere with academic freedom; to perpetuate the hated Land Apportionment Act; and to clothe themselves in what Mr Heath, in one of his more candid moments, referred to as the trappings of a police state. And if Mr Heath's own right wing have now caused him to modify that view, let him read the report of Amnesty International on police methods and prison conditions for political prisoners and restrictees.

In short, nothing less than universal suffrage would provide adequate guarantees against retrogressive amendments of African rights, and nothing less will now enable us to discharge our responsibilities towards the four million Africans.

Next, we call for stronger measures to bring down the regime. It is plain that Mr Wilson, in company with that proconsular figure Mr Bottomley, having virtually guaranteed a rebellion by announcing in advance that in almost no circumstances would Britain intervene to prevent it, has been proved to have misjudged and misplanned his subsequent policies to end it! Had there been better contingency planning at the outset, the Smith regime might today be a short-lived memory, and we would certainly not have had to rely upon the brilliant diplomacy of the Liberal Prime Minister of Canada to prevent the Commonwealth itself from disintegrating completely.

At present we are set on a course of sanctions. But sanctions are valueless unless they are effective; they cannot be effective unless they are enforceable. The logic of this is surely self-evident except to those Conservatives who support sanctions provided they are not likely to hurt.

At present oil is flowing into Rhodesia from South Africa and Mozambique; Rhodesian chrome has crossed the Atlantic; thirty per cent of the tobacco crop has been sold, with buyers drawn from no less than four of our NATO partners. However, in one context, sanctions have been supremely effective. On 9 April last the British Government sought powers from the Security Council which in consequence 'calls upon the government of the United Kingdom to prevent by the use of force if necessary the arrival at Beira of vessels reasonably believed to be carrying oil destined for Rhodesia, and empowers the United Kingdom to arrest and detain the tanker, namely the *Joanna V*, upon departure from Beira in the event of oil being discharged there'. In this context therefore HMG has already threatened the use of force — and its very credibility off the coast of Mozambique has ensured that no resort has had to be made to the use of such force — nor indeed is it likely. It has even enabled HMG to stop payment of £50,000 per month to Lonhro, the British pipeline-owning company, in return for their not pumping oil to Rhodesia.

Force is an emotional word, and it is the duty of a responsible party to define what we mean by it. It does not of necessity involve mounting an operation calling for the deployment of troops and resulting in the shedding of blood. I believe — and fervently hope — that both can be avoided. There are at least two preferable alternatives.

First, HMG should now apply to the United Nations for mandatory sanctions under Article 42 of the Charter to cover all of Rhodesia's major imports and exports. It should then become the responsibility of an international naval task force to exercise the same right of search on the high seas as was adopted by the Allies during the war in respect of vessels making for neutral ports to ensure that they were not carrying cargo intended ultimately to fall into hostile hands. It should also be illegal for the ships of any nation to carry goods originating from Rhodesia. It may well be asked whether South Africa would herself use force to resist any such action. Well, faced with the determination of the world to end the illegal Smith regime; bound by a decision of the United Nations of which she is a member; realising that she exports £200 million worth of goods annually to the United Kingdom alone; compelled to provide naval escorts from the port of any exporting country to the South African port of arrival as the only guarantee of immunity from search; it would be for South Africa to decide whether this was a price she would be prepared to pay to maintain the Smith regime which the world was dedicated to bringing down.

But this is not all: there are only four routes through which supplies can reach Rhodesia — three by rail and one by road. The main supply of oil now travels on the rail line which crosses the border at Malvernia. If that supply were to continue it might be necessary to consider whether, with the backing of a United Nations resolution, it might be feasible for that line of communication to be nipped on Rhodesian soil by the use of high-flying planes, under United Nations command. It would merely involve the extension of the same degree of force as has already been provided for by the United Nations to prevent the Beira blockade being breached at sea. It would in particular exclude any international repercussions and would not involve the use of troops or the loss of blood.

Ultimately what will count is the determination of this country that sanctions will succeed and that Smith will be brought down. Once that has become plain, then the Prime Minister can with justification talk of ending the rebellion in weeks, not months, without the need for aerial intervention.

It will then be our responsibility, to quote the Commonwealth communiqué, to ensure that Rhodesia is based in the future on a 'multi-racial society in which human and political rights will be vested in all the people without discrimination and in accordance with the true principles of democracy'.

We are now writing the last major chapter in a long imperial history. Are we to allow it to be said that at that stage we destroyed the multi-racial Commonwealth which we had created; that we appeared to reverse our belief in a non-racial society; that we abdicated our responsibilities towards the four million Africans living in Rhodesia, all because we were too weak in resources and determination to prevent 200,000 people from setting up illegally a political system based on racial discrimination in its every aspect?

I cannot believe that that is the course of Britain. But if that is to be our fate then we lose not only the respect of the world, but worse, our own self-respect.

Background to the speech

All the information I was getting from South Africa suggested that the authorities there were anxious to take stock of the determination of the UK government to render sanctions effective. They were particularly interested in the supply of oil, which would come almost exclusively via them, and whilst they were prepared, if possible, to prop up a white minority government on their doorstep, they were not prepared to face the possibility of retaliatory oil embargoes being inflicted on them.

The railway line in question was in the middle of a desert, and bombing it would cause no risk to life or limb. It could no doubt be repaired very swiftly but a repeat performance would probably not be necessary to bring South Africa into line. Those of us who backed sanctions felt it was the best way of avoiding armed conflict, and it is sad to think that in retrospect there are people who regard it as an outrageous suggestion, whereas the alternative — force — produced 20,000 casualties ending UDI. My point was proved when, some years after the independence of Zimbabwe, the South African-backed Renamo terrorists based in Mozambique destroyed the railway line carrying oil to Zimbabwe, and within three days Harare was almost brought to its knees.

The next time I visited Rhodesia I had the experience of watching Rhodesian television news. The propaganda ploy was that I had advocated bombing city centres and men, women and children! I was shown complete with Nixon-type five o'clock shadow! As the result of this propaganda I was named as Prohibited Immigrant No. 8 by the Smith regime. Rhodesia gained its independence in April 1980 and on my first visit to the newly-named nation I asked Mr Mugabe, the new Prime Minister, if I could have a copy of my banning order.

Kariba Dam

In 1967, when I was on business in Zambia, I was staying in Lusaka with my colleague, Anthony Mitchley, a white Zambian with whom I had been an undergraduate at Oxford. I asked him one Sunday whether he would drive me down to see the massive Kariba Dam, which had created a lake 175 miles long on the Zambesi River in Southern Rhodesia.

Apart from the fascination of the dam itself and the lake, I was interested to see what security arrangements existed. There had often been wild talk about some extremist lunatics destroying the wall of the dam (which seemed pretty indestructible) or wrecking the pumping station. My assessment was that if the wall of the dam were to be broken, it would wash away thousands of miles of topsoil and leave a vast desert, to say nothing of the loss of life in the area — hundreds of square miles — within its destructive powers.

We duly arrived at the main gate and were the only traffic about. Tony was slightly apprehensive. I asked the guard on duty: 'Who is in charge of security today?' and was given the name of the officer involved. I asked the guard to telephone him at once to present my compliments and to say that Mr Thorpe was on his way up to the office. The gates swung open and we were on our way.

The chief of security was waiting for me, and gave me a warm welcome. I told him that I was not an engineer but would very much like to get a general idea of what was involved in this miraculous project. He took me up on the roof, which was guarded by a platoon of soldiers, and from there we got a superb view of the sheer scale of the dam and lake. I gathered that the force and speed with which the water fell had gouged a huge hole in the lower side of the dam, equivalent in depth to the drop of the fall.

On our way down to the pumping ststaion, the security officer asked me if I would mind waiting for a few moments, as he had an important telephone call to make. He came back and asked me for my Christian name, which I told him. 'In that case, I'm afraid I must order you to leave the premises at once, on instructions from Salisbury [the capital].' We withdrew, but I felt reassured that the threat of sabotage in the future was unlikely in the extreme.

Nkomo: should we form a Rhodesian government in exile?

Should we spring him from prison? Should we form a government in exile? In 1971 there was a very real fear that the constitutional settlement for Rhodesia negotiated between Smith and Home would be foisted on the Africans against their will. At the same time, there appeared in the British press a photograph of the leading African politician, Joshua Nkomo, behind the barbed wire at Gonakudzingwa prison camp near the Mozambique border. It occurred to me that if the press could get that close, so likewise could a group of commandos!

Would there be a case for springing Joshua Nkomo and flying him out of the country to form a government-in-exile? At that stage, he was probably the only African nationalist with the authority to influence Her Majesty's Government in a more determined direction. The first requisite would be to consult the front-line states surrounding Rhodesia, and this I did. The replies were sufficiently favourable to justify taking the project a stage further. I took the matter up at a fairly high level with the Israelis. I pointed out that, additional to the Africans' cause, Israel herself was surrounded by countries hostile to her continued existence, and by associating herself with the movement of African independence, she could gain the friendship of Africans everywhere.

We decided we needed to establish whether there was an airstrip suitable for a jet or four-seater plane or helicopter to land near the prison. We needed to assess the disposition of the prison guards and the best way to dismantle the radio and telephone links which the prison had with the outside world. Here again the response was sufficiently favourable to justify taking things further. In September 1971, Judy Todd, daughter of Garfield Todd, one-time Prime Minister of Southern Rhodesia, and now under restriction on his farm, and Judy's husband, Richard Acton, came to see me in my room in the House of Commons. I outlined my plan to them.

The next vital requisite was to learn Joshua's reaction. The idea was to spring him from prison, fly him to Francistown in Botswana, on to Lusaka in Zambia and either direct to the United Nations in New York or to the UK. There would be some delicacy about the timing of the announcement of the government-in-exile. If Nkomo declared the creation of such a government in the UK, would the British government prevent him from going to New York? Conversely, if he made a declaration in New York, would the British government prevent him from entering the UK? Judy, who was to be in charge of the Francistown location, was enthusiastic. She subsequently consulted Josiah Chinamano, Joshua's deputy, who had just been released from Gonakudzingwa, to find out Joshua's reactions. Chinamano informed her that some women were shortly to visit the prison and would report back. Joshua's reaction was one of gratitude but he insisted that he would not come out and leave his colleagues behind. They must all come out together. Alas, our capacity was a maximum of six, depending on what sort of aeroplane was used. Interestingly, Joshua said that there was now a spokesman for the Africans in the shape of a bishop called Muzorewa. The bishop was prepared to put the African case but wished to stand down when the African nationalists were released and could campaign themselves. The fact that Muzorewa subsequently clung to power partly accounted for the bitterness which Nkomo and Mugabe felt towards him. In short, the rescue operation was abandoned. Chinamano and Judy Todd were both arrested and assumed that the details of the jailbreak project had been discovered. Happily, no details ever leaked out. This is probably the first occasion that the matter has been mentioned.

Flying down to Salisbury

My last visit to Rhodesia during UDI was in January 1975. Marion and I were taking a few days off in Mombasa, where we had a fascinating meeting with Jomo Kenyatta, President of Kenya. As we left we saw waiting in the garden outside his office three Africans — Joseph Savimbi, Holden Roberto and Agostinho Neto. They were the three leading figures in Angola, which was in turmoil following the departure of the Portuguese rulers. If Kenyatta's influence could make them work together, Angola could become the richest country in black Africa. Kenyatta attempted to get a measure of cooperation between them, but tragically civil war raged in that country for many years to come.

Jim Callaghan, then Foreign Secretary, was touring Africa, and I thought it was only courteous to let him know that following a planned visit to Zambia, I proposed to go down to Salisbury from Lusaka to find out the current political situation as a freelance. He naturally would be unable to visit Rhodesia whilst it was in a state of rebellion against the Crown. He tried to dissuade me on the grounds that it might raise false hopes amongst the Rhodesia Front. I thought this was unlikely and decided to try to make the journey.

From Lusaka I telephoned Roy Welensky in Salisbury, asking him what would be my chances of being allowed into the country to see Ian Smith and those African nationalists not in detention. I indicated that if my entry were permitted, I would charter a plane from Lusaka to Salisbury. He

Jomo Kenyatta, President of Kenya 1964–78

expressed extreme surprise, and said he would enquire, but was not hopeful about consent being given, since I was a prohibited immigrant.

When I rang him back, he said that for some unknown reason the authorities had agreed, provided that the press was not alerted and that the visit was kept secret. The plane on arrival was to taxi into an aircraft hangar, and transport would be arranged from there. I readily agreed. But the cat was out of the bag when it so happened that a photographer of the *Rhodesia Herald* was taking a flying lesson and was visiting the control tower when we drew into the hangar. 'Isn't that Jeremy Thorpe?' he exclaimed, and the press was alerted and on the hunt. We managed to get to Ken Mew's house at the Education Centre in Salisbury without being followed. There I met and had a session with the Reverend Sithole, one of the very few African nationalist leaders out of prison, along with some of his colleagues. He confirmed what I already knew, that opposition to the independence of Southern Rhodesia on a limited franchise based on white supremacy was as profound as ever, and that the white minority regime was becoming more and more repressive towards anyone holding such views.

Before I left Ken Mew's Centre, I thought I would telephone Garfield Todd, who had been the last 'liberal' Prime Minister of Southern Rhodesia, now confined on his farm. I got through to his wife, Grace, to say that I was ringing to wish Garfield well, and to tell him that he was not forgotten. She told me that she knew that he would love to speak to me, but was forbidden to talk on the telephone by the restrictions. I told her that I planned to be at Ian Smith's office at 4 o'clock that afternoon and would telephone Garfield from there between 4.30 and 5 P.M.

My next talks were with Ian Smith and several members of his Cabinet. I told him that whilst I was relieved to see that interim agreement had been reached between the Zambian and Rhodesian negotiators on eight points, there seemed to be a genuinely held difference of opinion as to the interpretation of these points. Would it not be advisable to have a reconvened meeting with, say, one person per side to try and reach agreement as to what the new agreement really meant? Mr Smith's reply was revealing: 'I am not aware of the existence of such points'. I pointed out that it was not often that the Zambian and Rhodesian newspapers carried the same story, but today's editions of *The Times of Zambia* and the *Rhodesian Herald,* referring to the eight points as the lead story, had done precisely that. Mr Smith replied: 'Well, I've been away on my farm'. I was not certain whether he expected me to swallow that, but in the unlikely event of my having believed him, it would have been a devastating indictment of his contact with day-to-day affairs.

At the conclusion of our meeting, I asked whether it would be in order to telephone Garfield Todd at his farm, 'Well', said Mr Smith, 'this is a free country, there is freedom to communicate unless there are specific reasons to the contrary'. He asked the Permanent Secretary to put through a call. He duly returned, somewhat embarrassed, saying that there were long delays to Shabani and it was unlikely that I would be able to get through before my plane took off. I replied that Shabani had gone on to automatic dialling that very morning, which had enabled me to get through instantly, and I had spoken to his wife; as to my plane, there was agreement with the airport authorities that I could leave at any reasonable hour and I had previously arranged to leave two hours hence. Was it permissible to speak to Garfield Todd?

The Permanent Secretary disappeared, and reappeared to say that it was not possible to speak to Garfield Todd, since he was under a Restriction Order. 'In that case', I said, 'I must ring Mrs Todd to explain that I was unable to speak to her husband, who has been awaiting my call'. I duly put through the call, which was answered by Grace Todd. I said that I was ringing from Ian Smith's office, and would she apologise to Garfield about my inability to speak to him, which I had just learnt, and to say that he was not forgotten. I heard laughter in the background, which was Garfield registering the situation.

This experience prompted me to advise David Owen, when he was Foreign Secretary, that when he was negotiating with Ian Smith he should get him to initial and agree the minutes of matters discussed and agreed on the previous day before starting a fresh day's work.

I was ready to fly back to Zambia, and the final drama was to be played out at the airport. An army of press men had tracked me down, and were waiting to converge on me at the main terminal building. I was anxious to honour my undertaking not to give a press conference, and was aware that if I had answered questions from the media I would be accused of having broken my word. Fortunately the Rhodesian Foreign Office representative who was accompanying me had a key to the side gate leading directly to the tarmac. Once we were through the gate we drove at immense speed towards the plane, and boarded it and drew the curtains. In what seemed only like a matter of three or four minutes we were taxiing down the runway and taking off for Zambia.

Coincidentally, Roy Welensky was in Lusaka for his first visit since the end of the Central African Federation. As former Prime Minister of the Federation of Northern and Southern Rhodesia and Nyasaland, he had been deeply unpopular amongst African opinion in these countries which were seeking independence and majority rule. However, by this time North-ern Rhodesia and Nyasaland, as Zambia and Malawi, had achieved their independence — one man, one vote, irrespective of colour — but it re-mained for Southern Rhodesia to follow suit. Roy had paid great tribute that evening to Zambia's achievements since independence. By the time I arrived in Lusaka, Roy and Kenneth Kaunda, President of Zambia, had established a firm rapport. Needless to say, we exchanged views on my day's visit to Salisbury, Rhodesia — now Harare, Zimbabwe.

Roy was to become a close and valued friend. He came in for some very rough treatment after UDI. Since the altitude of Salisbury was bad for his heart condition, he settled in the UK. The first Lady Welensky had died, but he happily remarried and started a new family who were with him when he died in Dorset.

Chapter Seven

Europe

Of the three major political parties, the Liberal Party alone has been consistent on the question of Europe.

On 1 and 2 June 1955 the six founder countries, Germany, France, Italy, Belgium, the Netherlands and Luxembourg, plus the UK, met at Messina. The object of the talks was to consider the possibilities of closer integration within Europe. Eden had refused permission for a minister — Anthony Nutting — to attend, and the UK was represented by an Under-Secretary from the Board of Trade, Mr Russell Bretherton. The Messina proposals were to prove the birth of the European Common Market. These proposals were subsequently studied in Brussels under the chairmanship of Spaak and the UK was again represented by Bretherton. In November 1955 Bretherton was withdrawn.

The attitude of the government prior to Messina was borne out by the briefing which Bretherton was given by Peter Thorneycroft, the President of the Board of Trade, which laid down the guideline: 'Be as helpful as you can, and don't seem to want to make us want to stop things — but no commitments'. The real attitude of the Foreign Office was expressed by Sir Evelyn Shuckburgh, Eden's Principal Private Secretary. In the course of an interview conducted by Michael Charlton in his book, *The Price of Victory* (1983), Shuckburgh says: 'I think I probably said I don't believe the French and Germans are really going to do it, or would not be able to bring it off, and we had better keep our options open and our hands clean'. It was generally thought — I think rightly — that this represented the views of Anthony Eden.

At the time, the Liberals said that we should join the EEC and it would be better to do so as a founder member rather than as a latecomer. The six pressed on and signed the Treaty of Rome on 25 March 1957, giving effect to matters agreed upon at Messina. It set up the European

Common Market — an economic grouping of nations with a total population of sixty million, to be developed in stages over fifty years. It aimed
at free movement of people, goods and money among the member states.
Tariffs were abolished. Rab Butler, thinking that the British electorate
might regard this move as a Papist plot, said: 'This is a Treaty of Rome, *not*
with Rome!'

As it was, successive British governments made increasingly hostile noises
until the great somersault of Harold Macmillan, when he announced in
the House of Commons in 1961 that we had applied to join the European
Common Market, and negotiations would start. It is right to recall that
eleven years earlier the Liberals, led by Clement Davies, had urged that
Britain should join the European Coal and Steel Community. Liberals
went on to back the proposed European Defence Community, which was
effectively scuppered by the opposition of the British government. The
French followed with their opposition but only because in their view the
absence of the UK from the European Defence Community would give
Germany an unacceptably predominant position. Liberals subsequently
supported the Monnet plan to create a European Coal and Steel Community, which again was opposed by the government.

When a Conservative and later a Labour government became converted
to the prospects of full British membership of the European Economic
Community, the Liberals backed the governments of both parties.

European debates

Two votes in the House of Commons that took place on the Common
Market in 1959 and 1972, thirteen years apart, epitomise the consistency of
the Liberal Party on this issue. On 14 December 1959, the Prime Minister
(Harold Macmillan), with senior Cabinet colleagues, tabled a motion for
debate: 'That this House welcomes the resolution adopted at the ministerial meeting in Stockholm on 20 November and the action of Her Majesty's Government in approving the Convention establishing the European
Free Trade Association contained in Command Paper No 906'. In our
view, EFTA was a very poor substitute for the political and economic
integration of the six EEC members, and many regarded EFTA as an at-

tempt to bypass the EEC. In practice, we could and should have been founder members of the EEC.

An amendment to the proposed motion was tabled in the names of Grimond, Clement Davies, Wade, Bowen, Holt and Thorpe. We sought, in the first line of the government's motion, to substitute 'Regrets the failure of Her Majesty's Government to associate Great Britain with the countries comprising the European Economic Community'. The names listed represented the sum total of the Parliamentary Liberal Party of the day. The amendment was not selected for debate, but as evidence of our disapproval we forced a division on the Prime Minister's motion. Jo Grimond was grounded in his constituency of Orkney & Shetland and so there were only three Liberals in the lobby, plus two acting as our tellers. The Labour Party abstained and we were defeated by 185 Tory votes to three Liberals. The result was treated with derision. Although it was not recorded in *Hansard,* in the general hubbub Arthur Holt shouted out to the Tory front bench: 'What you should be doing is to make application under Article 237 of the Treaty of Rome for negotiations to join the Community'. I was to hear this repeated two years later, on 31 July 1961, by Harold Macmillan to a tense House when he announced that we had applied to join the Common Market, and would now negotiate terms under Article 237 of the Treaty of Rome!

Before dealing with the 1972 vote, I must mention the vote on Europe on 28 October 1971, on a motion: 'That this House approves Her Majesty's Government's decision in principle to join the European Communities on the basis of the arrangements which have been negotiated.' The Prime Minister (Edward Heath) announced that there would be a free vote on the Tory side. When the vote was cast, thirty-three Conservative MPs voted against the government, with three abstentions. The Labour opposition were similarly split and no less than sixty-nine Labour MPs voted in the government lobby, with three abstentions. The House of Commons, by a decisive majority of 112, cutting across party barriers, including all but one of the Liberal Members, had declared themselves in favour of the principle of joining the EEC on the basis of the terms negotiated.

The 17 February 1972 vote was for the second reading of the European Communities Bill, to give effect to joining the Common Market, which of course had already been agreed in principle. However, the Labour opposition, disregarding their own prior position, decided that in view of the likely Conservative defections there was an opportunity of bringing down the government and causing an election. Accordingly, Labour Members were bound by a three-line whip to vote against the second reading.

At this stage, it was clear that the Liberal vote could be crucial. The Liberal Party, with the exception of Hooson, was ready, willing and enthusiastic to vote for the second reading of the Bill. My colleagues and I were not, however, prepared to vote for the motion if it was claimed to be a vote of confidence in the government or the Prime Minister. If that was the issue, at best we would be compelled to abstain, and some of us would have wished to vote against the government. Given a straight vote on Europe, the party could deliver four votes for and one against.

On the day of the debate David Steel, who was Chief Whip, set off to see Francis Pym, Government Chief Whip, whilst I went to talk to Willie Whitelaw, then Leader of the House. In my view, it was necessary that there should be an agreed passage in the Prime Minister's closing speech, and I put up a suggested draft. This was to the effect that: 'in October 1971, this House, by a large majority, decided in principle to join the Common Market. Today, that same House of Commons is being asked to give legislative effect to that decision. If the House of Commons defeats the means to achieve the end they had endorsed by a majority of 112 last October, this Parliament cannot sensibly continue.' As the Prime Minister reached this passage in his speech, Willie Whitelaw gave me the thumbs up, and I did likewise. The reference to a vote of confidence in the government did not feature. I told my colleagues that I felt that all hell might break loose after the vote as far as we were concerned, if the Labour Party failed to defeat the government. I therefore asked my colleagues to remain in their places to face whatever music was going to be played. My instinct proved correct. Heath obtained a majority of eight, with fifteen Tory MPs voting against, and five abstentions. The entire Labour Party voted against, with five abstentions, gallantly led by Christopher Mayhew.

If the Liberals had abstained, Heath would have had a majority of four or less; if we had voted against, at best there would have been a tie, and more probably a defeat not only for the government but for the European cause as well.

All hell broke loose. Labour MPs swarmed round the Liberal bench, jeering and shouting. A usually mild-mannered Labour MP, James Hamilton (Bothwell), grabbed the lapels of my jacket and pummelled me. Lena Jager nearly deafened me as she was shouting in John Pardoe's ear — God knows what it must have sounded like to him! Bob Mellish, Opposition Chief Whip, rushed into the fray, seeking to restore order. Obviously carried away, he bitterly commented: 'They are a gutter party, these Liberals'. It was a very ugly scene.

After the division I put out a statement:

> This is not a matter of arithmetic, but one of principle. This is not the first time we in the Liberal Party have borne the brunt of Europe, nor will it be the last. The Liberal Party is not concerned with the bitterness displayed by sections of the Labour Party at the conclusion of tonight's vote.
>
> What was tragic was that the failure by the Tory party to convert sufficient of their followers to joining the EEC led the Labour Party to indulge in arithmetical exercises, which ignored the principles which were also involved.
>
> The fact that men like Roy Jenkins, Michael Stewart and George Thomson — who voted for Europe on 28 October 1971 — should choose to stand on their heads on 17 February 1972 is a matter for them. But there is no reason why they should expect the Liberals to do likewise.
>
> The Liberal Party pioneered the movement towards European unity in this country, and it is a sign of the cynicism to which politics has now sunk that we should have been expected to throttle it tonight.
>
> We are proud once again to have been the spearhead of the movement towards Europe and of consistency in politics.

What a sea change between the Liberal votes in December 1959 and February 1972! The three Liberal votes on the first occasion produced a mocking reaction from the Tory and Labour Parliamentary Parties. The four Liberal votes on the second reading of the bill released a furious response from the Labour benches and relief on the Tory benches. The principle was unchanged: we should be full members of the EEC.

It is only fair to say that Roy Jenkins and George Thomson went on to serve the EEC with conspicuous skill: George as a Commissioner and Roy as President of the Commission.

The French veto

Successive British governments, with justification, have been haunted by the spectre of the French veto of our application to join the European Community. When the government under Macmillan finally decided to apply to join in 1961, President de Gaulle exercised France's veto in January 1963, and the first application was aborted. It may therefore be of interest to know how the UK became aware of the French intention to lift the veto at the time of the second application by the UK to join, in the autumn of 1969.

In the first week of November 1969, I visited Paris to address a luncheon hosted by the French diplomatic press. The suggestions I made in my speech were thought to be very avant-garde. I called for the convening of a new Messina Conference that would discuss matters which had not been dealt with by the Treaty of Rome, but which were, nonetheless, essential to the unity of Europe. The conference should take place at the same time as

Caroline and Jeremy Thorpe with Maurice Schumann, French Minister for Foreign Affairs, at a reception given by the Franco-British Society in London, January 1970

negotiations were held on the completion and broadening of the Common Market to accord membership to the United Kingdom and the other applicants. The conference should bring together the original six, the candidate countries and, perhaps with the status of observers, representatives of the neutral countries of Western Europe. They should consider the creation of a common European currency and the revival of the European Defence Community which would make it possible to formulate a common policy towards Eastern Europe — 'the precondition of a real relaxation of tension'. Such a Defence Community should be non-nuclear. I also suggested a Franco-British treaty along the lines of the Franco-German Treaty, so long as it was understood that through such a Franco-British understanding the broader objective of European unity was in fact assisted.

During my visit I stayed at our magnificent Embassy, with Christopher and Mary Soames, who elegantly and effectively discharged their duties as Ambassador and Ambassadress. During the morning of 7 November 1969, Christopher and I visited the French Foreign Minister, M. Maurice Schumann, at the Quai d'Orsay. Christopher Soames, in his usual forthright manner, came straight to the point and said: 'Well, Maurice, on what issue or issues are you going to veto our new application to join the EEC?' To which Schumann replied that, as far as France was concerned, she had no intention of exercising the veto. 'What you mean', said Christopher, 'is that this calls for real optimism about our application to join the enlarged Community?' 'That is correct', said Schumann. After the meeting Christopher rightly assessed this to be a vitally important landmark. It was the first indication we had that France would do nothing to obstruct our application, and we returned to the Embassy, where the staff were called in to the Duff Cooper Library when Christopher and I debriefed ourselves. Christopher immediately drafted and dispatched a telegram to the Foreign Secretary in London. France was as good as her word and I felt that we had both been in on an historic moment in the cause of European unity.

As a parting shot, Maurice Schumann, who incidentally spoke faultless English, told me that during the war he belonged to my club, the National Liberal Club in Whitehall, a club which 'overlooked the river and its food!' I was able to assure him that the food had improved and the river was cleaner.

Trouble with George

During the EEC renegotiations set in train by the Labour government — in 1974 — the Prime Minister, Harold Wilson, invited the Prime Ministers and Foreign Secretaries of the existing six members of the EEC to come, country by country, to London to discuss outstanding problems. There were the usual Downing Street dinners and to these Ted Heath and myself were invited, enabling Wilson to say, with truth, that all three political parties in the UK backed the European ideal.

One nearly fatal incident occurred at the dinner given for the Belgian Prime Minister and Foreign Secretary and their wives at No. 10. George Brown was sitting on the left-hand side of the Belgian Foreign Minister's wife. George had wined well — rather too well — and to my horror I saw his right hand moving relentlessly towards the left breast of the unfortunate lady. I could visualise a fearful scene, with her remonstrating either forcibly or by word of mouth; her husband storming out in protest; the future of Britain and the Common Market would lie in ruins. 'Thorpe', I said to myself, 'act quickly and decisively'. Fortunately, George's wife, Sophie, was close by and I called out: 'Sophie, look, act quickly!' 'George', said Sophie, 'stop it'. 'All right', said George, and his hand fell back into place. I said to myself: 'Thorpe, you have saved Europe!'

Treaty of Accession — January 1972

On Saturday, 22 January 1972, Ted Heath, as Prime Minister, signed the Treaty of Accession in Brussels by which the UK, along with Ireland and Denmark, became full members of the EEC. The Prime Minister invited an all-party delegation to accompany him. The passengers were Harold Macmillan, who when Prime Minister had made the original application for membership of the EEC; Alec Douglas Home, Foreign Secretary; Geoffrey Rippon, Chancellor of the Duchy of Lancaster, in charge of the negotiations; Duncan Sandys, an indefatigable worker for European unity; George Brown, who, following the rejection of an invitation extended to Harold Wilson to come on board, nominated himself as the representative of the Labour Party; and myself, representing the Liberal Party. Ted had gone ahead of us to receive in West Germany the Charlemagne Prize and we were to meet up in Brussels.

Signing the Treaty of Accession of the UK to the EEC: Brussels, 24 January 1972
From right, front row: Alec Douglas-Home, Edward Heath, Geoffrey Rippon; second row: Harold Macmillan, George Brown, Duncan Sandys, Jeremy Thorpe; third row: Christopher Soames

Apart from the historic significance of the event, the trip produced two vintage Harold Macmillan remarks. George Brown leaned across and said to Alec Douglas Home: 'Alec, why don't you move back into the official Foreign Secretary's residence looking on to the Mall? Sophie and I were only moved out because they wanted to decorate the place. Now it is occupied by civil servants and filing cabinets.' Alec replied: 'It may well be that one of our successors will move back but for the present, Elizabeth and I are very happy with the existing official residence.' 'Well', said George, 'There is no view and very little sunlight.' At this point, Macmillan, who, I suspect, had heard every word of the conversation, asked what all the discussion was about. Alec deferentially replied: 'George was saying that I ought to move back into the Foreign Secretary's previous official residence. Do you know it?' 'Oh yes', replied Macmillan. 'I know it well. It is a very pretty house. As a matter of fact, when my father-in-law (the Duke of Devonshire) sold Devonshire House, he bought it in order to have somewhere in London to store the furniture!' 'Christ!', said George — and that was the end of that.

Before the ceremony in Brussels, we lunched at the British Embassy, where the guest of honour was Jean Monnet, often referred to as the Father of Europe. At the conclusion of lunch, Ted said he had been asked to carry out a very pleasant duty on behalf of the Queen, namely to confer an honour upon him. Appropriately, Monnet was made a Companion of Honour. I later remarked to Ted that, in view of the dire warnings that we had been given by our opponents that membership of the EEC would wreck our Commonwealth links, it would have been tempting to confer upon him the GBE (Knight Grand Cross of the British Empire). 'Oh', said Ted, 'He had that years ago!'

The signing ceremony was delayed by a woman throwing an ink bottle at Ted, which scored a direct hit. Her protest had nothing to do with the Common Market, but arose out of a development plan for Covent Garden. The Treaty was duly signed and I remarked to the Irish Taoiseach that I had seen, to my consternation, that the copies of the Treaty were bound in orange ribbon. I was fearful that this might cause a point of order and consequent delay!

Our departure was very grand: four Rolls Royces were lined up, each flying the Union Jack, belonging to the UK representatives to Brussels, Paris, NATO and the EEC. Ted thanked them briefly, whereupon Macmillan stepped forward and said: 'As the back-bencher of this delegation, I would like to thank your Excellencies for the admirable way we have been looked after. We have had available to us secretaries, Rolls Royces and glittering hospitality. We have lived like Russian commissars. When I get home the only question I am asked is: "Do you have a good daily woman?" That's how the rich live!'

On the return journey, we broke open a bottle of champagne and with George's approval and complete understanding whom I had in mind, I proposed a toast to 'absent friends', in which everyone joined.

Referendum 1975

The EEC referendum campaign was an unique experience for those taking part in it. Apart from anything else it was a brilliant tactical manoeuvre by Harold Wilson, then Prime Minister. First, he was able to let members of his cabinet disagree with each other, thus suspending the doctrine of collective responsibility. Second, he pitched the Tory party into a battle in which they found themselves seeking approval from the nation for Labour's renegotiated terms of entry. Third, he was able to get money for the campaign to underpin the foreign policy of a Labour government from companies and industries who would not normally so subscribe. After a few teething problems the three-party campaign for a 'yes' vote settled down. In particular we rather enjoyed inter-party rallies. I appeared with Roy Jenkins and Willie Whitelaw at Liverpool; Ted Heath and Harold Lever in Harrogate and Ted Heath and Roy Jenkins in Central Hall, Westminster, and also in the great televised debate at the Oxford Union, in which Ted Heath and I took on Barbara Castle and Peter Shore. I deal with my exchange with Barbara Castle in Chapter Four.

The biggest attendance at any rally was in Barnstaple Pannier Market in my own constituency of North Devon. Ted and Roy were unable to accept my invitation to speak — in fact I suspect meetings were hurriedly organised for them in other parts of the West Country, it being widely thought by the party bosses that their presence in North Devon would underpin my political standing as local Member! I therefore decided to gather together the best possible box-office draw, and in this I succeeded, with Quintin Hailsham, George Brown and Vic Feather in the chair. There was an audience of over 2,000. We left the mayor's parlour to go into the Pannier Market and were confronted by a noisy group of protesters, one of whom held aloft a placard saying: 'Don't sell out the Com-

Keep Britain in Europe

COME AND HEAR

JEREMY THORPE M.P.

LORD HAILSHAM

LORD GEORGE-BROWN

Chairman: LORD FEATHER

IN

THE PANNIER MARKET BARNSTAPLE ON SATURDAY 31st MAY at 2.30. P.M.

Tickets available from your local Britain in Europe Groups and local Party Agents

Britain in Europe, 149 Old Park Lane, London W1Y 3LN. Printed by Bradleys, Portman Road, Reading

Referendum campaign: rally at Barnstaple, outside the Guildhall, 31 May 1975
From left: Jeremy Thorpe, Lord Hailsham, Lord Feather, Lord George-Brown

monwealth'. Quintin turned to me and said: 'Who is that idiot?' 'That', I
replied, 'is your former Conservative parliamentary candidate!'

The whole campaign was a most enjoyable operation. In contrast to
Liberal campaigns, where I had myself to raise much of the cash to pay for
initiatives such as closed–circuit television, enabling me to take my London
press conference from North Devon, the 1974 hovercraft tour, which reached
60,000 people, or part of the expenses for the hire of a helicopter, in this
case the referendum money was raised centrally and it rolled in without
too much effort. The result was decisive. Nearly 26 million people voted,
of whom 67.2 per cent voted 'yes' and 32.8 per cent voted 'no' — or
17,378,581 said 'yes' and 8,470,073 'no', making a majority of 8,908,508.

In the campaign we held a crowded and highly successful meeting in
Birmingham Town Hall, in Powellite country, addressed by the President
of the Canadian Liberal Party, Senator Stanbury, two former Liberal Prime
Ministers of Denmark, Poul Hartling and Hilmar Baunsgaard, and myself.

It was refreshing to take part in a campaign which was organised by someone else, and to be on the winning side!

Conclusion

When Harold Macmillan announced on 31 July 1961 that the UK would apply to join the EEC, this represented a complete, but welcome, somersault. Harold Wilson changed his views on the EEC no less than four times. Europe is one of the most divisive issues within parties and between parties. Unhappily there is no doubt in my mind that our relations with Europe will represent a political football between government and opposition, and within government and opposition, for many years to come. Europe could be the cause of a split, either in the Labour Party or, more probably, in the Tory party, which would be as significant and dramatic as the events following the repeal of the Corn Laws.

The Tory party have got themselves into a terrible muddle over the euro. They have polled their paid-up members and come up with a policy of saying: 'no' to the euro in this Parliament; 'no' again in the next election and possibly 'no' in the Parliament after next. It is the first time that a political party has sought to bind the vote of those who may become MPs but who have not yet been selected, still less elected. This will remain a divisive issue in the Tory party for several years to come.

At the end of the day, I believe that the European case will prevail and that the UK will remain a member of the European Union. There will be occasions when the government of the day will need rebel votes from the opposition to win the European debate. However, having said that, I also believe that the issue of the European single currency will cause tremendous bitterness within and between political parties, all the way down to individual families. It could change the whole face of British politics.

Chapter Eight

Britain

The Trial

On 14 December 1978, at the Minehead Magistrates' Court, I was committed to stand trial at the Old Bailey. With three co-defendants I was charged with conspiracy to murder one Norman Scott, and in my case alone, with incitement to murder Scott. The trial took place almost twenty years ago, relating to allegations of events upwards of thirty-five years ago. The jury acquitted all defendants — an outcome of which I never had any doubt.

I do not intend to rake over the embers of the trial. Its proceedings were exhaustively covered by the media, both at the committal and the trial itself, day after day, week after week, month after month. However, there are one or two reflections that I wish to set down.

The arrival of the co-defendants at the Minehead committal proceedings was not without irony. Under English law it is possible to conspire with someone whom one has never spoken to or met. It is sufficient that one link in the chain joins the next link in the chain, and so on. I had, in fact, never met, nor spoken to, the second or third defendants (John le Mesurier and George Deakin), and since the waiting room was filled with solicitors, plainclothes policemen and others with duties to perform, I did not know which were my two unknown co-defendants, and they had to be introduced. At the far end of the room there was a distinguished, white-haired man; I asked who he was, to be told that he was the Chief Constable of Avon & Somerset Police. 'Sir', I said, 'you do us much honour'.

Originally there were apparently to be five co-defendants, but the fifth (David Miller) opted to give evidence for the Crown, as a result of which he was warned in writing that he should say nothing in his evidence which might incriminate him!

At the inception of the trial, the prosecution would probably have held the view that Peter Bessell was the chief Crown witness. Bessell had been a Liberal MP for the Cornish seat of Bodmin, and was therefore a parliamentary colleague. Had the prosecution been aware of how he would stand at the end of the trial on the question of honesty and reliability, they might well have taken a different view of the case.

Bessell's businesses had failed, in consequence of which he did not stand for re-election. He was living in California when the British police visited him in connection with the case. Bessell was only prepared to make a statement if two British investigative journalists were at all times present during the interviews by the police, including in particular the compilation of Bessell's statement. In practice, at the conclusion of each session with the police, the two journalists would remain with Bessell. However, none of this inhibited the police from continuing their interviews with Bessell in these unusual circumstances. At the trial, Mr Challis, the policeman in charge of the case, agreed under cross-examination that this was a profoundly unsatisfactory and almost unheard-of arrangement.

What method of preparing the statement was used we do not know. Bessell was told that if he were to return to the UK to give evidence, he would be granted an immunity, in writing, from any criminal proceedings, the grounds for which might arise out of his evidence to be given at the trial. Bessell insisted that he had not asked for the immunity, nor did he ask for the reason it was offered. Mr Challis took a similar line, whilst the Crown, for their part, thought it necessary to adhere to the arrangement. Mr Challis admitted that it was the most widely-drawn immunity in his experience. At least we were able to establish in advance, as the result of my application to the High Court, that the immunity would not cover perjury arising out of evidence given at the trial. It is rash to speculate on the grounds on which the immunity was granted. However, Bessell very probably knew for a start that two letters purporting to come from me addressed to him would be challenged as forgeries at the trial. They were not, in fact, produced. In any event, it would be revealing to know against which crimes Bessell was given such an unique immunity.

Private Eye disclosed that Bessell had entered into a contract with the *Sunday Telegraph* newspaper, who had offered him £25,000 for articles if I was acquitted and £50,000 if I was convicted. It was referred to as the 'double-your-money contract'. The trial judge, Mr Justice Cantley, ordered the *Sunday Telegraph* to show good reason why they should not be committed to prison for contempt of court. In the end he ruled that Bessell's evidence had crystallised by the time the agreement was drawn up, but nonetheless criticised the behaviour of the *Sunday Telegraph* and referred to the contract as 'deplorable'. To indicate the extent to which Bessell's motives were coloured by commercialism, it was further discovered that Bessell's solicitor's wife was his literary agent. Payment by the media to witnesses involved in criminal cases remains relevant today in view of the publication by the Lord Chancellor of a consultation document on payment to witnesses. The document makes clear that the practice of paying witnesses still represents a threat to the administration of justice.

Early on, under cross-examination, Bessell agreed that he had difficulty in differentiating between fantasy and fact, and nowhere was this more apparent than his position in regard to the first count, which was that of incitement to commit murder, for which proposition he was the only witness. His recollection of an allegedly highly incriminating conversation with me was remembered in intricate detail in court: the venue where the conversation was said to have taken place was described at the committal proceedings to be in my flat in Ashley Gardens, whereas at the trial, he claimed it was in my room in the House of Commons. No such conversation ever took place, which may explain why Bessell so glibly shifted its location.

Another example of his Walter Mitty world was that within days of being elected as the Liberal MP for Bodmin, he had inquired of Willie Whitelaw, the Chief Whip of the Conservative Party, about the possibility of taking the Tory Whip, and made a similar inquiry of John Silkin, the Chief Whip of the Labour Party. Bessell conceded this, and in fact both Whitelaw and Silkin have confirmed this as well.

Perhaps the most damaging accusation made by Bessell was that there had been a long, and as far as I was concerned, highly incriminating telephone conversation, when he claimed that he rang me in Devon from Cornwall on Monday morning, 15 June 1970. It was put to him that this could not have taken place, since I was touring the Bodmin and North Cornwall constituencies in the company of Bessell on that morning, and had spent the previous night of 14 June in Bessell's home with my wife. This he denied. My solicitor, Christopher Murray, had painstakingly undertaken the task of reading through all my press cuttings. He remarked to me that it was a pity that the press cuttings books had been returned to Devon, since he distinctly remembered a photograph appearing on the front page of the *Western Morning News* on Tuesday 16 June 1970, recording the Bessell, Pardoe, Thorpe tour in *Cornwall* the previous day (i.e. the day on which Bessell claimed that the alleged telephone call had taken place). My mother-in-law found the relevant press cuttings book on my shelves in Devon. Thanks to a very helpful young farmer, the evidence was brought to London by car through the night.

The next morning in court, George Carman, my QC, asked that Bessell be recalled. This was granted. Bessell was confronted with the press photograph on the front page of the *Western Morning News,* which showed that he was with me in Cornwall at the time when he claimed to be telephoning me from his home. Carman remarked: 'Mr Bessell, it has taken us a long time to nail your lies, but we have done so at last, have we not?' 'You have a point', said Bessell. At that moment, if indeed not before, Bessell's credibility had been totally destroyed. Where Bessell had gone wrong was that he forgot that whilst I *had* been due the previous week, on 9 June 1970, to do a tour of Cornwall on the 10th, arriving by helicopter, weather conditions were atrocious and when we got as far as Eggesford the pilot insisted we turn back, and the projected tour was therefore cancelled. It was, however, reinstated the following weekend, when I arrived by car on Sunday evening, 14 June, and spent the night at Bessell's house, leaving for the Cornish tour the next morning. Had the original tour taken place, I would indeed have been in North Devon to take a call on Monday 15th. As it was, we could prove that I was not in Devon but in Bessell's company in Cornwall.

Some years earlier, during the mid 1960s, bankruptcy stared Bessell in the face and he came to me in desperation to ask if I could rescue him. Since he was a colleague and constituency neighbour, I said that I would do my best. Not to put too fine a point on it, Bessell's bankruptcy would have led to a by-election in Bodmin, which the Liberals would probably have lost with potentially dangerous consequences for John Pardoe's North Cornwall seat and my own in North Devon. I managed to raise £20,000 and in retrospect it was to become clear to me that Bessell was schizophrenic: on the one hand he seemed to be almost pathetically grateful, but on the other, he would be consumed by bitterness towards me, resentful of the fact that I had seen behind his façade as a successful tycoon. He was to become desperate again and asked me to help further. I indicated that it would be much more difficult this time, but I would try. It became clear at a later stage that he was hell-bent on making as much money as possible and in this case at my expense.

Bessell's fantasy was paralleled by that of Scott. Scott made no secret of his lack of mental stability, his delusions, his suicidal tendencies and his treatments in hospitals. Scott claimed that there had been a homosexual relationship with myself — a claim that I have always totally denied. According to Scott this 'affair' had started with a chance meeting at the stables of a friend, when I had spoken to him at the most for five minutes. Many months later he arrived unannounced at the House of Commons. It was after this second meeting that he alleged our relationship began. The defence had discovered from two Thames Valley police officers that many years before they had been called to a house at Church Enstone where a young man was threatening suicide — he turned out to be Norman Scott Josiffe. It was difficult to tie Scott down to the date of his first meeting with me, at the stables where he was employed as a groom. It either took place after the Thames Valley police incident or shortly before. At the most, Scott's contact with me when seen by the police from Thames Valley was a five-minute meeting at the stables. Scott then proceeded to describe me as a 'friend' to the police officers, but had to accept under cross-examination at the trial that he had also asserted to those officers that he had had a homosexual relationship with me, which he then had to agree was a lie.

Furthermore, Scott had to accept that having consistently told Penrose and Courtiour, two investigative journalists, and anyone else who was prepared to listen to him, that his sexual experience with me was after he called on me at the House of Commons some time later, he had now to admit that he had formerly been telling people that he had had a sexual relationship with me before the House of Commons visit. This was based solely upon a brief meeting in the presence of others, or if his timing was wrong, his timescale suggests that he was making the allegations before he had even met me! This was brought out when George Carman was cross-examining Scott:

Carman: 'You met Mr Thorpe (at Van der Vater's stables) and talked to him for five minutes or less. He hadn't written you a single letter before you went to the House of Commons. Neither had you written a single letter to Mr Thorpe before that. Why did you say that Mr Thorpe was a friend of yours when all you had ever done was to speak to him for less than five minutes?'

Scott: 'Because I had had the therapy at the hospital. I was going through a delusion, and I had had these letters. I was using them to say that I had a relationship with him already ...'

Carman: 'You were saying you had a sexual relationship with Mr Thorpe before you went to the House of Commons?'

Scott: 'Yes.'

Carman: 'Quite obviously, that was not true?'

Scott: 'No, it wasn't.'

Carman: 'You were suffering from a delusion?'

Scott: 'Yes.'

Carman: 'And you had suffered from other delusions, had you not?'

Scott: 'Yes.'

As far as I know these exchanges were not reported in the press, nor were they given their full significance by the media.

Another example of the workings of Scott's mind was that he informed me that his father had been killed in an air crash in South America. I suggested that he might be able to obtain some compensation. Accordingly I requested a solicitor friend to initiate some inquiries in this connection. In due course the solicitor reported that the story told by Scott was quite false. There had been no air crash in South America, and in fact his father was at that time a hospital porter living in Bexleyheath in Kent, where his mother also lived. Even the name Scott itself was a fantasy. Wishing to claim that he was a close relation of Lord Eldon, he adopted the family name Scott.

An investigation and prosecution had been mounted substantially on the allegations of Scott, Bessell and Newton (another Crown witness). They had destroyed their credibility and confessed to having fantasies. All three had further been destroyed in cross-examination, and the prosecution's case at its close was shot through with lies, inaccuracies and admissions to such an extent that the defence decided not to give evidence.

To have done so would have prolonged the trial unnecessarily for at least another ten to fourteen days. The defence took the view that it was time to bring down the curtain, and as George Carman put it in his closing speech, the time had come for the Crown to: 'Fold their tents like the Arabs and as silently steal away'. (Longfellow)

One of the more bizarre events of the trial was the intervention by Mr Peter Taylor, who led the prosecution; following the acquittal by the jury on all charges against all defendants, he volunteered the opinion that the police were to be congratulated on their work and that the prosecution had been properly brought. I thought to myself: 'Methinks he doth protest too much'. George Carman, who for the first and last time I saw mystified, replied: 'Very properly brought, but very properly concluded'. In one sense, the fact that the prosecution had been brought, and its consequent outcome, had largely silenced the campaign of rumour and innuendo that had gone on for three years. But apparently there still seems to be some money to be made by repeating the prosecution's flawed case! Where congratulations were unquestionably due was to the staff of the Old Bailey for their consideration and courtesy towards all the defendants.

I was asked whether I was disturbed by the fact that the jury were out for two days. On the contrary, I felt they would be open to criticism if they had reached a decision more quickly than they did. There were four separate cases to be considered, and evidence to be gone through which had been given during the four weeks of the committal proceedings and the six weeks for the trial itself — in other words, material that covered almost two and a half months.

At the risk of sounding vindictive, if Bessell could have been shown to publish in the UK any of the major allegations which he was making, he should have been prosecuted for criminal libel, if not by the Crown, by myself. The Crown would then have been able to make a better evaluation of the merits of the case, and the taxpayer might have been saved a great deal of expense.

As it was, I never had any doubt about the outcome of the case.

Bessell's 'double-your-money contract' with the *Sunday Telegraph* gave rise to a heated debate in the House of Lords a few weeks later, on 16 July 1979. Lord Wigoder moved the second reading of the Dealings with Witnesses Bill and said:

> ... The third instance was 13 October 1978, when the Daily Telegraph Ltd, and a company called Milbest Publications Incorporated, acting for another witness called Mr Bessell, entered into a contract, the effect of which was — and I stress 'the effect of which was' — that Mr Bessell would be paid £50,000 if there were a conviction for certain writings, and £25,000 if there were an acquittal. Let me say at once that, of course, the lawyers who drew up that contract did not indulge in crude language of that kind. It was disguised very simply in this way. In clause 1 of the contract it was stated that, in consideration of the sum of £50,000 sterling, the licensor granted to the publisher exclusive world rights to publish extracts from his book. Then in clause 4 it was stated: 'If, on the advice of his legal advisers, the publisher is not able to publish the extracts, then instead the publisher will pay £25,000 for up to six articles.'
>
> What that meant was what Mr Bessell understood it to mean, that in the event of an acquittal the book he was writing could not be published because of the laws of libel, and therefore, in effect, the substance of the contract was that Mr Bessell stood to gain very handsomely if there were a conviction. I should add in relation to that contract that it was entered into after Mr Bessell had made his statement to the police. That was a matter which Mr Justice Cantley referred to specifically in taking the view that it might not amount, therefore, to a contempt of court. In view of the evil that was created by this form of activity by various newspapers, which I shall come to in a moment, I am bound to say that it seems to me to be wholly irrelevant whether a contract of that nature is entered into before or after a witness makes his statement to the police.

Lord Hartwell (editor-in-chief of the *Sunday Telegraph*) replied:

> ... The proposed deal raised two question. One was the propriety of the financial terms. The other was the propriety of agreeing to any such deal with a prospective witness. As to the first, we consulted our own legal adviser, who said that in the circumstances he thought the terms were unexceptionable. Bessell consulted his own London solicitor, who gave him similar advice, but went significantly further. He spoke to a senior official of the Director of Public Prosecutions and explained to him the nature of the proposed agreement. 'Would the DPP's Department', he asked, 'see anything objectionable

in the precise financial terms outlined?' The answer was that the Department would raise no objection and did not think it would prejudice the case.

Lord Wigoder intervened:

My Lords, if the noble Lord will forgive me, is that contained in a written communication from the Director of Public Prosecutions, or is that what Mr Bessell has said?

to which Lord Hartwell replied:

No, my Lords, it is not what Mr Bessell has said; it was his London solicitor, a man of standing, who, if necessary, is prepared to swear an affidavit to that effect. I know the name of the official, but I do not want to name him in this place.

This allegation, however, was flatly denied by the Lord Chancellor, on behalf of the Attorney-General, two days later, on 18 July 1979, in a written answer to a Parliamentary Question tabled by Lord Wigoder.

Lord Wigoder asked Her Majesty's Government:
Whether (as was asserted in the Hosue on Monday 16 July), prior to the trial of *Regina* v. *Deakin and others* at the Central Criminal Court, the solicitor to the witness Mr Peter Bessell explained to a senior official of the Department of the Director of Public Prosecutions the nature of a proposed agreement between Mr Bessell and the *Sunday Telegraph* concerning a book, asked whether the Director of Public Prosecutions department would see anything objectionable in the precise financial terms, and received a reply that the department would raise no objection and did not think it would prejudice the case.

The Lord Chancellor:
I am informed by my right honourable and learned friend the Attorney-General that the only approach made by Mr Bessell's solicitor to the Department of the Director of Public Prosecutions concerning such a matter was on 2 October 1978, when he had a telephone conversation, a note of which was made immediately after, with a Principal Assistant Director. On that occasion, the solicitor said that Mr Bessell had received an offer (the terms of which he did not specify) from a national newspaper (which was not named) to serialise a book which, in part, dealt with the 'Thorpe case'. The solicitor made it clear that such publication would be after the trial, so there was no question of possible prejudice (in the sense of contempt), but he thought the Director

should know of the proposal because of the ammunition it could afford the defence to discredit Mr Bessell.

The Principal Assistant Director told the solicitor that his department would be concerned by anything which could be used to discredit Mr Bessell, financial or otherwise, but that he did not think it was for him to advise as to the offer.

The Principal Assistant Director was not told any of the terms of the offer, much less that it involved a contingency payment, and it is clear from his contemporary note that he neither gave his approval to the course proposed or expressed the opinion that it would not prejudice the case.

Parkinson's Disease

I was diagnosed as having Parkinson's Disease in 1979, and had probably suffered from the complaint for at least two years previous to this. The first symptom, which sounds strange, was a difficulty in doing up shirt buttons, which brought on a feeling of nausea. At that early stage, tremor of hands and arms was minimal, but would gradually increase. Another early symptom was the progressive deterioration of my handwriting.

In the early nineteenth century, Dr James Parkinson had noticed from the window of his consulting room in Hoxton the shuffling gait of various people passing by, and by 1817 diagnosed this as one of the symptoms of a clearly definable disease, which was to bear his name. Other symptoms can be weakening of the vocal muscles, which can produce voice inaudibility. This is accentuated by the fact that although the average person swallows unconsciously up to 2,000 times a day, the Parkinson patient needs to make a special effort to clear saliva, and failure to do so can make him dribble like a dirty old man. Rigidity of the jaw accentuates the difficulties of speech. Very often there is a delay in the Parkinson patient replying in conversation, due to the building-up of saliva which he has difficulty in swallowing before being able to speak. This leads the conversationalist to deduce that either the Parkinson sufferer is deaf or gaga or both, or suffering from cancer of the throat; hence, more often than not, he decides that the way out is to do what the average Englishman does when speaking to a foreigner — he shouts! Having done their best, the conversation is at an end. Another consequence of these difficulties is that there may be a problem over swallowing food, and in such cases it is necessary to prepare food to a puréed consistency in almost liquid form. The Parkinson sufferer can often be recognised by a rigidity of facial expression and a lack of blinking to moisten the eyes, which produces a staring look. Another aspect is a total 'freeze-up' of movement, accompanied by the sensation of feeling nailed to the floor. Fortunately the person's intellect remains unimpaired. All in all, Parkinson's makes the sufferer very tired during parts of the day.

One of the dangers connected with Parkinson's is a loss of balance: this is particularly caused by turning too sharply, but it is also possible to lose balance for no apparent reason. I began to dread the crunch which follows a fall, since in all probability this represents a breakage: in my case, a fracture of the left femur, fracture of the right hip, and a hairline fracture of the little finger of my right hand on three separate occasions. The first two breaks resulted in a six-week and a two-week stay in hospital. On one occasion following a fall (without breakage) in the street, I hailed a taxi, who assumed I was drunk and needed reassurance! He brought me home, and although I had bled copiously over his floor, he refused to accept any money for the fare.

Parkinson's is a disease which affects a hundred thousand people in the UK, and it is estimated that one out of every hundred over the age of sixty-five will develop it. The disease is not infectious, is probably not hereditary — and at present there is no known cure. However, let me qualify this bald statement: there is medication which can and does control the condition by a wise balance of drugs. The danger here is that too little medication has minimal effect, whilst a large dose can be more than the body can sustain, with unpleasant results such as clenching of the jaw and writhing of the limbs, which is known as dyskinesia. Each case needs different dosages and produces a wide variety of experiences. To complicate matters even further, each patient may have variations in their condition from day to day.

The cause of the disease has yet to be definitively established, but it is known that what is involved is an attack on what are known as the basal ganglia of the brain, particularly on the part known as the substantia nigra. The result is a reduction of the chemical dopamine, which controls muscular activity from the brain. This can in part be ameliorated by dopamine substitutes and other agents, but it is as yet not physically possible to make up the natural deficiency to produce a cure.

The mainstay of treatment for Parkinson's Disease remains L-Dopa. However, it may be necessary to take a second agent in order to enhance the effects of the drug or modify some of the side effects such as dyskinesia. Anti-cholinergic drugs like Disipal block the chemical substance acetylcholine, thereby reducing tremor. Another class of drugs is the dopamine agonists, like Eldepryl. These have the advantage that they stimulate dopamine receptors directly and to an extent bypass the neurones which have become depleted as a result of Parkinson's Disease.

A further group of drugs (COMT) are emerging at the centre of research. These aim to prolong the action of L-Dopa by inhibiting the enzyme catechol-o-methyl transferase, and maintaining the blood levels for a longer period of time, resulting, it is hoped, in a smoother, more beneficial effect from each dose. Tolcapone is the most potent COMT inhibitor under trial at the present and is to be followed by others in the group.

Much research has been carried out, particularly in the field of experimental surgery. One such example is the implanting in the patient's brain of dopamine-secreting tissue from an aborted foetus. This is an attempt to step up the supply of the chemical in which the patient is deficient, and it is hoped that the tissue will grow and reproduce. This treatment is bound to produce controversy and strong opposition on ethical grounds, although individual district ethics committees have reached agreement with various hospitals on a working pattern. In this country most of the experimental implants were performed by the late Professor Hitchcock at the Birmingham Centre for Neurology at Smethwick. I myself underwent the operation on the basis that I would never have forgiven myself if I didn't try all reasonable cures on offer. The operation involved boring two holes in the skull in preparation for a bilateral implant. One's head is put in a frame to control tremor, and the three-quarters-of-an-hour operation takes place under local anaesthetic. One remains conscious throughout, and the surgery is painless. The most incredible precision is called for and the operation is preceded by a brain scan. For me this was the most unpleasant aspect: fans which cool the computer had broken down and with the well-established rule that computers take precedence over humans, the scanner fans were transferred to the computer, leaving the scanner itself with the qualities of the Black Hole of Calcutta! It produced in me claustrophobia, and when some days after the operation I was due to be scanned in a £1 million nuclear scanner, which (as before) involved being pushed in a capsule into the machine, I was unable to stay the course and had to be retrieved. Another incident was when in mid-operation the surgeon said: 'Damn, the clutch has gone'. The sensation I was experiencing at the time was as though a pneumatic drill was going through my head. I asked him what was the effect of the clutch going. 'Oh', came the reply, 'I had to push harder!' I did, however, gain immediate relief for a short period after the operation.

It would seem that the answer lies in the use of more and younger foetuses in each case. Ideally it is hoped that the patient's own tissue from another part of the body can be engineered to act as a generator to increase the supply of dopamine from the brain to the body. This would remove any risk of rejection and hopefully would not meet with ethical opposition. It is also hoped that in the future, chemical engineering may produce an artificial substitute for the tissue.

Revival of interest has been shown in the operation known as pallidotomy. This involves the surgeon passing an electric probe into the globus pallidus area of the brain with the object of destroying those cells, or neurones, which, deprived of an adequate supply of dopamine, become over-active and result in the involuntary movements of Parkinson's Disease.

The operation takes a minimum of three hours and is carried out under a local anaesthetic with the patient fully conscious. A hole is drilled in the skull and a dye is injected for the purpose of taking X-rays of the brain, and individual cells are electrically stimulated to ensure that the right cells are destroyed. However, the operation carries certain dangers. If the wrong cells are attacked, this could involve bleeding, possibly leading to a stroke. It could also possibly cause blindness.

The Swedish neurosurgeon Lauri Laitinen has carried out more than 400 pallidotomies and claims definite benefits, lasting for years. British reaction is more cautious. The Institute of Neurology in London is carrying out a long-term trial involving six patients a year, whilst Mr Carl Meyer is carrying out a number of pallidotomies at Smethwick. He also claims a good measure of success.

Another line of research is the pacemaker, involving the fitting of an electrode into the globus pallidus of the brain through the neck. This is controlled by a 'power pack', i.e. a pulse generator containing a battery. This is fitted inside the chest. A computer unit is placed on the skin next to the power pack to control the electrical impulses which stimulate and control the diseased area of the brain. The battery needs replacing every five years. The operation is long and can take up to eight hours for one side of the brain; it is expensive and probably involves bilateral devices to act on both sides of the body. This procedure still needs further research.

Much dedicated research is going on, particularly in Sweden, America and the UK. I am confident that a cure will be found, and I hope that it will be sooner rather than later!

North Devon

North Devon is one of the most beautiful and varied areas in the world. It includes part of Exmoor; the rugged coastline of Lynton and Hartland; the golden beaches of Saunton and Woolacombe; the seaside resort of Ilfracombe and the market town of South Molton; the unspoilt inland villages and the dramatic meeting point of the Taw and Torridge rivers.

It continues to be a great joy to find friends in every town, village and hamlet whom I have known and worked with over the years. The forty-five years in which I have been associated with North Devon are a large part of my life. Certainly I should never wish to leave North Devon for anywhere else. It is home.

Landkey Stores and Sub-Post Office
At a Liberal 'do' in Landkey, North Devon, in the autumn of 1966, the question of who had been where and when for their annual holidays came up. I asked my friend Leslie Farrell, the Landkey sub-postmaster, whether he was going on vacation. 'I am not, I can't', was the uncompromising reply. It turned out that he felt there was a security problem involved and that it was almost impossible to find anyone who would take on the re-sponsibility of running the post office and store while he was away. On almost every occasion that sub-postmasters had attended a national con-ference there was on average at least one sub-post office burgled. He said

to me by way of a challenge: 'Will you take over and run the store?' I rashly and immediately said: 'Yes, provided you and your wife go away together for a holiday'. The deal was agreed.

In the course of the next few days I happened by chance to see Tony Benn, then Postmaster-General, in the Members' Lobby, and thought he would be interested to hear my proposal. Indeed he was, and an hour later telephoned me to say that there were problems if I took on the responsibility of acting as a sub-postmaster. I would be holding an office of profit under the Crown and as such could be unseated, thereby plunging my constituency into a by-election! The only solution would be for me to run the shop with the assistance of a retired sub-postmaster — if a willing candidate could be found — one of whose main functions every morning would be to change the date stamp. I learnt that if the date stamp was stolen it would enable unscrupulous people to validate a vast number of stolen but undated postal orders. The stamp might also be used to pre-date football pools coupons, arguing that the date marked was proof of their posting dates. Otherwise there were no objections about running the shop. Fortunately, a willing retired sub-postmaster was found, and we were back in business.

Our day started at 5.40 A.M. when the post arrived for sorting and collection by the postman for delivery. We opened to the public at 9 A.M. The village store is a wonderful meeting place, although it is now under threat from competition from the supermarkets. I found it most instructive to learn about people's shopping habits. I also discovered that one or two people postponed withdrawing their old age pen-

Sweeping the floor at Landkey stores

sions until after I had left, out of a sense of embarrassment lest I should learn that they were of pensionable age!

The takings were roughly the same as average, which I thought was a good sign and showed that it was business as usual. I was also of course a sitting duck, as Jehovah's Witnesses discovered who came to convert me!

It was a highly enjoyable week and a valuable experience. The Farrells returned with their batteries recharged to resume the administration of my Landkey emporium.

Lundy

In the spring of 1969, the Harman family announced that with great regret they had to sell Lundy, the remote island off the north coast of Devon in the Bristol Channel. From that moment, differing rumours spread like wildfire. First, it was suggested that it might turn into a Butlins-type holiday camp; next, that a local syndicate was to be formed to run a casino, and last but not least, that the scientologists would make it their headquarters.

Lundy is renowned for being totally unspoilt and I took the view that it must be rescued. Accordingly, I approached the late Peter Mills, then MP for Torrington, in whose constituency it fell. I also approached David Owen, then MP for Devonport. I suggested that we form a three-man all-party team to launch an appeal to raise the necessary funds to purchase Lundy for the nation. They both readily agreed. The first step was to approach the National Trust and ask whether they would launch an appeal. They said, quite fairly, that there was a limit to the number of appeals they could launch but if we three MPs launched the appeal and were successful, they would accept ownership of the island and all that that implied.

Shortly after the news of the intended sale of Lundy broke, John Smith, then MP for City of London & Westminster and founder of the Landmark Trust, made contact and asked whether we would be interested in having the Landmark Trust take a full repairing lease of the island. Needless to say, we were delighted.

John Smith, shortly afterwards, took Mills, Owen and myself over by helicopter. His wife confided in me that what had finally hooked John was the Georgian fog cannon on the west side of the island!

On the strength of this development we launched the appeal to the nation, and received helpful coverage in the press. A few days later Jack

Lundy Island

Hayward, a philanthropist living in the Bahamas, rang my flat in London at about midnight while I was still at the House of Commons. He said he would ring back in half an hour and Caroline passed on the message.

The call duly came through and Hayward asked what our intentions about ownership were. I told him that we wanted to buy Lundy and vest the ownership in the National Trust, and prior to this John Smith MP of the Landmark Trust was interested in taking a full repairing lease of the island. Hayward mentioned that he was a neighbour of Smith's in Sussex and this was welcome news. 'How much is being asked? £100,000?' asked Hayward. '£150,000', I replied. 'I'll buy it', said Hayward. 'Where shall I send the cheque?' I promptly rang John Smith to tell him the news; he said: 'A promise from Jack Hayward is as safe as the Bank of England'. The cheque came through two days later.

The National Trust were anxious to give a press release. I was opposed to this since I felt that the announcement of the purchase of Lundy for the nation should be the launching pad of a new appeal for £75,000, which was needed for immediate repairs. Over and above this, the Landmark Trust would meet the cost of other repairs, and on the expiry of their lease would help to raise an endowment fund, to spare the National Trust further calls on their resources. We moved very fast: Major-General Fergus Ling was appointed to run the appeal and did a superb job. Rio Tinto Zinc gave us free office space and we were off.

There was a slight hiccup before completion. The National Trust indicated that the cost of the livestock had not been included in the total. This amounted to £12,000. Would Hayward meet the increased amount? I replied that I was sure that he would, but that it would be wholly wrong to make a further approach to him; nor would it be popular to launch an additional appeal, since we were launching an appeal, in any event, for immediate repairs. The Trust must meet the sum involved out of their own reserves — and this they did.

To mark the transfer of ownership to the National Trust, a thanksgiving service took place at St Helena's Church on the island. Campbell Steamers had to work overtime bringing literally hundreds of well-wishers from the mainland. The church was not large enough for them all and so the Bishop of Crediton (Wilfred Westall) decided to give the blessing from the steps of the church. The weather was magical and one could see the coastlines of South Wales, North Somerset, North Devon and North Cornwall.

Recently, £40,000 was donated to repair and re-hang the church bells at St Helena's, which for decades had remained silent. They now ring out over the Bristol Channel, after a dedication service by the Bishop of Crediton in October 1994.

From the mainland, Lundy is eleven miles from Hartland, twenty-three from Ilfracombe and twenty-five from Bideford. The island is a quarter of a mile wide and three and a half miles in length. It has a magic of its own, which is enhanced by the hazards of reaching it by often very rough seas. The granite rocks (which were used to build the Embankment in London) have taken their poundings from the Atlantic Ocean. The sea in fine weather can be a translucent blue, and the waters around the island are now a marine park. The countryside is totally unspoilt. At the time of the hand-over, the population consisted of ten permanent residents and six lighthouse keepers in the two lighthouses.

I remember on one visit seeing a head and shoulders appear as if from nowhere. The intrepid climber looked familiar, and suddenly the penny dropped — it was Lord Hunt of Everest doing some practice climbs!

The island has had a long and fascinating history. First references date back to the twelfth century, when Jordan de Marisco and his family inhabited the island and built Marisco Castle. Lundy was one of the last places to surrender in the Civil War to the Parliamentarians. Much involved during this period was Thomas Bushell, who had been in the household of the Lord Chancellor, Sir Francis Bacon. Bushell mined silver in Combe Martin and South Wales and minted money to pay the King's army. Lord Saye and Sele claimed the island, backed by the Parliamentarians. Bushell agreed to surrender, provided he obtain the written authority of King Charles II in exile, and provided also that he was given an immunity for the garrison under his command, of approximately twenty-two in number. He also asked for the right to carry on mining his silver mines. A package was agreed.

Another character was Thomas Benson, a Bideford merchant. In 1746 he became Sheriff of Devon and in 1747 was elected MP for the Borough of Barnstaple. He leased Lundy from Lord Gower around 1750. He obtained the contract to transport convicts to the American colonies. In fact he landed them on Lundy and put them to work as slave labour, building many of the walls that still stand. A boatload of convicts escaped and landed at Clovelly. Benson was sued for breach of contract and successfully ran the defence that his obligation was to take the convicts overseas and that by landing them on Lundy he had fulfilled his contract, thereby winning the day.

A less successful activity of Benson was to load a ship, the *Nightingale,* bound for Virginia with a valuable cargo of linen and pewter. He landed the cargo on Lundy, gave orders for the ship to be burnt and then proceeded to claim the insurance. This time he faced prosecution for fraud but before the High Sheriff arrived to arrest him, Benson took a ship at Plymouth bound for Portugal, where he stayed. The captain and first mate of the *Nightingale* were hanged and others were imprisoned or transported.

The island was bought in 1834 by William Hudson Heaven. He built Millcombe House and the road leading up the cliff from the landing beach. His son, the Reverend Hudson Grosett Heaven, built the church of St Helena in 1896. Not surprisingly, the island was dubbed the Kingdom of Heaven! A centenary service was held in the church in 1997, at which the Bishop of Exeter preached.

Martin Coles Harman bought the Island in 1925. In 1929 he produced his own coinage — one puffin and a half-puffin, which appeared on one side of the coin, with his head on the other. 50,000 coins of each of the two denominations were minted by the Birmingham Mint. He was tried at Bideford Petty Sessions for unlawfully issuing a piece of metal as a token of money under Section 5 of the Coinage Act of 1870. His defence was that Lundy was outside the jurisdiction of the mainland, although it was a dominion territory of George V. He was found guilty and fined £5 plus costs. He appealed to the King's Bench Division, where the decision of the magistrates was upheld. Puffinage can be bought as tokens but not as legal tender.

Lundy stamps are still lawfully issued and since the Royal Mail does not deliver mail to the island the stamps serve as a receipt for the cost of transporting the mail to and from the mainland. The proviso is that the stamps are on the back of the envelope or the left-hand corner of the postcard so as not to compete with the Queen. This compromise on stamps may be an indicator of how best to play the issue on the European currency!

Codden Hill

The west side of Codden Hill adjoins the village of Bishops Tawton. It climbs eastwards to the highest point, which is known as Codden Beacon. It was probably one of a string of beacons crossing the country to be lit as a warning of a Napoleonic invasion. It is generally thought that the mound itself at the top of the hill was a Bronze Age burial ground. The mound is 629 ft above sea level and one gets an uninterrupted view of a full 360 degrees. On a clear day one can see Exmoor, Dartmoor and, forty-four miles away, Bodmin Moor in Cornwall; also the Island of Lundy, twenty-two miles out in the Bristol Channel — the lighthouses and church are clearly visible.

Prior to 1970 the beacon was in an appalling state: rusty, with broken-down wire fencing, an abandoned lookout post, an unsightly concrete plinth which served as a trig point and a variety of dumped rubbish. After one visit to the site, Caroline and I decided that one day we would try to buy the site and tidy it up, so that it could be enjoyed by the public. She died in a road accident in June 1970 when we had been married for twenty-five months. I determined that I would create a permanent memorial to her on Codden.

There was one man who I knew would design something worthy of Caroline and worthy of the Hill: Clough Williams-Ellis, of Port Meirion fame. He had designed Lloyd George's grave at Llanystumdwy, and the Lloyd George stone in Westminster Abbey. Clough readily agreed. Negotiations began with ministries, councils, Royal Ordnance Survey people and surrounding farmers — the latter being unusually complicated, since the tenure on which Codden Hill was held was a pre-1925 settlement, and therefore three different parties jointly and severally enjoyed title. However, the owners could not have been more helpful, although one of them, Bert Verney, had, I thought, some reservation. Fortunately he raised it: his brother used to ride his horse over Codden Hill. He had been killed in the RAF during the war. The family had always wanted to erect some memorial to him, and still hoped that they might be able to do so. I suggested that they should incorporate their tribute with mine, and I would ask Williams-Ellis, one of the leading landscape artists alive, to design something which would blend with our plans. Additionally, Michael Ramsey, then Archbishop of Canterbury, had agreed to conduct the dedication

Codden Beacon

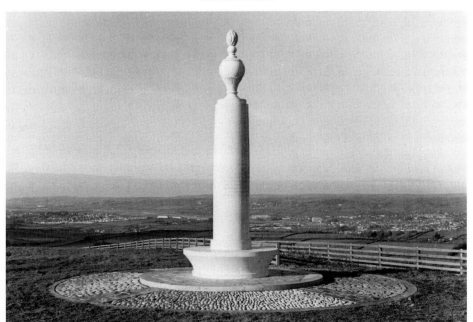

service, and again, we could join forces. Bert was delighted. Clough designed a handsome stone seat on the far side of the monument.

What I find moving is that these two young people, who had both died in their prime, should now share pride of place on Codden Hill.

The monument has taken the form of a column, which grows out of a circular stone seat and is crowned by a sculptured flame, all in Portland stone. The seat of the column was to rest on a base of cobblestones from the shore at Clovelly, appropriately by courtesy of Asquith's granddaughter. The site is completed by a circle of stone slabs, indicating in which direction one is looking and the places involved. The Portland stone is glistening white, and came from the same quarries from which the stone to build St Paul's Cathedral was supplied.

Round the column is a collar in stone, recording the names of the craftsmen who had been involved in building the project.

The day of the dedication in December 1971 was misty, and one did not get the full view. But one had the feeling of being up in the clouds, on top of the world. The service itself was taken by the Archbishop, assisted by the Bishop of Crediton, Wilfred Westall, both of whom had married us in the chapel at Lambeth Palace. Also present was my old friend Subdean Andrews of Chittlehampton.

I was lent an aeroplane which flew Michael and Joan Ramsey from Canterbury via North Wales to North Devon, picking up in Wales Lady Olwen Carey-Evans (Lloyd George's surviving daughter) and Clough and Amabel Williams-Ellis. The return journey was in reverse order. I noticed that Michael and Clough arrived with identical suitcases. I didn't give it another thought — but disaster! Clough opened his suitcase when he got home, to find that he had the Archbishop's vestments, bible, prayer book, notes for a sermon and several letters. When he reached Canterbury, Michael found Clough's yellow stockings and breeches, his famous hat and plans and drawings. Secretaries, chaplains, wives, all made the telephone red-hot, and in due course an appropriate exchange was made. I apologised to Michael when I next saw him, and indeed to Clough. Michael's eyebrows started to twitch in their inimitable way, and he said: 'Don't bother, don't apologise. I could use all Clough's things walking around Canterbury, but I had very great difficulty in visualising Clough scaling Snowdon in my vestments!'

The Hill is now much-visited and, I believe, appreciated and that is the intention.

Higher Chuggaton

My home in North Devon is known as Higher Chuggaton and you may well ask: where is that? Higher and Lower Chuggaton, Chuggaton Farm and Chuggaton Cross, along with Traveller's Rest, are part of the hamlet of Cobbaton. The postal address, however, is Umberleigh, the parish is Swimbridge, the telephone exchange was Chittlehamholt and the nearest village is Chittlehampton. I came to buy Higher Chuggaton by an amazing piece of luck. During the summer of 1968 I rented part of a farmhouse in Cobbaton from my close friend and neighbour, Jim Isaac. I mentioned to him that I was anxious to buy a property in the immediate area. He told me that there was only one house on the market, and this was down a long, unmade-up lane, and needed a lot doing to it. I was standing in Jim's orchard, from which one could see the thatched roof of a cottage three fields away. I said: 'That's the sort of house I am looking for', to which Jim replied that it was not on the market. He said that the house was in good condition, had central heating and a converted barn. Three days later it came on the market, and within five days I bought it.

Caroline and I moved in in January 1969. She

Rupert and Jeremy Thorpe on the bridge at Chuggaton, 4 September 1972 was six months pregnant, and was to lift nothing. A group of friends and supporters fifteen-strong awaited us and the removal van, and within two hours the furniture was in place, the drawers had been lined, china and glass unpacked and most of the curtains and pictures were hung. It was an instant move, which I recommend!

The top of the garden was completely wild and one could only reach it in the winter months when the brambles had died down from their six-foot height. An old boy called Reg Rice had agreed to cut the thicket and remarked: 'T'was like a bloody jungle, the only things missing were tigers!'

In due course we had to rethatch the barn and the cottage. Traditionally farmers used to set aside a field for growing thatching straw, but this nowadays occurs very rarely. Wheat now grows much shorter for economy of handling, and even Norfolk reed is affected by chemicals and pesticides which have reduced its lifespan. On two occasions, therefore, we ordered thatching reed from Austria and Hungary. It cost a third more, but lasts more than twice as long. I remember my anger, having just organised this source of supply, when I read in a well-known gossip column that I was using plastic thatch!

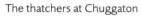

The thatchers at Chuggaton

The cottage dates from about 1630 and is built of cob, a mixture of clay, gravel and straw. The walls are three feet deep and retain the heat in the winter and keep the house cool in the summer. An inspector from the Department of the Environment

Rupert and Jeremy Thorpe at a carol concert in aid of Help the Aged, 11 December 1977

visited the house, as a result of which it was listed. He went into the roof space and there found some of the original thatch, which had been blackened by the smoke of an open fire. As it is the practice to lay the new thatch on the old, the darkened straw, caked with soot, showed the existence of an open fire which dates that part of the house back to the fifteenth century. Some original beams remain, and we have uncovered others which had been plastered over.

On one side of the fireplace a traditional bread oven is built into the thick cob wall. When one day I was showing a step-grandson the mysteries of baking bread, I noticed for the first time, rolled up into a ball at the very back of the oven, a partly-scorched newspaper. Still legible was the report of the speeches of David Lloyd George, then Chancellor of the Exchequer, and Sir Rufus Isaacs, then Attorney-General, in the two-day debate which took place on 18–19 June 1913 on the Marconi affair. It had lain there undisturbed for eighty-four years.

Within a few weeks of moving in, Caroline discovered that on her father's side she had a close connection with Chuggaton, and even more so with the neighbouring village of Chittlehampton. Her great-great-aunt, the late Mrs Lewis, had in my time been president of the local Liberal Association. Many years ago, John Richard Howard of Chittlehampton married Amelia Huxtable, whose father had bought Lower Chuggaton from the Duke of Bedford. Mr Howard's sister, Mrs Annie Hobbs, had a daughter Winnie, who married an Allpass; their son, Caroline's father, is my father-in-law, Warwick Allpass. Caroline also had second cousins living in the area. This was a splendid surprise.

The garden has grown and matured over the years. When it wakes up from its winter slumbers, it bursts into a sea of daffodils; one bank is planted out with daffodil bulbs given to Marion and myself as a wedding present by Alec and Elizabeth Home, and we call it 'Home Hill'. Chuggaton has always been part of my son's, Rupert's, life, and the three of us spend as much time there as possible. It is also a favourite visiting place for Marion's sons and eleven grandchildren — although there are occasionally casualties to the flowerbeds, not unconnected with football sessions!

For me it is the nearest thing to paradise on earth.

Jeremy and Rupert Thorpe at Chuggaton

Biographical notes

Idi Amin   1924/25–

Ugandan soldier, staged coup against President Obote on 25 January 1971. Noted for his abrupt changes of mood, from buffoonery to shrewdness, gentleness to tyranny. Expelled Asians in 1972, wrecking the economy. Tortured and murdered an estimated 100,000–300,000 Ugandans. Overthrown by Tanzanian invasion in 1978–79; now lives in Saudi Arabia.

Lord Avebury (Eric Lubbock)   1928–

By-election victor at Orpington, 14 March 1962; held the seat until 1970. Liberal Chief Whip 1966–70, leadership candidate 1967, led general election campaign February 1974. Succeeded to title 1971. Active in Parliamentary Civil Rights Group as MP; founded Parliamentary Human Rights Group in 1976.

Hastings Banda   1902–97

Doctor, practised in London and Ghana 1945–58. Returned to homeland of Malawi (then Nyasaland) to lead the nationalist movement; imprisoned by British colonial authorities 1959–60. Ruled Malawi from 1963 (as independent state from 1964), becoming steadily more totalitarian. Under pressure from domestic protests and aid donors, called first multi-party elections in 1994 and was voted out of office.

Sir Max Beerbohm   1872–1956

Caricaturist, writer, broadcaster and wit — 'the incomparable Max' (G.B. Shaw). Selected works: *Zuleika Dobson; Lytton Strachey* (Rede Lecture); *The Poet's Corner; Rossetti and his Circle; Things New and Old* and *Selected Essays.*

Married, in 1910, the American-born British actress Florence Kahn (died 1951), and moved (permanently, apart from wartime) to Rapallo, Italy.

Peter Bessell   1921–85

Liberal MP for Bodmin 1964–70. Early exponent of community politics, and instrumental, with Jeremy Thorpe, in re-establishing the Liberal Party as the main challenger to the Conservatives in south-west England; but maverick views isolated him from mainstream Liberal politics. Moved to US with large debts; featured as chief prosecution witness in the Thorpe trial, where he admitted that he was a compulsive liar.

Aneurin Bevan   1897–1960

The son of a miner, Labour MP for Ebbw Vale from 1929; editor, *Tribune* 1940–45. Minister for Health 1945–51, responsible for creation of National Health Service. Resigned from government in protest against rearmament and cutbacks in social spending, and became leader of the Labour left against Gaitskell. A brilliant spontaneous debater and orator, he could also be exceptionally rude to his opponents.

William Beveridge (Lord Beveridge)   1879–1963

Helped to lay the foundations of the post-war welfare state as author of the 'Beveridge Report', *Social Insurance and Allied Services* (1942). Civil servant 1908–19, Director of LSE 1919–37, Master of University College, Oxford, 1937–44. Liberal MP for Berwick-upon-Tweed 1944–45, led general election campaign 1945, elevated to peerage 1946.

Mark Bonham Carter (Lord Bonham Carter of Yarnbury) 1922–94

By-election victor at Torrington (March 1958), the first Liberal by-election gain since the 1920s. Lost the seat in 1959, made life peer 1986; central figure in party management under Grimond. First chairman of the Race Relations Board 1966–71, then of its successor, the Community Relations Commission, until 1977. Son of Violet.

Violet Bonham Carter (Lady Asquith of Yarnbury DBE) 1887–1969

Daughter of Liberal Prime Minister H.H. Asquith, she became his 'champion redoubtable' (Churchill) and the voice of Asquithian Liberalism after his death. President, Women's Liberal Federation 1923–25 and 1939–45, and the first woman to be Party President (1945). Given life peerage 1964.

Benjamin Britten (Lord Britten of Aldeburgh CH OM)   1913–76

Leading composer, pianist and conductor. His operas, including *Peter Grimes, Billy Budd, The Turn of the Screw* and *Death in Venice,* are considered the finest English operas since those of Purcell. Other major works include the *War Requiem, The Young Person's Guide to the Orchestra* and the Symphony in D Major for cello and orchestra, written for the Russian cellist Rostropovich. Co-founder of the Aldeburgh Festival in 1947. Created life peer in 1976, the first musician or composer to be elevated to the peerage.

George Brown (Lord George-Brown)   1914–85

Labour MP for Belper 1945–70; Minister of Works 1951; Secretary of State for Economic Affairs 1964–66 (responsible for the national economic plan), Foreign Secretary 1966–68. Often in conflict with Harold Wilson, and frequently offered his resignation — finally accepted in 1968. Able, but explosive in temperament, often aggravated by alcohol. Created life peer in 1970, left Labour Party in 1976.

Frank Byers (Lord Byers of Lingfield)   1915–84

Liberal MP for North Dorset 1945–50, Chief Whip 1946–50; key figure in post-war reorganisation of the party. Party Chairman 1950–52 and 1965–67, campaign manager at general elections. Created life peer in 1964; Leader of Liberal peers 1967–84. Director of Rio Tinto Zinc, 1962–73.

Colonel Sir Geoffry Christie-Miller   1881–1969

Uncle of Jeremy Thorpe: married to Olive Thorpe, Jeremy's father's sister. Director of Christy's, hat manufacturers in Stockport.

Sir Noel Coward   1899–1973

Playwright, actor, and composer best known for highly polished comedies of manners, including *Hay Fever, Bitter Sweet, Private Lives, Design for Living, Present Laughter* and *Blithe Spirit*. Rewrote one of his short plays, *Still Life,* as the film *Brief Encounter.* Directed and acted in films, including *In Which We Serve.* Songs include *Mad Dogs and Englishmen* and *Poor Little Rich Girl.*

Sir Dingle Foot   1905–78

Liberal MP for Dundee 1931–45, Vice-President of the party 1945–54. Believed the party was drifting to the right under Clement Davies, and followed Megan Lloyd George into the Labour Party in 1956; Labour MP for Ipswich 1957–70. Solicitor-General 1964–67, resigned over weakness of government policy towards Rhodesia, and opposed immigration restrictions. He began life as a Liberal (son of Isaac Foot) and 'there his heart remained' (Hoggart).

Isaac Foot   1880–1960

Liberal MP for Bodmin 1922–24 and 1929–35; fought thirteen parliamentary elections in all. Plymouth councillor 1907–27, and Lord Mayor 1945. Party President 1947, and a key figure in Liberalism in south-west England. A staunch Methodist and passionate reader, he left school at fourteen and mainly taught himself from his books. Four of his five sons became MPs and/or peers.

Philip Fothergill   1906–59

Liberal Party Chairman 1946–49 and 1952, President 1950–52, Treasurer; instrumental in keeping the party alive, and fighting on a broad front, at its lowest point; described in one of the papers as the 'Liberal Party's fiery little war-horse'. Woollen manufacturer and keen temperance reformer; President United Kingdom Alliance 1952–59.

Jo Grimond (Lord Grimond of Firth)   1913–93

Liberal Leader 1956–67, largely responsible for the first post-war Liberal revival; under his leadership, the Liberal Party and what it thought and said, became politically relevant in a way in which it had not done for over twenty years. Modernised party organisation, and attracted new policy thinkers; argued for realignment of the left, but his hopes were dashed by the Labour victory of 1966. MP for Orkney & Shetland 1950–83, interim leader in 1976, after Jeremy Thorpe's resignation, created life peer in 1983. Married to Violet Bonham Carter's daughter Laura.

Sir Edward Heath KG MBE MP   1916–

Conservative MP for Old Bexley & Sidcup since 1950. Chief Whip 1955–59, Minister of Labour 1959–60, Lord Privy Seal 1960–63 (responsible for negotiations on EEC entry), Secretary of State for Trade and Industry 1963–64. Elected party leader 1965, Prime Minister 1970–74. Took Britain into EEC in 1973. Faced major economic problems; after miners' strike, called election on question of 'who governs Britain?' and lost. Replaced as leader by Margaret Thatcher in 1975.

Roy Jenkins (Lord Jenkins of Hillhead OM)   1920–

Labour MP 1948–76; Deputy Leader of the party 1970–72. Home Secretary 1965–67 and 1974–76, Chancellor of the Exchequer 1967–70; President of the European Commission 1976–80. In October 1971, led Labour rebellion to support entry into EEC. One of the founding 'Gang of Four' of the Social Democratic Party, and its first leader, 1982–83; SDP MP 1982–87. Made life peer 1987, led Liberal Democrats in Lords 1987–98. Author of many books, including biographies of Asquith and Gladstone.

Russell Johnston (Lord Russell-Johnston of Minginish)   1932–

Liberal MP for Inverness 1964–97; Chairman, Leader or President, Scottish Liberal Party 1970–94. Member of the European Parliament 1973–79; Leader, Liberal Democrat & Reform Group in Council of Europe 1994–99; President of the Council 1999–. Created life peer 1997. Inspiring and well-travelled speaker and writer.

Kenneth Kaunda   1924–

Teacher, founded Zambia African National Congress in 1959 and led country to independence in 1964. An astute leader, he helped defuse tensions between black and white communities; but neglect of agriculture, coupled with sanctions against Rhodesia, caused growing economic and social problems. He imposed one-party rule in 1972; eventually forced to legalise opposition parties and was heavily defeated in elections in 1991.

Jomo Kenyatta   1894–1978

African statesman and nationalist, the first prime minister (1963–64) and then president (1964–78) of independent Kenya. His policies made Kenya one of the most stable and economically dynamic of the ex-colonies, though with large disparities of wealth; he also became increasingly authoritarian.

Seretse Khama   1921–80

The grandson of Khama III ('the Good'), chieftain of the Bamangwato people 1925–56, when he renounced the post because of his marriage to a white woman. Founded Democratic Party 1962, Prime Minister of Botswana (then Bechuanaland), 1965; on independence, elected as President for successive terms until his death. Promoted multi-racial democracy and free universal education.

Harold Lever (Lord Lever of Cheetham)   1914–95

Barrister; Labour MP, various Manchester seats, 1945–79. Paymaster-General 1969–70, Chancellor of Duchy of Lancaster 1974–79. Created life peer 1979.

David Lloyd George (Earl Lloyd-George of Dwyfor)   1863–1945

Liberal MP for Caernavon Boroughs 1890–1945. President of the Board of Trade 1905–08, Chancellor of the Exchequer 1908–15, Minister of Munitions 1915–16, Prime Minister 1916–22. Deputy Leader of the Liberal Party 1923–26, Leader 1926–31. Raised to the peerage in 1945. Dynamic and radical thinker, helped to put New Liberal policies of social reform into practice before the Great War, and fought 1929 election on highly imaginative proto-Keynesian manifesto; but helped split the Liberal Party in 1916, and was loathed by the Asquithians ever after. Two of his children became Liberal MPs; Megan eventually joined the Labour Party, and Gwilym the Conservatives (via the National Liberals).

Megan Lloyd George   1902–66

Liberal MP for Anglesey 1929–51, Deputy Leader of the party 1949–51. Seeing herself as a radical increasingly out of sympathy with the Liberals, she joined Labour in 1955 and was Labour MP for Carmarthenshire 1957–66. An eloquent orator, she remained true to her father's passionate radicalism and love of Wales.

Edward Martell   1909–89

A journalist and publicist, Martell was one of the small group who kept the Liberal Party alive during its darkest years. An effective election organiser, and founder of *Liberal News,* he was one of the two Liberal London county councillors for SW Bethnal Green 1946–49, their victory being the first for Liberals on the LCC since 1931. With Byers and Fothergill, he was an advocate of fighting general elections on the broadest possible front. Left the Liberal Party in 1956 and drifted well to the right.

Golda Meir   1898–1978

Born in Kiev, emigrated to US in 1906 and then to Palestine in 1921. Head of the Jewish Agency 1946–48, elected to Knesset after Israeli independence, Minister of Labour 1949–56, Foreign Minister 1956–66, Prime Minister 1969–74.

Yehudi Menuhin (Lord Menuhin of Stoke d'Abernon KBE DM)
1916–99

One of the leading violin virtuosos of the twentieth century. Born in the US, his performance of Mendelssohn's Violin Concerto at the age of seven caused a sensation. Moved to London in 1959 and in 1963 opened the Yehudi Menuhin School for musically gifted children at Stoke d'Abernon, Surrey. Became a British citizen in 1985, knighted 1965, ennobled 1993.

Sir Robert Menzies   1894–1978

Lawyer, member of Victoria state parliament 1929–34, Australian federal parliament 1934–66. Attorney-General 1934–39, Prime Minister 1939–41 (United Australia Party), 1949–66 (Liberal Party). Strengthened military ties with the US, fostered industrial growth and immigration from Europe. Supported Britain's intervention in Suez, and US involvement in Vietnam.

Herbert Morrison (Lord Morrison of Lambeth)   1888–1965

Labour MP for South Hackney 1923–24, 1929–31, 1935–59. Minister of Transport 1929–31, Minister of Supply 1940–41, Home Secretary 1941–45, Deputy Prime Minister 1945–51, Foreign Secretary 1951. Created life peer 1959. A pragmatic reformist, he was a key figure in Labour's 1945 election victory.

Sir Andrew Murray   1903–77

Edinburgh councillor 1929–51 (except 1934); City Treasurer 1943–46; Lord Provost 1947–51. Instrumental in founding the Edinburgh Festival in 1947. A National Liberal for twenty years, Murray rejoined the Liberal Party and served as its President, 1960–61, and Treasurer, 1962–66.

Joshua Nkomo   1917–

Railway worker and trade unionist, became a leading black nationalist in Rhodesia. Held in detention by white minority government 1964–74. Helped lead guerrilla war against white rule, but after 1979–80 was increasingly eclipsed by Robert Mugabe. Defeated in 1980 elections, dismissed from Cabinet in 1982, but the two leaders agreed to merge their parties in 1987; became Vice President in 1990.

Sir John Norton-Griffiths   1871–1930

Maternal grandfather to Jeremy Thorpe. Conservative MP for Wednesbury, and subsequently Central Wandsworth. Civil engineer. Founder, the Tunnellers' Regiment, and also the Comrades of the Great War, which became the British Legion.

Lady Norton-Griffiths   1873–1974

Maternal grandmother to Jeremy Thorpe.

Sir Peter Pears CBE   1910–86

Singer (tenor) of outstanding skill and subtlety. Met Benjamin Britten in 1936, and the two men became life-long companions. Created the title role in Britten's *Peter Grimes* and sang in the first performances of all Britten's operas. Co-founder of the Aldeburgh Festival in 1947.

Mstislav Rostropovich   1927–

Conductor and pianist and one of the best-known cellists of the twentieth century. Professor of cello, Moscow Conservatory; as a pianist, accompanied his wife, the soprano Galina Vishnevskaya. Supported the dissident writer Solzhenitsyn and in 1975 decided not to return to the Soviet Union; Soviet citizenship was removed in 1978 (restored 1990). Khachaturian, Prokofiev, Shostakovich, Britten and Foss, amongst many others, wrote works for him.

Herbert Samuel (Viscount Samuel)   1870–1963

Liberal MP for Cleveland 1902–18, and for Darwen 1929–35. Cabinet minister (various posts) 1909–16, Home Secretary 1916 and 1931–32. Helped introduce much of the Liberals' social reform programme, but stood by Asquith in 1916 and left office with him. High Commissioner for Palestine 1920–25. Leader of the Liberal Party 1931–35. Raised to peerage 1937, leader in the Lords 1944–55. A respected statesman, a formidable mediator and administrator, and a notable political philosopher.

Ian Smith   1919–

Founded Rhodesia Front in 1961, won 1962 Rhodesian election on platform of independence and white rule, became Prime Minister in 1964 and unilaterally declared Rhodesia's independence in 1965. UN economic sanctions and the strains of fighting nationalist guerrillas forced Smith to negotiate with black leaders from 1977, stepping down as Prime Minister in 1979. He remained in Parliament until 1987.

Christopher Soames (Lord Soames)   1920–87

Conservative MP for Bedford, 1950–66. Churchill's son-in-law and Parliamentary Private Secretary (1952–55). Secretary of State for War, 1958–60, Minister for Agriculture 1960–64. Ambassador to France 1968–72, played major role in persuading French government to accept British entry to EEC. European Commissioner 1973–77. Created life peer in 1978, Leader of the Lords 1979–81. Governor of Rhodesia 1979–80, successfully overseeing transition to black majority rule.

Roy Thomson (Lord Thomson of Fleet)   1894–1976

Canadian-born newspaper and radio station owner. Moved into British media in 1952, owning, among others, *The Scotsman, the Sunday Times* and *The Times.* In 1963 he became a British citizen and set up the Thomson Foundation, and in 1964 was created a life peer.

Caroline Thorpe   1938–70

Married Jeremy Thorpe in May 1968, in Lambeth Palace; mother of Rupert Thorpe (born April 1968). Daughter of Warwick Allpass and Marcelle Williams. Worked at Sotheby's and a firm of interior decorators. Killed in car crash, June 1970.

Jeremy Thorpe   1929–

Son of John and Ursula Thorpe, educated in US, Eton and Oxford. Called to the Bar in 1954 and practised until 1959; also, briefly, a television interviewer. Adopted as Liberal candidate for North Devon in 1952, won seat in 1959, at second attempt. Elected as party Treasurer in 1965, and Leader in 1967. Took Liberal Party to highest ever vote in February 1974. Resigned as Leader in 1976 after publicity given to the 'Scott affair'. Lost seat in May 1979, cleared of conspiracy to murder in June. Currently President of North Devon Liberal Democrats; received standing ovation at 1997 Liberal Democrat conference.

The Venerable John Henry Thorpe   1857–1932

Paternal grandfather of Jeremy Thorpe. Born in Dublin, the eldest of nineteen children. Ordained in Church of Ireland 1879 (Dundalk, Cork), moved to Church of England in 1892 (Nottingham, Stockport, Macclesfield, Chester). A powerful and persuasive preacher, he became a canon of Chester Cathedral and died while presiding over a meeting of the Chester Diocesan Assessment Appeals Committee. In 1884, he married Martha, the eldest daughter of Robert Constable Hall, a prominent corn merchant in Cork.

John Henry Thorpe   1887–1944

Father of Jeremy Thorpe. Barrister-at-Law; Bencher of the Inner Temple; Recorder of Blackburn; Deputy Chairman, Middlesex Quarter Sessions. Conservative MP for Manchester Rusholme 1919–23. Chairman of the Price Regulation Committee.

Marion Thorpe   1926–

Daughter of Erwin Stein, musicologist; born in Vienna. She married (1) the Earl of Harewood (three sons); (2) Jeremy Thorpe (one stepson). A pianist, writer, teacher, lecturer and musical administrator, she co-founded, with Fanny Waterman, the Leeds International Pianoforte Competition, and was first President of the Friends of Covent Garden, Governor of the Yehudi Menuhin School and President of the South West Arts Association. Chairman of the Britten-Pears Foundation.

Ursula Thorpe   1903–92

Mother of Jeremy Thorpe. One of the four children of Sir John Norton-Griffiths. Married John Henry Thorpe in 1922. A JP, member of Surrey County Council, and Chairman, Medical and Special Schools for Surrey, Oxted County School and Nutfield School for the Deaf.

Sir Garfield Todd   1908–

Prime Minister of Southern Rhodesia 1953–58. Arrested by Smith regime in 1965, confined to his ranch for a year; arrested again and detained 1972–76. Member of Zimbabwe Senate 1980–85.

Pierre Trudeau   1919–

Lawyer and Canadian Liberal MP. Minister of Justice 1966–68, Prime Minister 1969–79 and 1980–84. His terms of office were marked by improved relations with France, the defeat of the French separatist movement, independence from the British parliament, and the formation of a new Canadian constitution.

Roy Welensky   1907–91

Trade unionist, founded Northern Rhodesia Labour Party in 1941. Helped to establish federation of the two Rhodesias and Nyasaland in 1953, and served as Prime Minister of the Federation from 1956 until it was dissolved in 1963. Tried to promote a multi-racial society in gradual stages, but heavily defeated in Southern Rhodesian elections in 1964.

Harold Wilson (Lord Wilson of Rievaulx)   1916–95

Labour MP for Huyton 1945–83. President, Board of Trade 1947–51 (youngest cabinet minister since Pitt the Younger), resigned his post in 1951 in protest against the introduction of NHS charges. Elected Labour leader in 1963, Prime Minister 1964–70 and 1974–76. Created life peer 1983. Won four elections out of five, but his adroit political tactics, while keeping the Labour Party together and ending divisions over the EEC (through the 1975 referendum), masked a lack of strategic direction.

Ralph Wood   1870–1945

Great-uncle of Jeremy Thorpe; brother of Lady Norton-Griffiths. Worked in India and South Africa, and became a chartered accountant in the City. He was a noted collector of *objets d'art* and lived in a Queen Anne cottage (Flint Cottage, which at one time belonged to George Meredith) at the foot of Box Hill. He married Violet Ruffer.